School Children At-Risk

School Children At-Risk

Virginia Richardson,
Ursula Casanova,
Peggy Placier and
Karen Guilfoyle

 The Falmer Press

(A member of the Taylor & Francis Group)
London New York Philadelphia

UK   The Falmer Press, Falmer House, Barcombe, Lewes, East Sussex, BN8 5DL

USA   The Falmer Press, Taylor & Francis Inc., 242 Cherry Street, Philadelphia, PA 19106-1906

First published 1989

British Library Cataloguing in Publication Data
School children at risk.
   1. United States. Primary schools. Disadvantaged students.
I. Richardson-Koehler, Virginia.
371.96′7′0973
ISBN 1-85000-514-1
ISBN 1-85000-515-X (pbk.)

Library of Congress Cataloging-in-Publication Data
School children at-risk / Virginia Richardson-Koehler . . . [et al.].
   p. cm.
  Bibliograpy: p.
  Includes index.
  ISBN 1-85000-514-1: $44.00; ISBN 1-85000-515-X (pbk.): $20.00
  1. Socially handicapped children—Education (Elementary)—
United States—Case studies. 2. Underachievers—United States—
Case studies. I. Richardson-Koehler, Virginia, 1940–
LC4091.S35 1989
371.96′7′0973—dc19 88-26770

Typeset in 11/13 Bembo by
Input Typesetting Ltd, London

Jacket design by Caroline Archer

Printed in Great Britain by Taylor & Francis (Printers) Ltd, Basingstoke

Contents

Preface   vii

Chapter 1   The Meaning of At-Risk and the Design of the   1
            Study
Chapter 2   The Students and How They Were Identified   16
Chapter 3   School Contexts and the Schooling of At-Risk   40
            Students
Chapter 4   The Classroom Within the School   63
Chapter 5   Home and School   80
Chapter 6   Special Populations of Students: At Risk and LD   98
Chapter 7   The Social Construction of the Identification at At-   118
            Risk Students and the Dilemmas of Schooling
Chapter 8   At-Risk Status: An Interactive View   138

Appendix 1   Interview Guidelines   155
Appendix 2   Case Studies of Children   167
References   270
Index   281

Preface

This study of at-risk elementary students was funded, in part, by the Exxon Education Foundation. We would like to thank the Foundation for its financial support and L. Scott Miller, the Program Officer, for his interest in the project and his deep compassion for the problems of at-risk students.

A study such as this cannot be completed without the involvement of a large number of people. In particular, we would like to thank Gary Fenstermacher, Dean of the College of Education, University of Arizona, for his intellectual guidance of the project and the financial support of the College. In addition we thank Patricia Colfer, who participated in our weekly meetings while she was conducting a similar study of at-risk students at the middle school level. Lee Ann Seitsinger spent many hours transcribing our tapes of interviews with teachers, parents and students, and Leticia Green transcribed our bilingual interviews.

We particularly wish to thank the school personnel, students and parents at Plaza and Escalante schools for participating so willingly in the study. Strong motivation and willingness to improve schooling for at-risk students were evident in all of our interactions with teachers, principals, counsellors, nurses and specialists at both schools. Knowing that these dedicated professionals are in our schools makes the solutions of schooling for at-risk students seem both possible and probable.

Virginia Richardson
August 1988

Chapter 1

The Meaning of 'At-Risk' and the Design of the Study

Because my dad quit his job and a long time ago, like more than two years ago when I was in kindergarten, my dad molested me and I don't know who told the patrols and that, but somebody told them when we were living in a trailer. I had lots of friends there and it was good and I remember one time that . . . and then my mom really cared about me and that, it was really good cause I remember one time, she loved my hair. My mom was doing my hair and she took so long to do it that I missed the bus and I didn't get to school that day and I was so mad because I love school. It's one of my favorite things. (Ann)

Ann[1] was 10-years-old and in the third grade. She was described by one of her teachers as a 'beautiful student, academically — always does what she's supposed to do'. That same teacher considered Ann to be at-risk[2] because of her problems outside of school. Ann was in a foster home; she, her younger sister and two brothers had been taken from her parents. The new environment had not proved to be a positive experience for her either. The foster home had been reported by the school to the Child Protective Agency for the 'terrible treatment [counselor's words]' that Ann received there. Ann, in her writing, indicated that she had very negative feelings about herself concerning all these events. Her teacher considered her to be 'tormented', a 'perfect candidate for teen suicide'.

Gilberto, another third-grader in a different school, was also considered at-risk by his teachers although for different reasons. Gilberto had attended four different schools during his short career as a student. He was considered to have limited English proficiency. He

1

had been diagnosed as learning disabled. In the second grade he had been referred for language therapy. He was placed in programs to remediate these deficiencies, and on a typical day Gilberto divided his time among six different classrooms. One of his teachers felt that this movement from teacher to teacher brought out his 'sparkling personality', but she could not say how it benefited him academically.

In an interview, Gilberto described his school day in the following way:

> I start with Spanish language, later come back and go to recess, then . . . I go to music, then I go to this class to talk . . . English, and then to lunch. After lunch I go to play and then I go to another class Ms.—'s class (learning disabilities), and then go back to another class, a little one (language therapy), and then go back to the classroom to do some work and then go home.

When asked about what he did in all those different classes, he gave the following responses:

> —in the English class: 'we play games'.
> —in music: 'a test and some instrument . . . [we learn] a bunch of stuff'.
> —LD: 'how to read but I already know how to read'
> (Why are you there then?) 'I don't know'.
> —math: 'I'm already doing those that have the two little sticks together, like this' [as he draws an 'x' on the ground].

The reason Gilberto said he was learning in school was 'so I can pass grade'. His opinion of himself as a student was 'the worst in the class because I only get 'B' or 'C', I never get 100'.

Students At-Risk in School

The study described in this book examined at close range the experiences of twelve elementary school students, of which Ann and Gilberto are two, considered by their teachers to be at-risk. As we shall see, these two students each represented a particular perspective on 'at-riskness'.

One perspective shared by the school people we interviewed, was that the children's home environment placed them at-risk; this could certainly be argued in Ann's case. Some might say that Gilberto's home environment also predisposed him to be at-risk. It was poor, crowded and linguistically different; and yet, his mother was supportive of Gilberto and his education. Gilberto, in contrast with Ann, seemed confident and happy with himself. The risks for Gilberto appeared to occur at school. Frequent moves had interrupted his early progress in school, and he had fallen into the precarious 'below grade level' zone. This condition had motivated his teachers to seek resources to help him. The program he described above — fragmented, repetitive and difficult for him to fathom — was the result of those well-meaning efforts. He was, within that environment, at-risk.

But what does at-risk mean? And what does it mean for a child to be at-risk? The first question will guide the discussion that follows in this chapter. The second question was the motivating force behind this study. It will be addressed in the chapters that follow through our discussion and analysis of the data collected on the twelve students.

The Meaning of At-Risk: Two Models of School Success and Failure

The term, at-risk, has appeared with increasing frequency in educational documents and discourse in recent years. For example, in one recent issue of *Education Week* the term appeared in five different articles.[3] Many conferences have been held on the topic, and it is the subject of policy at state, district and school levels.

In educational research, the term, at-risk student, is relatively new, and has not warranted a separate ERIC listing despite the current spate of publications employing this descriptor.[4] In the ERIC *Thesaurus of Descriptors* (ERIC, 1987), the reader is referred from 'at risk students' to 'high risk students', a descriptor which has only been in use since 1980. However, 'related terms' under this heading, such as low achievement, underachievement, and disadvantaged, have been used since the ERIC data base was created in 1966. Therefore, the term, at-risk, appears to be simply a new label for phenomena which are as old as public schooling itself. What purposes are served by using this new label?

The Epidemiological Model

In most educational discourse, use of the term, at-risk, is indicative of what may be called the epidemiological model of school success and failure. In this model, education is analogous to medicine, and school failure or dropping out is analogous to disease. Epidemiology is the branch of medicine that 'is concerned with the patterns of disease occurrence in human populations and of the factors that influence these patterns' (Lilienfeld and Lilienfeld, 1980, p. 3). Risk factors in epidemiology are characteristics of persons — demographic, biological, socioeconomic, or behavioral — which are associated with a higher-than-expected probability of being afflicted with a disease or other dangerous condition.

Used alone, the term, at-risk, does not have much meaning in epidemiology. The linguistic rule for the use of at risk in this field is that the population-at-risk and the condition for which they are at risk should be specified.[5] Some educational researchers, especially those from medically-related fields such as clinical psychology or special education, have followed this rule in their usage. For instance, Walker and Emory (1983) refer to 'infants at risk for psychopathology'.

The purpose of medical-epidemiological research is to find ways of identifying categories of persons who are the most at risk for certain medical or quasi-medical conditions so that something can be done to prevent or ameliorate the conditions' occurrence. It is this identification-and-prevention/treatment sequence which the term at-risk seems to carry when used in non-medical areas of education, such as the study of school failure and dropping out.

Another principle of epidemiology is that risk is always *relative*. Everyone in a general population may be at-risk for a condition to one degree or another. What the would-be preventor of this condition seeks are the sub-populations who are at greatest risk, in comparison with others. Therefore, using the term, at-risk, alone leaves unanswered the questions: Who is at-risk? At-risk for what? and in comparison with whom? In educational research, the answer most often seems to be that certain identifiable students are at-risk for failure or dropping out in comparison with students who succeed or stay in school. But who exactly are the students most likely to drop out or fail in school? and how are they identified?

The 'risk factors' or predictors that are statistically most often associated with school failure or dropping out are student background characteristics such as minority status, poverty, and language difference. Schools are not in a position to prevent or alleviate the socioeconomic and cultural conditions that make such characteristics risky for persons in this society. Thus school people see their function as that of an intervening treatment.

Compensatory programs have been used as a form of preventive treatment for school failure. For example, the development of the federally-funded Head Start program[6] was based on the statistical association between poverty and school failure, theories about poor families that were developed to explain this association and educational interventions designed to compensate for the supposed home deficits.

However, epidemiologists admit that the identification of those at-risk for medical conditions based on social characteristics is an inexact enterprise, based on complex chains of inference.[7] Similarly, in the case of social phenomena such as school failure and dropping out, early identification and treatment of those at-risk based on social character-istics such as race, class or language are not only inexact, but highly controversial. Compensatory preschool programs have been widely criticized for these reasons, among others (Baratz and Baratz, 1982).

Therefore, many educational responses to at-risk students are being based on later identification of these children through school-related behaviors such as low grades, suspensions, absenteeism, etc. However, even then, the *ultimate* cause of such behaviors is still often attributed to background social characteristics. The student's problems are seen as manifestations or symptoms of those characteristics that the student brings to school.[8] Figure 1 illustrates this approach to the identification and treatment of at-riskness. Compensatory programs may identify students for treatment solely on the basis of background characteristics,

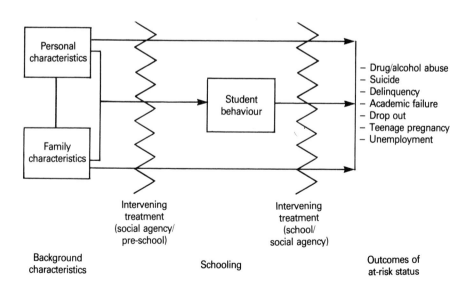

Figure 1: Epidemiological Model of At-Risk Status

whereas schools often treat students on the basis of inappropriate school behavior, thought to stem from background characteristics. The rationale for these treatments is that they are thought to break the seemingly natural relationship between at-risk characteristics and adverse outcomes.

The borrowing of epidemiological language from medicine to education may reflect a desire to infuse a sort of scientific or medical legitimacy into a very uncertain and politically-charged realm.[9] It also can serve as a justification for policy decisions such as expenditures of public funds. The use of the term at-risk conveys a sense of urgency suggesting that educators must quickly respond to the problems of students failing and dropping out. Unfortunately, the decision to employ an epidemiological model for the study of these problems limits educators' ways of thinking about these phenomena. Since the problem is believed to be inherent in the student, then the search for the cause is limited to the characteristics of the students themselves. Characteristics of our society and schools are left unexamined (Wehlage and Rutter, 1986).

Problems with the use of the epidemiological model in education are exacerbated by the current growing interest in at-risk students. The number of students being labelled as at-risk is dramatically on the rise (Brown, 1986). Both proactive early identification and reactive intervention programs have been proposed as solutions by educational policy makers.[10] Our review of the research and policy literature at the outset of the study revealed that the epidemiological model is the predominant way of thinking about and developing solutions to school failure.

Our initial concerns with this approach to the identification and treatment of students at-risk related to the effects of labelling. Since our focus was on elementary schools, we were particularly concerned with the effects of labelling children on the basis of background factors, such as socio-economic status (SES), minority or linguistically different status, and other characteristics over which children have no control. Therefore, rather than develop our own definition of the at-risk student, we decided to examine the identification process as practiced by teachers and other school personnel.

This initial focus on labelling and its effects, in addition to further reading and initial data analysis, led us toward a model of at-risk status that is profoundly different from the epidemiological approach. The alternative framework is helpful in several ways. First, it can better account for the beliefs and practices of educators, the interaction between students and school personnel, and the effects of different models of educational organization. It also helps to explain the discontinuities we found between the literature and what was happening in the schools, and in answering questions such as why some students, with similar predisposing characteristics as those who are failing, may succeed in school while others do not; and/or why a child could be at-risk at one point in time and not at another. It leads us to look at the nature of the context in which individual children were identified as at-risk, how that context affected both the at-risk status of a child and how the child was handled in school. This model, briefly described below, will be explicated more fully in the chapters that follow.

The Social Constructivist Model

The model that seemed to explain the concept of at-risk as practiced in schools better was the social constructivist model. It is an interactive view in which the perception of at-riskness is constructed within a particular social or cultural context. Nelkin (1985) described it this way: 'It is the social system, the world view, the ideological premises of a group or a society that shapes perceptions of risk' (p. 16). In the social constructivist model, the person considered at-risk, the reasons for this consideration, and the ways the school responds are viewed as being constructed in the context of the classroom. Figure 2 presents a graphic model of this concept.

The child brings to the classroom a certain number of characteristics that have been shaped by background and personal factors, and past experiences in school. This child interacts with a classroom context that includes other children, teacher(s) and materials. In addition, what happens in the classroom is shaped, in part, by school level factors that are often influenced by district level factors. The focus in this approach is not on the child alone, but on the interaction between the child and these nested contexts.

While this understanding of at-risk status has not permeated the popular and policy literature in the U.S.,[11] a growing body of studies of special student populations have been framed within it.[12] For example, Coles (1987) proposes an 'interactivity theory' to describe how learning disability (LD) is created:

The interactivity theory of LD proposes that while various features of an individual (including neurology), group and institutions, and social, economic and cultural forces each have their own characteristics, identify, activity, degree of influence and interde-

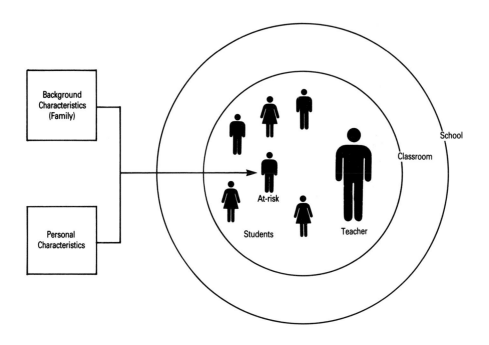

Figure 2: Interactive Model of At-Risk Status

pendencies, at the same time they all combine to create the processes and products of learning and disabled learning (p. 209).

Smith (1983) also looked at learning disabled students and Mehan, Hertwick and Meihls (1986) at special education students within the social constructivist framework. Page (1987) found that the model explained the differences in the organization of lower-track classes in two schools with quite similar student populations. And, in an attempt to develop a theory of student status as socially constructed, several case studies of 'problem students' were conducted by Erickson and his colleagues at Michigan State University.[13] While none of these studies used the term 'at-risk', they focused on students who could be identified as such. The Michigan State studies, by examining the child in relation to the social context of the specific school and classroom, indicated how each student's problem status was socially constructed within the classroom.

Our study focused on students identified as at-risk, but was not designed to 'test' the social constructivist model. However, the nature of the study's qualitative design allowed our thinking to move quickly in that direction as we considered our preliminary data and continued to review the literature. A brief description of the design follows. More information on the design will be provided in the individual chapters

The Study

The study described in this book focused intently on several students considered at-risk within the context of their specific classroom and school. We began by attempting to determine the meaning of at-risk status to the teachers and other school personnel. We studied the interaction between the context created around this meaning and the students who had been identified as at-risk. The students were the focus; their lives were examined in relationship to influences from the school and home environments.

Approach and Questions

Since the purpose of this study was to explore what happens to at-risk children in the context of a particular school, we chose a qualitative methodology and were guided in our enquiry primarily by Bogdan and Biklen (1982), Glaser and Strauss (1967) and Spradley (1979). We had no hypotheses to test, just a number of initial lenses through which we viewed schooling and at-risk children, and a set of guiding questions.

The assumptions that existed at the outset of the study were:

- The concept at-risk may be viewed as a combination of personal and background characteristics of a child and the social and academic context of the school. It is therefore necessary to look at the interaction between the school and the at-risk students as well as the child's background factors: socio-economic environment, ethnicity, language, family mobility, etc.
- The particular organization of the school and classroom, the norms of its teachers, the academic expectations held for its students and the academic tasks encountered by the students may affect the students' at-risk status.
- The labelling of children within a school setting as deprived, learning disabled, mentally retarded or at-risk could be more damaging to a child than the characteristics of the child that led to the designation.

Since our aim was to understand the nature, experiences and view-points of at-risk students in school, our guiding questions were as follows: (i) Who are the students designated as at-risk?; (ii) What is the organization of the schools and classrooms in which the students are operating?; (iii) What are the beliefs held by the teachers and other adults in the school setting about the term at-risk?; (iv) What happens to the at-risk students in their classrooms and schools?; (v) What perceptions do the at-risk students express about school?; and (vi) What do the parents of the at-risk students believe about their children and about school?

These questions were pursued with a research design that allowed for discovery within specific settings (Wilcox, 1982). The focus on individual students called for a case study technique (Yin, 1984), in which each child became a unique case. While we attempted to maintain commonality in data gathering protocols and techniques for all the cases and sites, it was often necessary to devise techniques for specific situations.[14] Since our twelve students were distributed in three classrooms, two schools and two school districts, it was possible to frame cases at these three levels as well as at the student level. Thus, our design could best be described as a nested case field study.

Sample and Data

In order to maximize our chances of discovering and describing school environments appropriate to the needs of at-risk students, we sought schools designated as effective by criteria used in the literature[15] and serving populations of students traditionally thought of as at-risk, such as minority and low SES students. On the basis of nominations, documentation and observation visits, two target schools, Plaza and Escalante, were selected. These two schools were similar on a number of dimensions and differed on others. They were both Chapter 1 schools;[16] one serving a largely Hispanic and one a mixed black, white and Hispanic population. One was located in a large city school district, Suroeste and the other, in a lower to lower-middle income suburban district, Raintree. Both had principals who were female and minority group members.

We asked the principals of the target schools to select two experienced grades 2 or 3 teachers who represented, in the principal's view, the philosophy and instructional approaches of the school. The four teachers thus selected were joined by a fifth when one of the teachers was appointed a team leader and her class was taken over in the afternoon by another teacher. Table 1 (Chapter 2) provides information on the five teachers and their classrooms.

The twelve target students were selected from a list of at-risk students generated by each teacher. Final decisions were made on the basis of the following criteria: consent of parents, inclusion of at least one female at-risk student in each class and inclusion of one 'marginal' at-risk student in each school. Marginal students were defined as students about whom the teachers were uncertain as to the degree of their at-riskness. The teachers were not informed of the final selection and, at least as indicated in the final interviews, did not discover who among the set they initially presented was being followed by the researchers. Chapter 2 provides further information on each of the children in the study, and Appendix 2 contains the complete case studies of the students.

The study relied on three forms of data collection: formal and informal interviews, observations, and documents. Figure 3 outlines the multiple data sources and the time during the school year the data was collected. Four researchers were involved in data collection procedures, two assigned to each school. All researchers had been teachers. One had also been a principal and all four were experienced in classroom observation techniques and ethnographic methods.

Teachers were formally interviewed two to three times during the study concerning their beliefs about at-riskness and their specific students identified as at-risk.[17] We also informally discussed aspects of the classroom and the students with the teachers. A feedback session was provided for the teachers to test the observations and inferences that emerged from the study (Sevigny, 1981). The principals were interviewed at the beginning and the end of the study. Interviews with other school staff were also conducted. All interviews were tape recorded and transcribed. One foster mother and one or both parents of all students were informally interviewed at the beginning of the study. At the conclusion, one or both parents of all but two students were formally interviewed.[18] Formal interviews of the students were conducted at the close of the study using a semi-structured interview schedule, and informal discussions and comments with students were recorded during the course of the study. The interviews in one school were then conducted around the reading of Spanish books in several cases and the drawing of pictures in others (Enright and Tammivaara, 1984). The interview protocols are included in Appendix 1.

Prior to the selection of the target students, the two observers spent time in each classroom, noting the organization of the day, grouping patterns, transition procedures, use of materials, the format of lessons

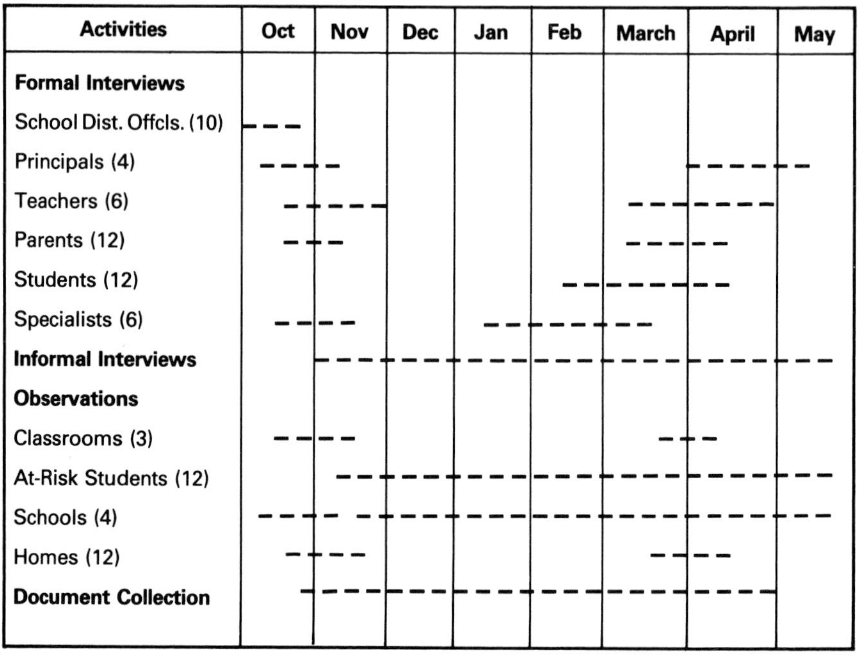

Activities	Oct	Nov	Dec	Jan	Feb	March	April	May
Formal Interviews								
School Dist. Offcls. (10)	— —							
Principals (4)	— —	—					— — —	—
Teachers (6)	— —	— —				— —	— — —	
Parents (12)	— —	—				— —	—	
Students (12)					— —	— — —	— —	
Specialists (6)	— —	—		— —	— —	— —		
Informal Interviews	— —	— —	— —	— —	— —	— —	— —	— —
Observations								
Classrooms (3)	— —	—				—	—	
At-Risk Students (12)		— —	— —	— —	— —	— —	— —	— —
Schools (4)	— —	— —	— —	— —	— —	— —	— —	— —
Homes (12)	—	— —				— —	— —	
Document Collection		— —	— —	— —	— —	— —	— —	— —

( ) Numbers of individuals or entities

Figure 3: Data Gathering Activities Timeline

and teacher/student interaction style. These observations focused on the classroom and the teacher. After the students were selected, the formal observations focused, in turn, on each of the at-risk students. The field notes recorded during the observations noted time, general classroom activity and what the target student was specifically doing during that activity. If the target student left the class to attend a special session with an LD teacher, the observer followed the student. Observations were also made in the students' homes and at other school functions such as the faculty and staff retreat in Escalante and the awards assemblies at Plaza.[19]

Analysis

Data analysis was guided by our goals for the project and by several approaches to qualitative data analysis. First, we were interested in developing, inductively, an understanding of what it means to be an early elementary at-risk student in a school context. We therefore relied on Glaser and Srauss' (1967) methods of constant comparative analysis and data collection. Data collection and analysis were carried on concurrently during the course of the study.

The initial analysis of the data consisted of a set of nested case studies. The largest unit was the school, each of which became a case with its specific organization, instructional programs and norms. These were derived from interviews with the principal, teachers and other specialists, observations at the school level and school documents related to school-wide aspects. Later, when it became evident that the district's influence was important, we added information on the school district as well.

Within the school setting, each teacher and her classroom was considered a case, and data were analyzed for that unit. Therefore, for example, each teacher's theory of at-risk was developed in two different ways: one by an analysis of answers to questions related to the concept of at-risk and one through their specific identification and descriptions of at-risk students in their classrooms.

The smallest units were case studies of individual at-risk students. These were developed by forming a triangulated picture of each child (Sevigny, 1981), in which the perspectives of the different participants were portrayed. The different perspectives included: the teacher's views and behaviors toward the student and the views of specialists, the parents, observers and the children themselves. All of these perspectives, of course, were filtered, as objectively as possible, through the researchers' own perspectives.

Organization of the Book

In the chapters that follow, we provide a brief description of the target students and how they were selected (Chapter 2). We then move into the analyses of the nested cases of schools (Chapter 3), and classrooms (Chapter 4) and the relationship between home and school (Chapter 5). Chapter 6 tackles the very timely issues of the identification and treatment of learning-disabled (LD) students and the heightening of a 'specialist' flavor in schools. Related to the LD problem is the concern that a higher proportion of LD students in our's and other studies conducted in the US were also children who spoke languages other than English, usually labelled Limited English Proficient (LEP).[20] Chapter 7 provides a summary of our theoretical understandings of the social construction of at-risk status as this construction operates within broader social constraints that create a set of enduring dilemmas for school people. Also in Chapter 7 is our response to the question: What is an at-risk student? The last chapter (Chapter 8) summarizes our conclusions and proposes a set of principles to be considered in reforming elementary schools to meet the needs of at-risk students.

Notes

1 The names of all children, adults, schools and school districts have been changed to protect their identities.

2 We will follow Coles' (1987) lead in this book and refrain from placing quotation marks around the term, at-risk, even though we sometimes question its validity. This should not be construed, as Coles also suggested for his treatise in learning disabilities, as 'approval of either the use or the meaning of the terms'(p. xviii).

3 *Education Week* is a weekly newspaper for educators and educationists, published in Washington, DC, that describes recent policies, discusses national trends and summarizes important issues in education.

4 *Educational Resources Information Center* is a nationwide information network, funded by the US Department of Education, to acquire, abstract, index, store, retrieve and disseminate education-related reports.

5 The psychiatric literature, for example, has used the term at-risk for some time. Again, the reason why the child is considered to be at-risk is always specified. See, for example, Garmezy (1974); and Werner, Bierman & French (1971).

6 The Head Start program is a federally-funded pre-school program designed to prepare poor and disadvantaged students for regular elementary schools. It combines medical, nutrition, academic and social approaches to preparation.

7 See, for example, Lilienfeld and Lilienfeld (1980) and Stacy (1981).

8 Examples of research that has attempted to link predisposing factors with later behavior such as low achievement, dropping out or truancy are reported in: Broman, Bien and Shaughnessy (1985); Hoffman (1979); Spivak, Marcuso and Swift (1986); and Vellutina, Steger, Moyer, Harding and Niles (1977).

9 See Carrier (1986).

10 For instance, one Arizona school district has developed a list of eight characteristics, including both background predispositions and behavioral

indicators, to identify at-risk students. Their policy states: 'existence of three or more of these factors designates a student as being at-risk for dropping out of school'. Monthly lists are generated to inform the school staff of all newly-identified at-risk students. In line with the epidemiological model, these students then become the target of school intervention programs (Phoenix High School District, no date).

11 In fact, the policy literature discourse is increasingly dominated by the epidemiological model, in part, because federal US policies require that specific and easily identifiable populations of students be the target of additional discretionary federal funds. Thus, SES, minority status and other background characteristics are discussed as identifying characteristics of at-risk students.

12 The tradition seems more established in Britain. See, for example, Birksted (1976), Ball (1981) and Davies (1983).

13 Erickson (1985); Boersema (1985); Lazarus (1985); and Pelissier (1985).

14 For example, in interviewing the Hispanic students at one school, the researcher used Spanish comic books to motivate several of the students to talk about reading.

15 For example, Cohen (1987); Corcoran (1985); and Purkey and Smith (1983).

16 Chapter 1 of the Education Consolidation and Improvement Act became a federal US law in 1981 and provides funds to states and school districts for poor and low-achieving students.

17 Interviews were conducted during lunch, or before or after school. On several occasions the interviews were completed at another time.

18 The parents of one of the students had moved twice during the study and could not be located after the second move. In the case of the second student, it was felt that the foster mother would not have the information needed and the natural mother could not be located.

19 In Plaza, the large classroom was observed for forty-two hours; in Escalante, one classroom was observed for twenty hours, one for nineteen hours.

20 We call these children Limited English Proficient (LEP) students in this book only because this is the 'official' term used in education in the U.S. However, we consider this term demeaning and prefer the term Speaker of Other Languages (SOL).

Chapter 2

The Students And How They Were Identified

Since we were interested in studying the interactive nature of the identification and treatment of at-risk students, we did not rely on our own criteria for identifying at-risk students. Instead, at the beginning of the study, we asked our sample of teachers to define the phrase 'at-risk students', and identify and describe the students in their classes who could be considered at-risk. (The interview protocol may be found in Appendix 1.) We interviewed the teachers again at the end of the study to determine whether the identified students were still perceived to be at-risk.

We were concerned with the labelling of students and whether such labelling established certain expectancies in teachers' minds that would affect the ways they dealt with the students.[1] Who were the students identified as at-risk by the teachers? Did they remain at-risk in the teachers' minds until the end of the year? Further, if one teacher identified a student as at-risk, would another teacher agree? Or, as Erickson (1985) suggested, is the notion of at-risk dependent upon the nature of the classroom context and the teachers' goals and instructional expectations? By determining the teachers' beliefs about at-riskness as well as observing the teachers and students in their classrooms and interviewing other school people and the students' parents, we were able to capture the process of the social construction of at-risk status.

In this chapter, we will describe the teachers and their ways of looking at the concept of at-risk students, describe the students they identified as at-risk and those we selected for study, and report our analysis of the degree to which students' at-risk status changed in the teachers' minds during the course of the study.

The Teachers

The two teachers selected as participants in our study by Ms. McGuffey, the Principal of Plaza Elementary School, team-taught in a large classroom of fifty-four second and third grade students. Ms. Jones had been teaching for twenty-nine years, and Ms. Green for thirteen. The Principal of Escalante Elementary School, Ms. Bolivar, selected two classrooms, one grade 2, the other grade 3. The third grade teacher, Ms. Santana, who had been teaching for three years, was the least experienced of our sample of teachers. The second grade teacher, Ms. Osgood, who became a team leader, had fourteen years of experience and Ms. Wilson, her afternoon replacement, had taught for seven years. The two teachers in Plaza were Anglo, and the three in Escalante were Hispanic. Table 1 provides information on the teachers and their classrooms.

Table 1 Sample teachers

School	Teacher number	Pseudonym	Sex	Minority status (Yes/No)	Grade-level teaching	Years experience	No. of at-risk students initially identified	Size of class
Plaza	1★	Jones	F	N	2–3	29	10	–
Plaza	2★	Green	F	N	2–3	13	10	54
Escalante	3	Santana	F	Y	3	3	7	21
Escalante	4★★	Osgood	F	Y	2	14	7	–
Escalante	5★★	Wilson	F	Y	2	7	6	23

★ These teachers team taught in same classroom
★★ Teacher 4 taught the class in the morning, teacher 5 in the afternoon

Their Beliefs About At-Riskness

The teachers' responses to the interview questions concerning the definition of at-risk reflected the general confusion about the term in everyday use today. Two were uncomfortable with the term because of its negative connotation. Ms. Green stated that she did not use the term because 'some parents are put off by it'. Another suggested that it should also have a positive connotation — 'there could be a positive at-risk, for example, of becoming a popular political candidate' (Ms. Santana). Some of the definitions were tied to outcomes ('at-risk for what?') and others to non-productive behaviors. For all but one of the teachers, the definition remained stable over the year.

What became clear in the analysis of the interviews was that the term, at-risk, is used in a similar way to the terms 'problem' students,[2] or underachieving or disadvantaged: in other words, for students who are noticed by teachers as not adapting. As Ms. Jones stated: 'Over the years so many terms have been used. Soon at-risk may be out because there are problems with law suits. I think the term replaced learning disability. First it was special ed, then gifted, then deprived, then high and low end of the scale, etc'.

There was a difference in teacher response by school. The teachers in Escalante thought about at-risk in terms of long-term problems. Ms. Santana stated: 'It's a matter of will they be at-risk when they grow up? Will they be able to function in society? Am I helping them? Can anyone help them?' Ms. Wilson stated: 'We are thinking of what's going to happen to these people as adults. With so many people homeless and unemployed, we ask "where did this all begin?" '. This approach to at-risk may have been related to the five-year goal setting exercise the school had just completed. In Plaza School, at-risk definitions were tied to school behavior. For Ms. Green, it was primarily academic problems or a history of failure that defined an at-risk student; however by the end of the year, she had changed her definition to include 'any kind of problem: academically low, low self concept, emotional problems that they bring into the class — that I haven't caused'. Ms. Jones suggested that there are two ways a child can be at-risk: 'one can be academic, and one socially or emotionally. A lot of times they are related in a child'. The manifestation of the latter, according to Ms. Jones would be behavioral: aggressive behavior towards other children.

For all teachers, the learning-disabled (LD) students in their classrooms would be considered either at-risk or, for two of the teachers, perhaps 'marginally at-risk'.[3] Nonetheless, by the end of the year, several LD students were considered not at-risk by the teachers.

All but one of the teachers felt that the cause of at-riskness in children was related, in large part, to the home situation. Family problems, divorce, parents who don't care, and high mobility were all mentioned by the teachers. Another attributed at-risk status to the lack of school-beneficial experiences that left the children behind when they entered school. One suggested that all students in foster homes were at-risk and another that all LD students were in bad family situations. Two suggested that school could cause a child to be at-risk: one explicitly mentioned basal readers and pushing children too hard, and another believed that she, as their teacher, could be a cause of their at-riskness.

In general though, the major problem in the teachers' minds was the home rather than the school or the child.

The Identification of At-Risk Students

When teachers were asked to identify their at-risk students at the beginning of the study, they each automatically selected those who had been identified as learning-disabled, as well as several others.

In the large classroom at Plaza, both Ms. Green and Ms. Jones identified ten students, although they agreed on only seven (see table 3). In the team-taught classroom at Escalante, Ms. Osgood named six of their twenty-three as at-risk, and Ms. Wilson named seven, agreeing on four students as at-risk. Ms. Santana named eight of her twenty students as at-risk. Thus, in the Plaza classroom, each teacher named 18 per cent and in Escalante it was closer to 35 per cent. The higher percentage of at-risk students named in Escalante may be related to the emphasis in that school on diagnosis of individual problems and referral of students to a large number of available experts. The differences between the two schools will be further discussed in Chapter 3.

All teachers identified more boys as at-risk than girls. In Plaza School, fourteen of all the students mentioned were boys and seven were girls. In Escalante fifteen boys and seven girls were identified. When asked about this finding, two of the teachers stated that it was a random event: 'something that just happened this year'. The two Plaza teachers had quite elaborate theories about how first-born sons develop problems because of parental and societal expectations. Ms. Osgood had an elaborate cultural theory about what goes on in Hispanic homes: Mothers do too much for their sons, and the sons are not expected to talk as much as daughters. This, she felt, places girls at an advantage when they enter school.

The Students

Table 2 presents demographic information on the at-risk students selected for the study. In the Plaza classroom, three of the six were minority students, proportional to the percentage of minority youngsters in Plaza. All of the at-risk students at Escalante were Hispanic, again proportional to the 90 per cent Hispanic population at Escalante. Nine out of twelve of the students had been designated as learning disabled, emotionally handicapped, or limited English proficient.

Table 2: Demographic Information on Students

Student	Date of Birth	Sex	Race Ethnicity	Position in Family	Number of Schools Attended	Number of Years at present school	Retention Record	Special designation	Grade Assignment
Plaza School									
Ann	11/77	F	Anglo	1st of 4	At least 3	New this year	No	–	3
Andy	3/78	M	Black	1st of 2	3	2½	No	LD	3
Brad	10/77	M	Anglo	3rd of 4	1	4	No	LD	3
Gary	10/77	M	Anglo	Only child	1	4	No	LD	3
Jerry	9/77	M	Vietnamese/Anglo	2rd of 3	At least 4	New this year	?	–	3
Travis	4/77	M	Black	1st of 2	2	New this year	2nd grade	LD	3
Escalante School									
Victor	3/79	M	Hispanic	1st of 3	1	4	No	LEP/LD	2
Mateo	8/79	M	Hispanic	1st of 2	2	2	No	LEP	2
Jose	4/77	M	Hispanic	4th of 4	4	1½	Yes	EMH/LEP	3
Carmin	9/77	F	Hispanic	1st of 2	4	1¼	Yes	LD	3
Gilberto	12/77	M	Hispanic	4th of 7	4	2½	No	LD/LEP	3
Lina	8/79	F	Hispanic	2nd of 4	3	1½	No	–	2

However, all but two of the Plaza students and one of the Escalante students were from low income situations.

An introduction to the at-risk students observed for this study is provided in the following short sketches. More information on these students will be found throughout the book, and complete case studies are located in Appendix 2.

Lina, Mateo and **Victor** were second grade students in a classroom shared by Ms. Osgood and Ms. Wilson. **Gilberto, Juan** and **Carmín** were third grade students in Ms. Santana's classroom. **Andy, Ann, Brad, Gary, Jerry** and **Travis** were third-graders in Ms. Jones' and Ms. Green's classroom in Plaza School.

Andy was a tall, quiet black boy in third grade at Plaza School. He had liked school since kindergarten and rarely missed a day, although his records indicated that it had not been a very successful academic experience for him. By third grade, both his teachers were concerned with his progress and considered him at-risk for academic reasons. They attributed his lack of success in school to his home environment. In discussing Andy, one teacher said: 'Very much below level, goes to LD, but a real interesting kid. He's the one who never gets out of bed at night because his mother tells him that there are snakes on the floor.' The counselor was also concerned with his home life and in discussing the snake story said, 'Kids always have an imagination' but 'some things that stem from the home [Andy's] that are almost cult, in thinking'.

Andy lived in a single-parent home with his younger sister, his aunt and her children and his uncle. His mother worked long hours at a convenience store to support the family. She said: 'It's kind of hard for Andy — cause he doesn't have a father or a father figure'. She indicated that she was doing as much as she could when she said, '. . . course my kids have probably had some little problems in school, but as far as keeping a roof over their heads and feeding them, I think I've done pretty well'. She did wish that she could do more for him but she was always working and had no transportation.

Since Andy's mother did not attend conferences or meet with the teachers, they took this to mean that she was not interested. They did not know about her transportation problem. This was one of several misunderstandings that appeared to exist between the school and the home and contributed to Andy's problems.

Andy was not succeeding academically, and it appeared that the school accepted this as fact. The teachers emphasized the development of his self-concept and social skills, although there were indications that he had the potential for progressing were he to receive appropriate instruction. As an example, the aide reported that after hearing a story read, Andy could 'just stand up and literally tell you the whole story — every little detail'. Apparently Andy had a good auditory memory but in his LD program the teacher was working on 'his visual processing'.

At the end of the school year, he was still below grade level in reading and math and considered at-risk for academic reasons by both teachers. Ms. Jones said, 'I love Andy. I don't think he's ever gonna be great in school work.' Ms. Green said that he 'probably will be [at-risk] for a long time'.

Ann was a sandy haired, chubby, 9-year-old Anglo girl in the third grade. She often came to school with her hair uncombed and in clothes that never quite seemed to match, looking as if she had gotten herself ready with no adult help. She appeared to be the perfect student and worked at portraying this image. When the study began, Ann had been in Plaza School for two months. She entered with school records that began with second grade and showed that she had perfect attendance and did well academically.

Initially, Ann was considered marginally at-risk for social reasons by one of her teachers, Ms. Jones. She was concerned about Ann being a loner, her lack of friends and a 'few strange things' that she did as a third-grader. Her other teacher, Ms. Green, saw her only as a good student and did not consider her at-risk.

According to Ann and her teachers, she had been molested by her father when she was in kindergarten. She was taken out of the home, sent to her grandmother's, returned to the mother and then placed in a foster home. The environment in the foster home did not appear to be supportive. In an initial interview, the foster mother shared only negative comments about Ann. Near the end of the school year, the school contacted the Child Protection Services[4] about the treatment Ann was receiving there. She was eventually removed from the home.

Ann apparently found school to be a haven. She needed the support that it offered to good students. And she worked to be one. Past experiences, however, and her present home environment continued to contribute to her poor self-image. By the end of the school year, both of her teachers were very concerned about her socially and emotionally and considered her to be at-risk for these reasons.

Ann is representative of students who cause teachers concern but to whom little help can be provided. She did well academically but was unstable in her social and emotional well-being, both of which had been, and were being, influenced by factors outside the classroom. She seemed to blame herself for the bad things that had happened to her and had suppressed any hostility she felt toward others. She may have needed intense counseling which is not generally offered in schools.

Brad, a third grader, had been in Plaza school since kindergarten and his teachers knew him well. He had been with Ms. Green since first grade and Ms. Jones since second. Due to problems in the home and problems he was having in school, they had often worked with both him and his mother. Ms. Green now felt that Brad was doing better academically and emotionally but, because of his poor self-concept and problems she thought he continued to have in the home, she considered him marginally at-risk. Ms. Jones had also seen improvement but considered him at-risk for social and emotional reasons because of his difficult home situation.

Brad's school records showed an irregular pattern and some discontinuities. In kindergarten, his teacher gave no indication that he was having problems. In first grade this pattern reversed. He was referred to speech and language in the fall and five months later he was referred to special education for testing. He had repeated absences. In second grade he was released by the speech pathologist but was placed in the LD program. The school counselor worked with him and his sisters. During that year, his report card grades began to show improvement as did his attendance.

Brad had mixed feelings about school, his ability, his teachers' perceptions of him and life in general. In an interview, he said he didn't like school and then said, 'I feel great about school but I don't know how school feels about me'. He said that his teachers didn't think he was smart; later he said that they liked his work. It was learned that he carried this ambivalence into his classroom work. He said he didn't like Silent Sustained Reading (SSR), but he always participated. He didn't like being quiet but he seldom talked in the classroom.

The school staff saw most of Brad's problems as being caused by the home. The mother felt that the home had contributed but that he also 'has a visual/memory problem that needed working on'. Regardless of the original causes, the home and school had worked closely together on Brad's behalf. Brad was able to change his behavior and become more successful. All those involved, including Brad, were aware of his improvement. He said, 'I didn't know how to read . . . now I do'. In the classroom his work was now satisfactory.

Interestingly, even with the progress Brad had made neither he nor his teachers could 'let go' of his past. Even though Brad reluctantly went to the LD class, Ms. Green was not recommending that he be taken out of the LD program. She said, 'Let's see how he's doing in fourth grade . . . it's very difficult to have them removed and then have them put back in.' There were still labels that could not be discarded even though they no longer seemed appropriate.

Nine-year-old **Carmín** was much smaller than her classmates in Ms. Santana's class, but seemed healthy and energetic. She expressed every feeling openly. In whole group lessons, she participated with enthusiasm, and seemed very pleased when she knew an answer. When she made a mistake, however, she appeared anxious, or even cried. Her whole body became tense when she was faced with difficult tasks.

Carmín liked being in charge of classroom duties, and always complied with classroom routines; in some ways she was a 'model student'. But she had to depend on teacher assistance to complete most of her 'independent' work. She told our interviewer that she needed help to read words, and was unable to recall the major elements of a story the interviewer read to her. Her favourite and most successful activity was handwriting, which entailed only copying.

Ms. Santana considered Carmín to be 'at-risk' because she confused English and Spanish, had difficulties with reading, spelling and math, and had limited attention and memory. There was also talk at school about Carmín's home life, that she was a 'relative foster child' living with her aunt. Things 'did not come easily' for Carmín, and she was becoming 'very frustrated' with school. Ms. Santana wondered why. To get some answers, she had decided to refer Carmín for a child study.

The child study team concluded, after assessments by the psychologist and a visit with her aunt, that Carmín was learning disabled. Her mother was contacted for permission to place her in special education. Carmín began receiving LD services in Spanish, with a small group (including Victor) three days a week. The LD teacher said that Carmín's disability had not been recognized sooner because everyone assumed she had a 'language of instruction' problem. Records showed that she had been instructed in English in pre-school, kindergarten and first grade, though her home language was Spanish. After an unsuccessful first grade year, in lieu of retention she had been placed in a bilingual second-grade classroom. But her problems persisted.

Carmín's mother reported that she had been a healthy, sociable baby who walked and talked early. She was very worried about Carmín, because she could not understand the contrast between her daughter's cleverness at home and her failure at school. She had intervened when the first grade teacher recommended retention. She had transferred Carmín to Escalante when this happened again at the end of second grade. Carmín's mother worked full-time and relied on her sister for after school childcare for Carmín and her sister. She made sure that Carmín did her homework and was more than willing to help at home.

In summary, the themes in Carmín's story were determining the language of instruction for bilingual students, the relationship between bilingualism and learning disabilities, and the difference between parent and school perceptions of a child's abilities. In addition, Carmín raised concerns about the emotional effects of the stresses of repeated failure.

Gary was an Anglo boy of average height and size. He had blonde hair, wore glasses and dressed in casual, conservative clothes. When observed in his Plaza classroom, he usually seemed on task, completing his work in minimal time, and producing a quality product. His grades in all academic areas were above average as were his achievement test scores. He was included in the study since he represented not only what teachers considered a marginal at-risk student but one with experiences that appeared to be quite different from the other students. He came from an upper-middle class family and both his parents were professional people. He was an only child and received an unusual amount of support and concern from them. They were often at school, especially his mother.

Gary's parents had been concerned with what they labelled 'perceptual problems' since he was in pre-school. They had him in special training with a local doctor. Based on the doctor's recommendation he had been placed in the LD program. The mother worked closely with Ms. Green concerning this problem and she was the teacher who considered him marginally at-risk because of the difficulty she saw him having with his writing/penmanship. His other teacher, Ms. Jones, who had been his teacher since first grade did not appear to share these concerns and did not consider him to be even marginally at-risk.

Gary liked school and thought the teachers, Principal and students were nice. He appeared to have an understanding of his problem. He said, 'I love writing'. When asked about his problems in writing, he replied, 'I had trouble with handwriting. Writing is something that you feel and handwriting is something that you do with your hand.'

Gary's school performance was so different from the other students in the study that it was difficult for his teachers to view his perceptual problem as serious. At the end of the study Ms. Green had come to the conclusion that his perceptual problems were not serious enough to identify him as an at-risk student, although she expected that he would remain on the LD roles.

Gilberto was a gregarious boy who celebrated his ninth birthday in December of our study year. Ms. Osgood and Ms. Wilson said that though Gilberto 'tried very hard' and was a 'sweetheart', he had been diagnosed as suffering from 'dyspraxia', a language disorder which limited his achievement. In addition, he was classified as learning disabled and limited English proficient. As a consequence, his school schedule was very complex; 'pull-out' programs had him travelling from classroom to classroom. He was beginning to comment on the repetition across his lessons, and at the day's end complained of being tired. When he attempted 'regular' classwork, it was clear that he did have academic difficulties and was dependent on teacher assistance. But despite all these challenges, Ms. Santana felt that he had a 'noble personality' and was at least making progress. Gilberto took his complicated school life in his stride and was a favourite of his teachers.

In addition to concerns about Gilberto's academic problems, his teachers also had concern about his home life. Their perception was that his large family had 'more than one father', and there were signs of possible neglect. Gilberto did come from the largest family in our study. He was a middle child, fourth out of seven. The family lived in a very small, crowded house, and obviously had few financial resources. His mother told us that Gilberto and his three older siblings were children of a young marriage which ended in divorce. Her ex-husband denied that he was Gilberto's father, and paid him little attention. There was tension between the father of the three younger children and the older children. The mother said she felt 'caught in the middle'.

Gilberto had been a healthy child, though his mother described him as difficult to handle. At home, he seemed very clever and so friendly that she worried about him taking up with strangers. He had an unsettled early life, moving often and attending several schools. At times they had been hungry. But through it all Gilberto's mother had tried to support his education. The previous year the teacher had given her work to do with him at home. This year she had limited contact from the school; she thought that his teacher might be 'too easy on him'.

Therefore, Gilberto was viewed as something of a success story at school. Despite the challenges in his life, he seemed very resilient. His teachers were concerned about his slow academic progress and his family, which they viewed as a liability rather than a potential resource. But they were delighted with his social adaptation to school.

Jerry was a tall boy, larger than most of the other students in his Plaza classroom. His appearance made him noticeable in the classroom. The teachers and classroom aide used the term 'unusual' when they described him. He often sat staring off into space and his eyes, which reflected his mother's Asian heritage, appeared sad. His clothes were too small and often unclean. He rarely smiled. He and his two sisters were new to Plaza School in the fall. Although he appeared passive, after one month in school, Jerry had already been in fights protecting his sisters from students who 'picked on them'.

Ms. Green and Ms. Jones were very concerned about him as were other school staff. Both teachers considered him at-risk for social and academic reasons because he was functioning below grade level and had a poor self-concept. School records had never been received from the school that his father said his children had last attended. The teachers, therefore, had no information about his previous educational experience. There was also little they could find out about his home life. His father did not volunteer much information when he enrolled the children at the school and he did not come to school conferences. The mother sometimes came, but she knew little English and the teachers were unable to communicate with her in her own language.

The teachers, together with the counselor and school nurse, worked intensely with Jerry to help him develop his social skills. By mid-year he seemed to be making progress. Then he began showing up at school with bruises which he blamed on bicycle accidents. He started missing school and was quiet and withdrawn when he was at school. One day he appeared with extensive bruises and two black eyes. The teachers reported it to the school nurse, who, after she had examined Jerry, called the Child Protective Services. The CPS tried to contact the parents. Possibly as a result of this, the family suddenly moved and placed the children in another school in the district. Shortly afterwards, they were withdrawn from that school leaving no forwarding address.

Much about Jerry reflected a culture different from that of most of the students in the classroom. He was different socially and academically. He was only 9 but he looked as if he had already lived a lifetime and had the weight of the world on his shoulders. His spelling skills were at the beginning level as were his reading skills. Although he had difficulty expressing himself verbally, he was able to express himself in writing, but lagged behind in most academic areas. Jerry represents a dilemma for schools. While the school people felt that they could make a difference in Jerry's life and set out to do so, they had no control over what happened to Jerry outside school. The school's response to suspecting child abuse, calling the CPS, could have been the cause of Jerry's family moving once again. Jerry was, indeed, at-risk through no fault of the school's.

Juan, who became 10 in April, was the oldest of the Escalante students. Like Gilberto, he had a complicated schedule of pull-out classes, and he too seemed tired by the end of the school day. In the regular classroom, he became almost completely stalled on reading and writing tasks without teacher assistance. His speech was somewhat hard to understand. Pale and thin, he appeared very sombre and distant, except when his imagination was engaged — then he lit up with ideas. Juan participated more freely in his small pull-out classes, especially his individual sessions with his language therapist.

Ms. Santana referred Juan to us as an LD student who was 'mainly monolingual' in Spanish and had a severe speech handicap as a result of a head injury. She wondered if Juan were going to 'keep striving' in school in the face of his difficulties. All of his work was below average, and he seemed unwilling to risk doing anything challenging. Sometimes he grew impatient with himself and others. Though the other children did not 'mock' him, he had few friends.

The language therapist found Juan 'delightful' and creative. But the LD teacher thought he had 'poor work habits', lied to avoid things, and insulted other students. The ESL teachers named him as one of their top contenders for 'at-risk', and seemed to have very limited expectations for him. Perhaps because his difficulties could be traced to a physical injury, Ms. Santana did not bring up Juan's home life as an issue. She found his mother cooperative. However, the language therapist had heard that his injury might have been the result of abuse. The LD teacher thought that he watched 'horrendous' movies at home, which gave him a preoccupation with death and violence.

In our visit with Juan's mother, she told us that his head injury resulted from a fall when he was 1-year-old. The doctor told her that his 'voice box' was damaged. Since then, he had attended Head Start and several schools. Each new school adjustment was emotionally hard for him; he cried and fought when other children teased him. According to his records, in each school the teachers recognized his learning problems immediately and referred him for special services.

At home, his mother said, Juan was somewhat difficult. His favorite activity was watching TV, especially horror movies. He generally refused to do anything to help around the house, because he was a 'man'. He liked being with his uncle and older cousin, rather than doing childish things. But she was not too concerned about him, since he seemed fortunate to be leading a fairly 'normal life' in spite of his injury.

The questions recurrent in Juan's case, then, were how to set levels of expectation for a student with a physical handicap, how to assess whether he was being challenged or avoiding risks, and how to keep him interested in school in the face of his very slow progress and interests in more 'grown-up' pursuits.

Seven-year-old **Lina** seemed quiet, isolated, unexpressive and often tired in her Escalante classroom. Seatwork tasks dragged on and on for her. She appeared preoccupied; for example, she examined little things on her desk, slowly added extra curlicues to her writing, or watched other children. But at other times she was active, excited and talkative. She especially liked socializing with other girls, though some girls seemed unwilling to interact with her. Boys seemed to like to tease her, and she in turn sniped back at them.

Ms. Osgood referred Lina to us as a child who was being ostracized. She thought that Lina provoked this rejection by being mean to others. She also cited some 'LD-type' problems in Lina's writing and a lack of work completion. Her team teacher, Ms. Wilson, agreed with this assessment. Ms. Osgood attributed Lina's social difficulties to her family; Lina had a brother who was also 'picked on' at school. She attributed Lina's academic difficulties to her first grade experiences as a Spanish-speaking student in an English-only classroom, a 'full year of failure'. Both teachers had talked with Lina about her problems and had contacted her parents.

Lina was the second of four children in what appeared to be a very close-knit, stable family. Her mother described her as irresponsible, messy, spoiled by her father and easily distracted. She blamed Lina herself for some of her school problems, but was also ready to intervene on her daughter's behalf if necessary. For example, there had been confusion over Lina's language of instruction in first grade. Her mother said she requested Spanish instruction, but school personnel thought she requested English, and Lina was placed in English. When Lina's teacher proposed to retain her because of her slow progress, her mother protested. Records show that Lina's language proficiency was reassessed, and she was found to be Spanish-dominant. The Principal decided to give her a chance in a bilingual second-grade classroom.

Therefore, this was a catch-up year for Lina. Ms. Osgood hoped that she would pull out of her slump and succeed, with the benefits of Spanish instruction and the cooperation of her parents. Ms. Wilson was less hopeful; she thought Lina would need two years to recoup her losses, and that she had fairly low potential.

Mateo, like Lina, was one of the younger students in his class; both had turned 7 in August. He was very low-key, somewhat unresponsive to his teachers, and rarely participated in class. When Ms. Wilson or Ms. Osgood talked for extended periods, or during independent seatwork, Mateo yawned and his gaze wandered. Quite often his gaze came to rest on other boys who were also not engaged, who were doing something fun. During seatwork Mateo would also initiate games or try to distract his classmates. It was clear that Mateo could succeed; when he did perform, he did well. He simply seemed uninterested in schoolwork.

Ms. Osgood considered Mateo to be only 'marginally at-risk'. He really had no academic difficulties; in fact, he was 'bright'. His problem was work completion — she said there was a 'three week lag' on his assignments. Ms. Osgood had a hunch it was because his mother did too much for him at home. She and the mother had been communicating through a journal that Mateo carried between home and school.

Ms. Osgood had also been concerned about Mateo's social isolation, but observed that lately he had been interacting, in a 'rumbling' way, with other boys. She and Ms. Wilson disagreed about the seriousness of Mateo's misbehavior. Ms. Osgood thought it was an acceptable trade-off for his former isolation; Ms. Wilson thought he was avoiding responsibility for his behavior, and that this could lead to serious problems in the future.

Mateo's home life appeared to be pleasant and unexceptional. He was the oldest of two boys. It had been a difficult birth and his mother seemed to have been concerned about him from an early age. She said that when he was a toddler she worried about his slow speech development. She had enrolled him in Head Start because she wanted him to learn to get along with others. She thought the program had also helped her to learn how to correct him without losing her temper.

School records showed a few concerns on the part of Mateo's kindergarten teacher, but Mateo had done extremely well in the first grade. This year his achievement had dropped, and his mother blamed his attitude toward school. She knew he was intelligent enough to do well, but thought that he 'played around' instead of doing his work.

In summary, Mateo was considered an 'underachiever'. He had no learning disabilities, had suffered no disruptions of his school career, and his home life appeared to be stable. Most of the teachers' efforts were being directed toward finding ways to motivate him to complete his work.

Travis was a 10-year-old, black boy in the third grade at Plaza School. He was tall, well-coordinated with handsome features. He was accepted socially, had many friends and appeared confident. Travis was new to Plaza School. He had come from another school in the same district where he had repeated the second grade. Comments made on his records from that school included: 'will not do any of his work' and 'will not participate in classroom activities'. Since coming to Plaza, Ms. Green had seen him 'shy away from an activity' but found that he would complete the task if given encouragement. The LD teacher was not as successful with him and had difficulty getting him to participate in her classroom.

Ms. Green considered him marginally at-risk at the beginning of the study for academic and attitudinal reasons based on his school records and the above incidents. She thought his work was 'below grade level but not tremendously below'. Ms. Jones did not mention him in her initial interview.

Travis was a student who did not appear to enjoy school and this perception was substantiated through his interview. He said that he didn't like school, couldn't think of anything that would make him like it and found it boring. It appeared that not many of the activities in the classroom motivated him. During most lessons he appeared bored and rarely was an active participant. He had difficulty completing tasks and responded to them with minimal involvement. This lack of participation was usually ignored by his teachers because he seldom acted out or caused discipline problems. He had no difficulty with reading but had problems in math, primarily, it appeared, because he had not learned his multiplication tables. The classroom aide said, 'Travis, he's really bright. He can read. He understands but there are times that — I don't know if he's a perfectionist or not — but he's slow getting his work done.'

At the end of the study, Ms. Jones still did not feel that Travis was at-risk: 'Travis is doing very well. I wouldn't consider him at-risk now.' But Ms. Green said that his work was 'probably low average, at best' and she thought that 'he had a poor self concept because he had been a retained child'. She added that 'he'll probably be at-risk forever because no matter what I say, his self-concept still comes through as very low . . .'. Ms. Green had not contacted the home about these concerns and his mother thought he was doing fine.

Victor, who had his eighth birthday in March, was one of the boys whose antics Mateo liked to watch and one of the boys who teased Lina. He was very articulate, quick and socially adept though sometimes aggressive. Most of his abilities seemed to be directed toward other-than-academic activities. It was apparent that he had great difficulty with reading and writing, and went out of his way to avoid school work. However, the LD lessons designed to remediate his deficits also seemed well below his level of comprehension. He expressed more interest in rewards for work completion than the intrinsic aspects of his school activities.

Ms. Osgood described Victor as a bilingual LD student performing below his grade level. She also had grave concerns about his home life; since his mother, in her view, was irresponsible and abusive. According to his teacher, the boy was expected to take care of his younger brother and sister, and to get himself up and ready for school. Worse than this, he had taken 'quite a few blows to the head'. The previous year, his teacher had reported her suspicions of child abuse to the Child Protective Services. Stories about his home life which he shared in class were upsetting, she said. Ms. Osgood communicated regularly with Victor's mother, but really doubted the sincerity of her concern.

Academically, Victor had reached a 'plateau'. At times he was also disruptive in class. Ms. Wilson was most concerned about this misbehavior, which she attributed both to his home life and to his frustration with not making academic progress.

Victor did tell scary stories about his home life, but he also spoke positively about his mother. The mother told us that Victor had been born in Mexico when she was only 15 and had no idea of the responsibilities of motherhood. Her parents had taken care of him, but both had died when he was only 2-years-old. Since then she had married, had two more children, divorced and moved to Suroeste to live with her older sister. She described Victor as very helpful around the house, though sometimes too bossy with his younger siblings. She knew that he had had school problems in first grade, and had noticed that when he 'read' he actually 'made up' stories. In her view he needed to stop being so feisty. But this year she thought he must be doing better, since he brought home so many prizes from school.

Victor's story was full of contradictions: between teacher and mother, between his apparent potential and his performance, between his social prowess and academic failure and between his interest in life and his disinterest in schoolwork.

The Stability of At-Risk Status

If schools operated within the epidemiological model that identifies students as at-risk on the basis of background and personal characteristics, we would expect teachers to agree on which students are at-risk. Further, unless background or personal characteristics of the students changed, once identified, a student would remain at-risk. On the other hand, if schools operate within a socially constructed framework, teachers would not necessarily agree on who is at-risk. The identification process would be quite fluid, with individual students considered at-risk in some settings and not in others. Our study afforded us the opportunity to investigate which of these models was operating in the two target schools.

We looked at the stability of at-risk student status in two ways. The first involved the degree of agreement between the two teachers on each team. The second was the degree of permanency related to the ascribed status. Since we interviewed each teacher at least twice, we could determine if and for how many students the teachers changed their minds about at-risk status.

Nine of the twelve students described above were in classrooms for which two teachers were responsible. Of these, only three — Jerry at Plaza and Victor and Mateo at Escalante — were named as at-risk by both teachers at the beginning *and* end of the study. All other students were named by only one teacher, or were no longer at-risk according to one or both teachers at the end of the study. Thus, it would appear that at-risk status was quite fluid in the three classrooms.

Further evidence of this fluidity is summarized in Table 3. Included are the numbers of students in each class, the numbers described as at-risk by each teacher in the first interview, the numbers of those who left during the year, those who were still considered at-risk at the end of the year, the new-to-the classroom students identified as at-risk, and those who were not mentioned at the beginning of the year who had been added to the list at the end. The 'overlap' category indicates the agreement on at-risk students between Ms. Green and Ms. Jones, and Ms. Osgood and Ms. Wilson.

Table 3: Numbers of At-Risk Students Identified by Each Teacher in Two Interviews

		PLAZA			ESCALANTE			
Category of student		Teacher 1*	Teacher 2*	Overlap	Teacher 3	Teacher 4**	Teacher 5**	Overlap 4&5
Total number of students in class			54		21		23	
Total number of at-risk first interview		10	10	7	8	6	7	4
Number named left school		1	2	1	–	1	–	–
Number still at-risk second interview		3	6	3	6	4	5	4
Number of new at-risk second interview		5	2	2	1	3	1	–
Number of old students, second interview newly named at-risk			1	1	1	–	3	1

*   Team teaching same class
** Teacher 4, morning; Teacher 5, afternoon – same class

While the numbers of at-risk students in each class appears to remain quite stable, the students themselves do not. Ms. Jones, for example, named ten students at-risk at the beginning of the study. Of those, one left the school. In the final interview, she identified only three of the original ten students as at-risk and one of those was questionable to her. However, five new students were placed on her list. She was responsible for the most changes in students' status; however, all of the teachers changed to a certain degree.

Further, it appeared that the concept was not stable across teachers. Team teachers Green and Jones, while espousing quite similar philosophies, each named ten students in their class as at-risk, but only agreed on seven. Teachers Osgood and Wilson who did not work as closely together as those on the Plaza team, after jointly naming thirteen students, agreed on only four of them in their class.

The changes in individual teacher's opinions can be explained to a certain degree by the high mobility of the students. New students arriving in the second semester seemed particularly prone to being identified as at-risk. Further, it may be that teachers can only pay close attention to a limited number of students. As Ms. Osgood stated: 'And you know what teachers do: we replace some with another. As we get kids that have real severe needs, we tend to bump up those that aren't as bad . . . until M . . . and S . . . came, I didn't realize how much Juan had grown . . . And teachers do that as a defense mechanism 'cause we can't handle it.' Thus, if a student enters in the second semester who does not understand the social rules of the classroom and therefore does not seem to adapt, quickly, that seems enough of a problem to the teacher to displace a previously identified at-risk student with a new one.

The lack of agreement between teachers reflects, in part, the use of different criteria for identifying students. For example, Ms. Jones identified five students as at-risk in the first interview on the basis of academic or learning disability, one as social/emotional, three on the basis of behavior and one received a mixed diagnosis. Her new at-risk students were all identified as behavioral or social problems. The behavior problems for this teacher were primarily aggression toward other students. Ms. Green, however, named no students in the first interview on the basis of behavior; she seemed to focus primarily on academic problems. Ms. Wilson appeared to focus more of her attention on behavior problems than on academics, whereas Ms. Osgood focused on academic lags due to learning disabilities. The two at-risk students identified for physical reasons were LD students for whom she provided clinical brain dysfunction reasons. The behavior reasons for Ms. Wilson related solely to students not finishing their work and/or not bringing in their homework. It would seem, then, that the teachers focused on quite different criteria for the identification of at-risk students, and that these criteria were related to the teachers' sense of what a smooth, well-run class should be like, and the student responses to school they considered most crucial.

The reasons for students being 'delabelled' as at-risk related most often to the students' adapting to the social organization of the classrooms, and to the teachers' expectations for classroom work behavior. Students were taken off the at-risk list if they improved in their social skills with other children, exhibited better working behaviors, demonstrated improved self-concept, and seemed reasonably adjusted to the particular environment of the classroom. While academic problems were stated as the primary criterion for identifying an at-risk student, improvement in academics was not used as the sole criterion in removing a student from the at-risk list except in two instances in which the students were named because of lack of English language skills. In those two cases, their English oral language skills improved during the year. In all other cases, students' social, personal and behavioral adjustments were noted as improved. A number of LD students were taken off the lists either because they seemed to adjust to their handicaps, or the LD problems had become minor. One teacher, for example, was asked in her second interview about whether a special education student who had been on her list in the fall was still at-risk. 'No, I wouldn't . . . because if she is doing the best that she can, so she is socially adjusted, and she seems to fit in well, then I would not consider her at-risk' (Ms. Green).

Discussion

The teachers in this study exhibited a fluid notion of the concept of at-risk. This contrasts with the epidemiological model in use today that assumes that a student's at-risk status can be determined easily on the basis of relatively stable enduring predispositions such as minority culture background, or generally agreed-upon problem behaviors such as high absenteeism. At the beginning of the study, the teachers identified students at-risk in their classes as those who were not fitting in socially, were performing poorly on tests or were not working as they should. At the end, students still at-risk were those who had not responded adequately to the attempts the teachers made to help them adjust.

Their strong feelings of responsibility toward all students in their classes and their high sense of efficacy concerning their own power to help students conform to their classroom norms, led to great tensions in dealing with their small number of 'problem' or 'at-risk' students. One tension they confronted related to labelling or stereotyping students, and making efficient and appropriate decisions about them. All teachers were concerned about stereotyping their students, and of behaving in such a way that it might seem to stereotype them. For example, Ms. Santana, in describing a student whom she wanted to refer for a child study (LD assessment), explained that she had heard from other teachers that this child came from a large family, and many of the children had been placed in special education. She was, therefore, hesitant to recommend him for child study because she thought that would suggest that he 'was following a pattern that runs in the family'.

The teachers were generally unwilling to attribute a student's lack of success to a characteristic inherent in the child, or to their own instructional programs[5]. They therefore moved outside the classroom to find the cause of the students' problems. These causes most often rested on their students' home lives and parents. Their frustration with the parents of at-risk students was repeatedly stated, and the assumption that the not-at-risk students came from strong families was universal. The teachers appeared to accept any negative statement about families of at-risk students from other teachers or adults in the building, or, in one case, from a relative of a teacher. For example, the myth that a student lived in a household with 'weird religious rites' was mentioned by two teachers, a nurse and a counsellor in one school in separate interviews on the basis of one comment that the student had made to a teacher about what his mother said to him when he went to bed. Some of these concerns were well-founded, others were not; but the assumed correlation was taken for granted in either case. However, never questioned was the fact that some non-at-risk students may come from similar family situations; in fact, given the nature of the complaints about some of the families, we would be hard-pressed not to find such conditions in any family.

In looking at the students who were identified as at-risk, the effects of this socially constructed identification process become clear. The identified at-risk students were primarily low income, minority and male. This was particularly clear in the Plaza classroom which was quite heterogeneous. Only two of the at-risk students at Plaza were from middle-class families; one was black, and the second had been named learning disabled on the insistence of his family and doctor. The rest of the students were, by-and-large, from minority, low income families, usually living with single parents, and bussed to the school. Most of the students at Escalante were Hispanic and lower middle-class; but the at-risk students were, by and large, from lower income, highly mobile and non-traditional, or single parent families. If the norms for acceptable social behavior in schools and classroom are middle-class in nature, children who do not grow up in that culture and are not socially adaptable will not fit in, and thereby may be labelled as at-risk.

What was not seen by the teachers was their own role in the creation of an environment and set of expectations that affected both the label-ling of at-risk students and the students' behavior; or that the concept of 'lack of success' or 'at-riskness' was defined by themselves and differed from teacher to teacher. The teachers saw, in part, the effect of the context on the behavior of their students, and they understood that a child may not be at-risk in another context. But they were not aware of the way in which they affected that context through the enactment of their beliefs and understandings about students. The teachers' strong sense of efficacy and feelings of responsibility for their students on the one hand helped them create a strong and unique learning environment in their classroom that was beneficial for many of their students. On the other hand, it was difficult for them to understand and question the effects of this environment on students who did not adapt to it.

Notes

1   See, for example, Keogh and Daley (1983).
2   See, for example, Brophy and Rohrkemper (1980), and Erickson (1985).
3   A marginal at-risk student was described by Ms. Green: 'they have a limitation on them because of a physical or mental handicap but their desire to learn far outweighs their handicap and so they do whatever they have to do to keep improving themselves'.
4   The Child Protective Services (CPS) in a government agency that investi-gates suspected cases of child abuse. Case workers in this agency have the right to remove a child from a home, with the understanding that, later, a hearing would be held to investigate the evidence in the case, and arrange for longer term solutions such as placing the child in a foster home. Teachers and others in the helping profession are required by State law to report suspected cases of child abuse to the CPS.
5   These findings match those of Medway (1979) who found that teachers did not attribute student learning or behavior problems to themselves, but they seem to contradict the findings of teacher attribution literature that

suggests that effective, high efficacy teachers take responsibility for what happens in their classroom (see, for example, Ashton and Webb, (1986), and Brophy and Rohrkemper (1980). The differences could, however, be attributed to the way in which questions were asked. Ours was a very global open-ended about question at-risk students and the causes of at-riskness.

Chapter 3

School Contexts and the Schooling of At-Risk Students

In the course of our study, we also collected information about school organizations and district policies in our two research settings. Social constructionists, particularly classroom ethnographers, have sometimes been charged with ignoring the influence of school, district and even broader social contexts on classroom happenings. Their studies have often failed to look beyond the microculture of the classroom for explanations of phenomena such as student success and failure. Such phenomena are presented as locally produced, through microinteractions between students and teachers.[1] Findings on the school context are often presented as a mere background to the *real* findings. As Mehan, Hertwick and Meihls (1986) have put it, 'Research, in its rush to the classroom, has sometimes been guilty of premature closure and tunnel vision' (p. 41). These authors argue that:

> Classrooms and other organizational units of the school are influenced by the bureaucratic institutions of the school and the society of which the school is a part. Administrative policy . . . is established by school boards and state departments of education at an organizational level above the classroom. The decisions made at higher levels of the bureaucracy impinge upon educational practices in the classroom. (p. 47)

Our study of at-risk students in two contrasting schools located in different districts prompted a comparative perspective on how district and school characteristics might influence the definition of, and responses to, such students. Though teachers play a powerful role in constructing the success or failure of individual students in their classrooms, their responses to at-risk students may be constrained by the options provided by their school and district environments. Because of differing school norms, students considered to be at-risk in one school environment might not be in another. In other words, students may be matched or mismatched to the organizational and cultural features of the districts or schools to which they are assigned. Moreover, students who do not 'fit' often have negative experiences at school which undermine their continued commitment to education — making them further at-risk as time goes on.

The Two Districts: Suroeste and Raintree

The two districts in our study differed in certain structural, demographic and political characteristics. Plaza School was located in Suroeste School District, a large district of over seventy elementary schools, twenty junior high/middle schools and fifteen high schools. The total student population of the district was over 55,000. Over half of the students were classified as white; Hispanics constituted the next largest group at approximately 30 per cent; black, American Indian and Asian students made up the difference.

Suroeste District was divided into several administrative regions, and included a wide diversity of school populations and programs — a veritable smorgasbord of educational options. Contributing to this was the fact that magnet schools[2] were the desegregation strategy which district leaders had negotiated with the Office of Civil Rights in the 1970s. The Suroeste Education Association had a history of activism and citizens' groups periodically formed to pressure the school board in one direction or another. As we began our study, the board had just been through a bitter period involving the hiring of a new Superintendent. A rejected candidate, a black woman, had brought a civil rights suit against the board. In short, Suroeste was a highly politicized district, characterized by pluralism and conflict, bordering (some said) on unmanageability.

Suroeste District had adopted few districtwide instructional programs. District authority over Plaza School was most evident in the areas of textbook selection, computer-assisted instruction (CAI), development of K–3 programs, a teacher mentoring program and requirements for teacher planning. With Plaza School as a referent, one could derive the impression that schools in Suroeste District were relatively autonomous.

Raintree District was much smaller, with eleven elementary schools, three junior high/middle schools and two high schools. It was located on the outskirts of Suroeste, bordering an Indian reservation. The student population was 60 per cent Hispanic, the remainder Anglo and American Indian. Raintree's drop-out rate was almost twice as high as that of Suroeste District. In response to the drop-out problem, during the period of our study the district sponsored an 'At-Risk' conference which generated recommendations about reaching potential drop-outs at a younger age. It was not surprising to Raintree officials that a study of at-risk students would be conducted in their district.

Public criticism over low student performance on standardized achievement tests had characterized Raintree District over the years. As a result of such pressure, the board and administration of Raintree seemed much more likely than Suroeste to follow the latest trends in educational reform and to import the most currently popular expert advice. Improvement efforts occupied a great deal of the school board and administration's attention.

For example, Madeleine Hunter's 'Essential Elements of Instruction' (EEI) had been a thrust of teacher staff development in recent years.[3] Increased emphasis was placed on curriculum coordination across schools through the development of district-wide objectives in both reading and mathematics. These objectives were accompanied by criterion-referenced tests intended to evaluate both pupil progress and the efficacy of instruction. The school board had decided to implement Outcomes Based Education,[4] a program sponsored by the Danforth Foundation as a result of the report *A Nation at Risk* (National Commission on Excellence in Education, 1983) on a school-by-school basis. Workshops for principals and teachers had been offered to encourage adoption of this model. Raintree leaders had also adopted a career ladder program for teachers which entailed closer evaluation of classroom performance and differential rewards based on these evaluations.[5]

To summarize, the contrasts between our two district contexts set the stage for some of the differences between the schools. In many ways, these contrasts are consistent with Weick's (1982) distinctions between loosely and tightly coupled organizations. Suroeste was a large, politicized district in which there was very loose coordination and great diversity among schools. It was often remarked that Suroeste's magnet schools received an unfair share of resources, but the trade-off was that magnet schools were more closely scrutinized and subject to higher expectations. In a small, relatively obscure school like Plaza, staff had the autonomy to create a unique school identity over time without much district interference.

It has been argued by some organizational analysts that loose coupling such as that found in Suroeste District is a generalizable character-istic of educational organizations (Weick 1982; Meyer and Rowan 1978). However, the thrust of much recent educational reform has been toward tighter coupling and closer top-down monitoring of elements of the system. This was true of reforms in Raintree District. The Raintree administration was very reactive to public criticism — grasping at just about every new educational reform that came along and aiming for close coordination among schools in curriculum, instruction and teacher performance. The direction of Raintree reforms was toward what Popkewitz, Tabachnick and Wehlage (1982) have termed 'technical schooling' — schooling dominated by norms of efficiency and control, often adopted in response to public demands for improved school performance. A large school like Escalante — long known, we were told, as the 'armpit of the district' — was likely to become the focus of such reform demands.

A View of the Two Schools: Plaza and Escalante

Plaza School and Escalante School were different in size, ethnic make-up and school organization. Table 4 summarizes the basic features of the two schools.

Table 4: Sample School Features

School	School district	Grade level	Pupil size	Ethnicity	Student/ teacher ratio	Free lunch	Special programs	Organiza-tion charac-teristics	Mobility
Plaza	Large urban	K–6	266	50% Anglo 28% Black 18% Hispanic 4% Other	23:1	65%	Chapter 1 Computer lab Music Business/ school partnership	Traditional, plus a grades 1–3 and a 4–6 classroom	High
Escalante	Subur-ban	K–6	760	90% Hispanic 7% Anglo 3% Other	25+:1	75%	Chapter 1 Computer lab/LD Magnet Music Art PE	3 teams, K–1, 2–3, 4–6	Moderate

The schools were, however, similar in an important way that undoubtedly led to their being recommended for study. Both schools exuded a warm and welcoming atmosphere, and their staffs were conscious of what is often called 'school climate' (Anderson, 1985).

For example, Ms. Jones at Plaza and Ms. Osgood at Escalante quite similarly remarked on the absence of vandalism and the sense of ownership children felt with respect to their schools. In both schools, children's work was exhibited around the walls, and we consistently observed relaxed, enthusiastic students. Both staffs frequently recognized positive student behavior and achievement through awards and incentives. There was also a sense of hope in each of these schools. In our contacts with the staff, they put forward a positive, 'can do' philosophy.

It was clear from our interviews that both schools had felt the impact of the 'effective schools' movement. However, though both schools were recommended to us as 'effective', they were not recommended on the basis most often used to define effectiveness: standardized test scores. What we heard was that these schools performed pretty well, *given* their student populations (an interesting observation in itself). In looking at scores from previous years, we could see a pattern of improvement. In fact, latest scores for the third grade at Plaza were well above the national average and student achievement did not appear to be a particular worry at this school. Scores at Escalante were still very low, and improvements in achievement were the central aim of school-level reforms.

The principals of both schools were similar in their personal characteristics and leadership styles. Both were female, minority group members who had worked their way up in the system. Both were doctoral candidates in education at the University. Further, both had been brought in, we were told, to reform their respective schools. However, the Principal at Plaza, Ms. McGuffey, had spent six years improving her school when the study began and seemed to be coming to the close of a cycle in her administrative career. Upon completion of her doctoral degree, she planned to apply for a promotion to the district level. Ms. Bolivar at Escalante, on the other hand, was only in her second year of a five-year plan of reform. The staff at Escalante stressed that it was unfair to assess reform efforts at their school, or to compare them with other schools after such a short time.

In addition, there were other differences between the schools which became important to our analysis of the school experiences of at-risk students in each school.

Plaza School

Plaza School, in Suroeste District, was a small school of only 280 students. For many years it had served as a neighborhood school for predominantly white, middle-class families. A portion of this neighborhood was quite affluent, in fact. The building of new schools, restructuring of school boundaries, and a desegregation order in the late 1970s caused major changes in the school population. In addition, gradual encroachment of the university on the neighborhood had made it less attractive to middle-class, homeowning families. By the time of our study, the school was marked by cultural and economic diversity. Students were 24 per cent black, 19 per cent Hispanic, 4 per cent Asian, 3 per cent American Indian and 50 per cent white and others.

Asked to describe their school, teachers Ms. Jones and Ms. Green both emphasized its diverse student population. Ms. Jones recalled that some measure of cultural diversity had characterized the school even before desegregation, since it was located in a neighborhood with a large number of university students and professors, many from other nations. After desegregation, she said, there had been some 'white flight' from the school; but an increasingly positive school reputation had drawn families back. Ms. Green said that a 'regular classroom' at Plaza was likely to be very heterogeneous; 'that's just the way it is at this school'. She remarked, 'It's a deseg school so we have a lot of low income families. We run the gamut.' The school population at Plaza was also quite transient; the Principal reported that over 50 per cent of the students were new to the school during the year of the study. Ms. Jones remarked that some children might 're-enter the school three times' in one year.

The Principal, Ms. McGuffey, described the school as serving an 'extended community' created as a result of desegregation. Half of the students lived in the immediate area, and half were bussed in from a predominantly black neighborhood which had been divided among several schools. She explained that family patterns in the school population varied widely, from nuclear to single-parent to extended, and that because of the proximity of the University the school had many foreign students. Although Plaza was a 'deseg' rather than a 'magnet' school, there was something magnetic about it. Fifty students attended the school with special permission, because their parents liked the school environment. A 'developmental' mixed-grade primary classroom headed by one of our participating teachers (Ms. Jones) had been especially popular with parents over the years.

Improvements in the climate and public image of Plaza School since desegregation had been the special concern of the Principal. Ms. McGuffey was a black woman who appeared assertive in her relationships and assured about her school. When she was first assigned there, Plaza had just been desegregated and was considered a 'problem school' in the district. From her reports, students fought, the halls were barren, and graffiti was everywhere. Ms. McGuffey had brought the school counselor from her previous school with her to Plaza. Together they had worked with faculty, parents and students to turn the school climate around. From all accounts, over a six-year period they had succeeded.

The school counselor acted mainly as a co-administrator but the therapeutic language and world view she brought to the school were different from the usual management perspectives of school administrators. She argued that 'when kids feel good about themselves, they're going to do well in school'. She had recently established several groups for students of newly-divorced parents, and was extremely optimistic about the ability of the school to help with such personal events in student lives. She worked with troubled students in the classroom, counseled them individually, and consulted closely with their parents. She was most proud of the positive school climate at Plaza, and reported that when people visited the school they told her they sensed 'a feeling of love and respect and high expectations'. All adults at the school took responsibility for all students. For example, the custodian played a special role at lunchtime each day, supervising children and interacting with them.

After six years of Ms. McGuffey's leadership, in partnership with the counselor, Plaza School gave the appearance of having arrived at a somewhat stable state. The two leaders had recently decided that it was time to move from improving school climate to tackling other issues. They had become caught up in the 'effective schools' movement, not through the district but through a state-sponsored improvement program called 'Success Schools'. Plaza's enrollment in the program meant that the staff had been willing to complete a lengthy application and assessment process through the State Department of Education and to develop an improvement plan. As part of their improvement plan, the administrators had decided to target 'parent-community involvement and communication'. For instance, Ms. McGuffey was trying to bring the surrounding business community closer to the school through a business/school partnership program.

While the Principal and counselor were preoccupied with public relations and taking care of the personal side of students' lives, the teachers at Plaza School had been given a great deal of autonomy to shape the instructional program. Ms. Jones told us that the leadership at Plaza gave teachers 'leeway to use each of our own special skills'. This very experienced teacher had exerted a strong influence over the shape of the primary grade program in her twenty-four years at the school. She described the philosophy of teaching at Plaza as 'child oriented', combining whole language[6] instruction with an emphasis on 'personal and social growth and responsibility. We feel these are just as important as math facts and learning the vowel sounds.'

As Ms. Jones remarked, the Plaza teachers had a 'kind of camaraderie'. 'We're a small school, therefore, we pretty much fight our problems so that we're of one mind about things. We don't have any separate cliques . . . everybody shares and helps each other out.' She held that parent confidence in Plaza was built on the 'family feeling' of the school and the fact that children were 'happy to come to school'.

Ms. Green described Plaza School as having a 'very positive approach to dealing with children'. The instructional emphasis was on teaching all the academic areas through the arts. Ms. Green also said that the teachers at Plaza favored a 'whole language' approach, and that this had been a collective decision:

> Basically we started doing it because we felt we were seeing too many children who were not successful [in the regular program, with basal readers]. A lot of us got together and really discussed it and a lot of us felt like we were failing too . . . we talked with our Principal and we really felt like what we needed to do was possibly investigate some other methods of teaching, some more positive forms, especially in our particular school. We found that a lot of our children did not have the background information that the basal readers assumed. So, we took the approach, that we would take the child from where he or she is and we would use whatever resources they have with them when they come to us and build on those.

Before coming to Plaza School, Ms. Green said, 'I was a basic skills kind of teacher, and I made sure I covered all the objectives and all the agendas that were given to me.' She attributed much of the change in her teaching to her teamwork with Ms. Jones. However, it is notable that Ms. Green argued for a whole language approach because she thought it was adaptive to the *particular* school population at Plaza, because it addressed certain problems or deficits she believed the students to possess. In Ms. Green's opinion, student diversity at Plaza was linked to the predominant mode of instruction, since diversity 'lends itself to individualizing' rather than 'worrying about covering material'.

While the staff at Plaza prided themselves on their ability to adapt to student diversity, as in any school there were students who diverged so far from school norms that they became the object of special attention. Teachers often seek outside advice in such cases, both to obtain extra assistance for their problem students and to share responsibility with other adults (Mehan, Hertwick and Meihls, 1986; Willig, 1986) At Plaza School, Ms. McGuffey and the teachers had established certain policies for teachers to follow in these situations.

Ms. McGuffey thought that some youngsters had not been given sufficient opportunity to use expressive language or to develop socially, and it was unfair to rush toward labelling such students learning disabled or handicapped. She wanted all students to be given an 'opportunity', and for teachers to modify their classroom environments if necessary to provide this opportunity. She advised teachers to 'try other alternatives' before making a formal referral for special education assessment. As she argued, 'You can take a student who is at-risk and work with the student and do a lot . . . You tell them they can achieve and they will achieve.'

If a teacher's own strategies did not succeed with a student, before referring the student to special services the teacher was expected to make use of a Teacher Assistance Team (TAT).[7] The TAT was a group of three teachers who met once a week to hear reports from other teachers on problem students and to recommend classroom solutions for the teacher to try. Only if these strategies failed was the student considered a candidate for special education referral (see Chapter 6 for more on special education policies and practices at each school).

Therefore, at Plaza School a developmental philosophy prevailed in the identification and treatment of problem students. Ms. McGuffey was cautious about permanently labelling students whose difficulties might be resolved given time and the right kinds of support from adults. She took conditions in the classroom into account as potentially contributing to a student's 'problem' status. Teachers had been empowered to use the knowledge that they had gained in the social context of the classroom to make appropriate decisions for each student. (Erickson, 1985). It seemed that as a result of this philosophy, proportionately fewer students were referred to special education at Plaza than at Escalante.

In summary, Plaza School was marked by small size, student diversity, a positive public image, an intimate school climate, a child-oriented developmental and therapeutic philosophy, and some consensus among teachers on a whole language approach to instruction. Plaza School was the collective construction of a group of experienced, committed, determined educators working together over several years in a setting in which they had relative autonomy from outside constraints. Perhaps because it was a small school in a very large, decentralized district, Plaza School did not appear to be particularly vulnerable to district control. As Ms. Jones put it, 'A lot of people will say, "Plaza School? Never heard of it," even though the school has been here for over forty years . . . we're not in the limelight.' There also appeared to be no major preoccupation among the staff with 'at-risk students' or the sense of urgency generated by that label. Proportionately fewer students, in fact, were named by their teachers as being at-risk at Plaza in comparison with Escalante.

Schooling such as that found at Plaza had been termed 'constructivist' by Popkewitz, Tabachnick and Wehlage (1982). In such schools, a broader range of learning activities have been legitimized, and not all adult-child interactions are task-oriented. Skills are developed in the context of the exploration of general concepts and there are efforts to integrate many kinds of knowledge, including the aesthetic. Interestingly, the constructivist school in the Popkewitz, Tabachnick and Wehlage study was a middle-class school with 'university kids', similar to Plaza School before desegregation. The school in their study was dominated by middle-class 'professional' teachers, highly dedicated and committed to their philosophy of education. Their critique of constructivist education was that it tended to emphasize the intellectual over the physical, to maintain a form of social control based on monitoring interpersonal relations and attitudes, and to consider knowledge and work to be properties of individuals. We shall return to this critique in our discussion of the school experiences of at-risk children at Plaza School.

Escalante School

Escalante School, in Raintree District, was a large school of 750 students in a rapidly growing, predominantly working-class area of Suroeste. The student population was 90 per cent 'Hispanic' (almost entirely Mexican American), 7 per cent Anglo and 3 per cent American Indian, Asian and others. The transiency of the school population was lower than at Plaza, but still moderately high. Many Escalante students had either been born in Mexico, or had parents or grandparents who were born there. These families often maintained close ties across the border. The school population also included immigrant students from other Latin American countries, such as El Salvador.

When asked to describe the students at their school, the teachers at Escalante responded positively, in terms of the social behaviors and attitudes of students and their families. They seemed to assume that their students were culturally homogeneous. Ms. Osgood said her students were 'eternally hopeful . . . and culturally rich', with many traditions they could share with others at the school. She said that recent immigrants had not yet experienced the 'polarization' in US society, and at Escalante they could feel at home and be 'fairly inconspicuous'. She also praised the Escalante parents' commitment to their children's success. Ms. Wilson, who had grown up in the Escalante area, remarked that 'They may be a bit too rambunctious, but for the most part, most of them are really kind. They've been taught that you treat people kindly.' She liked the neighborhood because people there were struggling with down-to-earth issues in their daily lives. Ms. Santana, who had been bussed to school as a child, thought that a neighborhood school promoted a community feeling and appreciation of the school. She described the children as very 'warm-hearted, very close . . . motivated and interested in school'.

The Principal, Ms. Bolivar, described the school population as having 'lots of children who are at risk' if defined in terms of low language proficiency (in both Spanish and English), poverty, single parents with little time to spend with their children, parents with little education, and child abuse or neglect. But she also argued firmly that 'schools control the conditions of success', and could adapt to meet children 'where they are at'.

Ms. Bolivar was both well-prepared and idealistic, primed for her role as a school reformer. She was a powerful supporter of Outcomes Based Education (OBE), and as the above quotations reflect, wanted to make her school an example of this model in action. There was a seriousness of purpose in her demeanor, and she often seemed very harried, but she also displayed a quick sense of humor. Her appointment to the school seemed to have been an intentional act by district administrators, who had high expectations for change at Escalante under her direction.

In her first year Ms. Bolivar had faced particularly strong opposition from some of the bilingual teachers at Escalante School. These teachers had had little supervision under the former Principal, and their commitment to bilingual education had waned. This had been a bone of contention with Ms. Bolivar in her former role as district director of bilingual education. She had used transfer and hiring practices in an attempt to build a strong corps of allies among the bilingual teaching staff. Her teacher allies emphasized to us, however, that the school's transformation was not complete, and there were still some teachers at the schools who were resisting change. At a staff 'retreat' we attended, tension among the staff, critical differences in instructional philosophies, and the near-burnout state of Ms. Bolivar were obvious.

Consistent with the OBE model, Ms. Bolivar struggled to overcome a school history marked by tracking of students. She argued that low-achieving students should be treated with respect and helped to feel 'no less than the others'. The self-concepts of her students, their feelings and personhood, were a recurrent theme in her interviews. Tracking by ability was one Escalante tradition which had wounded students' self-esteem. To change this pattern, students were now placed in heterogeneous groups for many activities. Though the teachers still formed reading groups based on achievement, students were graded relative to their level of placement, so that there were fewer 'failing' grades.[8]

Ms. Bolivar had implemented other organizational changes that gave teachers some measure of control over their day-to-day coordination of instruction. Teachers were grouped into three teams (K–1, 2–3 and 4–6), each with a team leader, and had every Wednesday afternoon free to meet for planning. Their major planning tasks were organizing ability groups for reading in two languages, and in the primary grades, teaming to provide bilingual instruction in content areas.

Teaming improved teacher communication, but it also complicated their worklives. 'Switching' groups (as they called it) among teachers could occur several times a day, and had to be well-coordinated or a great deal of instructional time could be lost. For example, with the advice of a university consultant, the 2–3 team had set up a reading program of incredible complexity which shuffled eight groups of students from one classroom to another, so that each teacher had only two skill levels in a single language to manage. The switching of groups at the beginning and end of the morning reading period could take as long as fifteen minutes.

Team leaders were teachers who had reached the top of the district's career ladder. As Ms. Bolivar explained, career ladder placement was based on 'experience, good evaluations within our system', and 'some kind of formula . . . in terms of [a teacher's] committee work, inservice training, contribution to districtwide efforts'. Ms. Bolivar's role in teacher evaluation meant that she played a part in determining career ladder placement and promotions to the quasi-administrative team leadership positions. This further complicated Ms. Bolivar's staff relationships, and at the staff retreat teachers expressed complaints about the fairness of the evaluation system.

In our earlier discussion of Raintree District, we argued that district reforms were aiming toward 'technical schooling' as described by Popkewitz, Tabachnick and Wehlage (1982). Technical schooling, as these authors describe it, is characterized by detailed sequencing of the curriculum for purposes of management and monitoring and an emphasis on efficient delivery of the curriculum. Considerable staff time is spent in identifying and arranging explicit, measurable objectives for each level in a hierarchy of skills for each academic area. Through cooperating in this enterprise, teachers overcome their isolation and find a simple way of defining their 'professional' role. Technical schools may be characterized by a supportive environment for students, an emphasis on positive 'self-concept', and rewards for students who observe the norms.

According to Popkewitz *et al.* (1982), the result of this approach is a reductionistic definition of school knowledge. Creativity and 'non-academics' are de-emphasized, especially for low-achieving students, who are limited to the 'piecework level'. The psychology of instruction guiding technical schooling is that children are deficient or lacking in 'mastery'. Instruction follows a diagnosis and remediation model analogous to the medical model, with continual assessment and adjustment of instructional 'treatments'. The so-called 'professional' discussions which preoccupy teachers in such a system are actually 'impoverished', since they concern only reified objectives, criteria, and measures — not the deeper purposes of schooling.

The norms of technical schooling were clearly reflected in principal and teacher descriptions of the Escalante program. Ms. Bolivar said that the 'number one' goal for the teams was 'assessing, diagnosing where children are within the area of reading'. Teams spent their time at the beginning of the year placing children according to the 'skills that they haven't mastered yet' and assigning them to teachers who wanted to teach those skills. She added, 'We have a list of essential skills from the district that need to be taught at each grade level'. These were in turn linked to criterion-referenced tests administered by the district. For children who 'still are not mastering those significant skills that need to be at each grade level . . . [teachers] work on corrective, prescriptive modes for these children'. Children 'above grade level' were supposed to receive 'enrichment' activities.

Ms. Osgood noted that teachers coming to Escalante were not expected to 'break the habits of a lifetime' or 'break out of the teachers' guide'. They simply needed to 'aim at objectives' set by the school.

Ms. Wilson said, 'I've noticed we're trying to have similar goals instead of everyone doing their own thing . . . to identify some positive objectives so that we all work toward the same ones at different levels . . .' At the staff retreat, teachers in each team reported on how far they had come in setting up agreed-upon systems of sequencing instruction and assessing students at each level. In April, Ms. Bolivar told us that it had taken half the year to write a curriculum guidebook of objectives in language arts, and it would probably take another year to further develop and 'articulate' the system.

The arts and other 'non-academic' areas were given short shrift at Escalante. Classes received three week sessions of art, music and physical education on a rotating schedule, which added to student movement around the school and further complicated the daily schedule. These classes lasted half-an-hour, three days per week. The skills-based reading program placed little emphasis on use of the library or on personal reading, and writing was taught through a step-by-step formula.

Another feature of Escalante contributed to its characterization as a technical school. It was the only school in the district that could provide bilingual special education services, and as a result it attracted many students who were classified both as limited English proficient (LEP) and handicapped. Therefore, though students may have been ethnically homogeneous at this school, they were diverse in terms of the myriad of 'special' student categories represented. The school provided bilingual LD services, a bilingual language therapist, and bilingual speech and hearing specialists. The presence of all of these specialists gave the school a clinical flavor that seemed more than anything else to influence teacher responses to problem students.

In the previous section on Plaza School, we discussed the policies and procedures which had been established for responding to problem students under Ms. McGuffey's leadership. Ms. Bolivar defined at-risk students in terms very similar to the ones Ms. McGuffey employed. She argued that 'if you don't. . . . take kids from where they're at . . . when a kid doesn't feel comfortable in a learning environment, or excited, or motivated or feel like the people with whom they have contact on a daily basis don't respond to whatever background they're coming from, I think you have an at-risk situation.' She argued that 'in some cases you have children who are not at-risk because they fit right into the mentality of the school', while children from certain communities or cultures have never met with success in school.

Ms. Bolivar wanted to create a system without failure, a system which adapted itself to the needs and culture of every student. However, at Escalante district policies and the influence of special education personnel at the school seemed to be limiting the possibilities of such adaptablility. District policies required more and more standardization in the delivery and evaluation of instruction. School autonomy and flexibility of the kind Ms. Bolivar wanted was controversial. For instance, her informal practice of out-of-grade achievement testing for some students was strongly opposed by district personnel, to the point where her position was threatened. But she felt that her practice was more consistent with OBE philosophy.

In addition, the teachers at Escalante were not delegated as much power over their responses to problem students as those at Plaza. If a teacher at Escalante had a student with persistent academic difficulties, the teacher generally called for a Child Study meeting. These meetings, facilitated by a district school psychologist and attended by the LD teacher and the nurse, followed a medical, diagnosis-and-treatment model. Teachers were considered the non-experts on the team, and parents rarely participated (cf. Mehan, Hertwick and Meihls, 1986). In their interviews with us the psychologist and the nurse both articulated an epidemiological definition of at-risk students based on background characteristics, and a rather hopeless outlook on our at-risk students and their families (see Chapter 6).

Further, though Escalante School had an abundance of special education personnel, there was no counselor (as at Plaza) to provide personal attention for students in trouble or an alternative viewpoint on the causes of poor student performance. The Principal, Ms. Bolivar, had no other administrator with whom to share the task of managing a very large school. The school was assigned only a part-time 'community liaison' from the district who made some parent contacts and organized parent activities.

To summarize, Escalante School was characterized by its large size, students' ethnic homogeneity, a negative-but-improving public image, anxiety over low achievement, a clinical atmosphere due to a special education emphasis, and a fragmented, complex instructional program. Plagued by a lengthy history of failure, and being a large school in a small district, the school did not exhibit the relative obscurity and freedom from district intervention which Plaza School enjoyed. At Escalante, student achievement scores, though improving, were still the lowest in the district. And district policies such as the career ladder program and criterion referenced testing, constrained school-based leadership by the Principal. The first policy heightened teachers' sensitivity to evaluation procedures. The second imposed external limits on teachers' pedagogical responses to individual students. In addition, as a former district administrator the Principal seemed to feel very vulnerable to district pressures. Her own school-level reform attempts, her personal interpretations of Outcomes Based Education, sometimes ran up against district constraints, producing contradictions and confusion.

There was a sense of urgency at Escalante that we did not encounter at Plaza. 'Risk' was in the air at the school level. The Principal often referred not just to 'at-risk' but to 'high risk' students among her school population. One of our participating teachers at Escalante had been involved in the at-risk conference held by the district. There seemed to be few political qualms about considering minority students at-risk in this district. After all, the vast majority of the students in Raintree and at Escalante *were* 'minorities'!

Popkewitz *et al.* (1982) criticized technical schooling such as that found at Escalante for conveying an image of competence and legitimacy to the school community, thus appearing to respond to improvement demands, while masking internal contradictions, inefficiency and uncertainty. They argued that the worldview underlying technical schooling defines a passive role for the individual. Classroom interactions are dominated by repetition, routine and the norm of 'time on task'. In the following discussion of the school experiences of Escalante's at-risk students, we will return to this critique.

The Schooling of At-Risk Students

In the introduction to this chapter, we suggested that it may be students who do not fit within the norms of a particular school context who are mostly likely to be considered 'at-risk'. In this section we shift our focus to consider this possibility, and also to examine how school norms shaped the daily experiences of the students in our study.

Plaza School: Community, Coherence and Individual Development

Plaza School has been described as a small, intimate school with a close 'family feeling' despite its diverse student population. The school enjoyed relative autonomy from district authority, and teachers had considerable autonomy to shape their overall instructional program. They appeared to have come to some consensus on a philosophy of education which proposed that children must be given time to develop without comparisons with others, and that children's feelings about themselves and their relationships with others are as important as their academic achievement. Students who did not fit within these norms, then, were not only those whose achievement did not improve as expected over time, but also those who appeared to have low self-esteem or who were uncooperative with others.

Ms. Jones, in particular, took a therapeutic approach toward her students, and had been influential in shaping the primary grade program at Plaza in this direction. At the school level, the school counselor was available to help teachers, students and parents resolve any social or psychological difficulties which were interfering with a child's schooling. The counselor had more time than teachers to make home contacts and to work with at-risk students individually. In her interview, Brad's mother talked extensively about the help that the counselor had provided her family in working through problems which had been interfering with Brad's school performance. Ann, who poignantly described to our interviewer her history having been abused and placed in a foster home, talked about how her visits with the counselor made her feel better.

To return to Popkewitz *et al.*'s (1982) critique, it will be recalled that they considered schooling of this ilk to exemplify middle-class values of individualism and personal growth. At Plaza School, however, these values were tempered by an emphasis on cooperation and acceptance of others. Social relationships and the psychological state of students *were* monitored, and at signs of problems, the staff intervened. The counselor even became involved in advising parents on their family relationships. This might be considered a form of sophisticated middle-class social control, but judging from the at-risk children's generally positive responses to school, the benefits may have outweighed any threats.

For instance, the emphasis on a balance between social and academic development, and encouragement of artistic talents, meant that students who were at-risk academically were provided with other means for retaining or building their 'self-esteem'. Andy, who was not meeting with academic success, was assigned to give drawing lessons to other students, since he was considered a good artist. Ann, who was perceived as depressed and in need of an extra boost, was assigned to be a student helper in the library. Jerry, who was having serious social problems, received individual counseling and assistance with his personal relationships in the classroom. At the school's periodic awards assemblies, all of the at-risk students were recognized for a wide variety of positive contributions to the school.

An important aspect of Plaza School was a spirit of friendliness and cooperation. The Principal, counselor and teachers remarked on how relaxed students were as they travelled around the hallways, how they felt free to talk with any adult at the school. Four of the six at-risk children remarked in their interviews about how much they liked the school. For example, Ann called it 'the best school I've been to in all my life'. Regarding interracial relationships at the school, she also commented that 'the kids here aren't prejudiced'.

Ms. McGuffey expressed the opinion that in a small school, an ungraded, developmental program allows for more flexibility and variety in programming. Ms. Jones had chosen over the years to remain with the same group of students from first through third grades. Such stability in teacher-student relationships seemed to provide additional support for at-risk students, and had been especially helpful for Brad. After three years in the same classroom, Brad appeared to be on the road to academic success, and he was doing better socially. (However, he still maintained that he did not like school, because 'I always have to do math'.) This arrangement also facilitated teacher-parent relationships, which did not have to be developed anew each year.

The intimacy and stability they experienced in the primary grades seemed to contribute to both students' and parents' positive attitudes toward schooling at Plaza. However, the benefits of such a school culture required time to take effect. Highly mobile students like Jerry, who attended the school for only a short time, were considered likely to remain at-risk.

Escalante School: Classification, Fragmentation and Production

The experiences of at-risk students at Escalante presented a contrasting picture. The dominant norms at this school were those of technical schooling. Students who did not fit were those who could not keep up with the pace of instruction, who did not complete their work because they were 'off-task', and who did not seem to be motivated sufficiently by the school's system of rewards.

Students who did not keep up with the pace were spoken of as falling 'below grade level', i.e. they became defined in terms of their test placement. The prescription was for them to practice the skills they were lacking until their test performance improved. That is, rather than trying a different tack with at-risk students, teachers subjected these students to more of the same.

The rapid pace of instruction and lack of work completion as a criterion of at-riskness were interrelated with the fragmentation of the daily schedule at Escalante. The schedule was divided into short periods of instructional time, due to patterns of classifying students according to language and achievement and 'switching' groups across teachers. By reducing student diversity through grouping, teachers reduced the complexity of their instructional tasks and were theoretically able to teach the specific skills each sub-group needed to master. The large population at Escalante actually made such a system feasible, since there were enough students in any particular classification to make a 'group'.

Another source of complexity in the overall schedule was the rotation of art, music and physical education classes. Here, too, school size was a factor. Even with the rotated schedule, the art teacher complained of large class loads and classes which were too short to accomplish very much. Students' artistic or physical talents were not valued nearly as highly as their academic production. Yet students seemed to yearn to exercise these talents. Ms. Santana complained that one of her at-risk girls always wanted to draw instead of doing her assigned seatwork. One day Gilberto carried a picture he had drawn in art with him to every class, and proudly displayed it to the classroom observer.

Teachers at Escalante consistently named lack of work completion as an indicator of at-riskness. Because of their fragmented schedules, students had to complete their assigned tasks within a short time period. But the personal pace of some students did not seem to match the required pace. For instance, both Mateo and Laura were recommended to us because they did not complete their assignments on time. Mateo was a bright boy who was also slow and quiet. He seemed to find watching or playing with other boys more interesting than his schoolwork, and whiled away his seatwork time to the frustration of his teachers. Laura appeared to lose her concentration, and 'daydream' during individual seatwork tasks. It took extra teacher efforts to keep these two students on track. Victor, who was adept at avoiding schoolwork, could easily fill up a short task period with trips to the restroom, searches for a pencil, etc.

In addition, Mateo seemed especially indifferent to the rewards offered for conformity to school norms. The general pattern at Escalante was to offer students small prizes such as stickers, pizza coupons, pencils, etc. for work completion. Certainly this system was more positive than the punitive atmosphere which reportedly had pervaded Escalante in the past. However, students like Mateo who were unresponsive to school rewards were considered to have a personal problem. Little effort was made to discover what *would* motivate Mateo, and why his schoolwork was uninspiring to him. Victor, on the other hand, was very interested in rewards, but expended his efforts in attempts to circumvent the prerequisite work and to negotiate with the teacher and other students to get his share.

Another feature of the fragmented schedule at Escalante was the multiple adaptations to different teacher-student relationships and patterns of classroom organization it required. Ms. Wilson in particular emphasized that good students were those who could make this adjustment easily. In a talk with the class about their behavior, she remarked: 'You have a certain way of behaving for Ms. Osgood, a certain way of behaving for Mr.– and a certain way of behaving for me.' Ms. Wilson thought that students who had difficulty with these behavioral adjustments were at-risk. However, Ms. Osgood and Ms. Santana both emphasized the positive side of the system — that students could find at least one teacher in their schedule with whom they were mutually compatible.

For Ms. Osgood's students, the district career ladder program had created a shift in organization and teacher expectations within the *same* classroom each day. Because she had reached the top rung of the ladder, Ms. Osgood had been appointed to a quasi-administrative position as 2–3 team leader. This meant that she left her classroom each day at 11.00 a.m. to spend the afternoon performing her team leader duties. Ms. Wilson took over the classroom for the remainder of the day. In the following chapter we will describe how this district policy affected the day-to-day classroom experiences of Ms. Osgood's students.

The students whose school experiences were most affected by the norms of Escalante were those whose daily schedules were further fragmented because they had been placed in special programs: special education, speech/hearing therapy, language therapy or English as a Second Language (ESL). For these students, the school day was divided into small periods, each with a specific function. The rationale for further fragmentation of the schedules of 'special' students was that such students needed to meet with specialists for individual remediation a few minutes each day, in order to succeed in the regular program. However, some students were pulled out of their homerooms so often that they no longer experienced even an approximation of a 'regular' school day.

At-riskness at Escalante appeared to be related to a 'special' student's ability to cope with the demands of a complex, fragmented schedule, and fragmented relationships with others. For students who especially needed teacher attention, scarce instructional time was lost in the switching and pull-out processes. For example, Victor, a second grade LD student, had a habit of becoming 'lost' on his way to his thirty-minute LD and ESL lessons.

Oddly enough, students who were not considered to have special needs had the simplest school schedules and the easiest adaptations to school. Because they were not pulled out for special classes, regular students had more time to complete their regular classroom tasks and more consistent relationships with their homeroom teacher.

When we interviewed our target students at Escalante they appeared to have very little understanding of the purposes of their fragmented schedules, of the connections between school activities and meaningful learning experiences. They had come to *define* school, in fact, as a schedule of activities. Carmín's school description was: 'First I go with Ms. Santana and I bring her all the homework. Then I go with the other teacher. Then I come back to play. Then we eat lunch and write and I stay with Ms. Santana.' Since Carmín was classified as both learning disabled and language impaired during the year of our study, her schedule became even more fragmented than this description (see also Gilberto's description of his school day in Chapter 1).

In summary, at-risk children were especially vulnerable to the effects of the technical style of schooling found at Escalante. For not-at-risk children, adaptation to the system was considerably easier. While they did not seem especially inspired by their schoolwork, they enjoyed the rewards offered at the school for good behavior and work completion. They participated in the sense of purposefulness which characterized their school culture. However, students as well as teachers at Escalante did not participate in defining the larger purposes of the system for which they worked so hard.

Summary

What we have described in this chapter are two very distinct contexts of schooling, two contrasting district and school cultures and their effects on definitions and treatment of at-risk students. Page (1987) has recently argued with regard to 'lower track' students in two contrasting high schools:

> . . . the meanings of the roles of lower-track student and teacher
> and of the lower-track curriculum are negotiated in classrooms.
> However, the classroom negotiations also translate principles of

membership and differentiation from the wider contexts of school and community. (p. 77)

Page argues against sole reliance on either reproductionist interpretation of stratification within a school, based on predetermined social categories; or an interactionist interpretation, based on individual teacher personality. Similarly, the meanings of 'at-risk', the roles of 'at-risk students' and institutional responses to these students are not based solely on predetermined social categories or external social/economic forces. Nor do they emerge entirely through microinteractions in the classroom. The norms or ethos of the school as a whole play a powerful role in constructing students' success or failure.[9]

'At-risk' appeared to be defined differently in these two school cultures, and the treatment of at-risk students varied with the organizational arrangements adopted by districts and schools for coping with student diversity. At Plaza School, fewer children were named at-risk and those who were seemed to be benefiting from a school program designed to adapt to student diversity through variety in the curriculum and individualized expectations. At Escalante, organizational arrangements of extraordinary complexity, and very specific expectations for academic performance, meant that more children were considered to be maladapted to school norms. It was ironic that attempts to transform the negative image of Escalante School were actually resulting in the creation of a larger number of problem students.

Notes

1   See Ogbu (1980), Lutz (1981), Wolcott (1982) and Barr and Dreeben (1983) for this critique of classroom studies.
2   Magnet schools have special programs designed to attract Anglo parents to enroll their children in schools with predominantly minority populations. Special programs range from 'back to basics' to fine arts curricula. Schools with predominantly Anglo populations were desegregated by bussing of minority students. Plaza School was one of these 'deseg' schools.
3   The EEI program involves instructing teachers in the use of a standardized sequence of instruction. In districts which have adopted this approach, its correct use often also becomes a basis for teacher evaluation. For descriptions of EEI, see Hunter (1976) and Stallings and Krasavage (1986).
4   Outcomes Based Education (see Rubin and Spady, 1984) is a system in which variability in student achievement is accommodated through flex-

ible grouping, with lessons for each group targeted toward development of specific skills. The curriculum is sequenced into a hierarchy of skills and concepts, and is to be delivered in this order. Student evaluations are directly related to skills specified in the curriculum.

5 Promotion on the career ladder was based on principal evaluations, continuing education and evidence of additional training or service. Teachers at the top of the career ladder were promoted to quasi-administrative positions as 'team leaders' in their schools. In addition, teachers on the ladder received differential levels of merit pay at the end of each year. For a critique of such career ladder plans, see Bacharach, Conley and Shedd (1986).

6 The 'whole language' philosophy is that learning to read is a natural, contextualized process. Children want to read if reading is important in their community and contributes to their personal understanding of life (see Goodman and Goodman, 1981).

7 See Chalfont and Pysh (1981) for a description of the TAT model for problem-solving at the school level for students with special needs.

8 This school policy seemed to confuse parents. From their children's grade reports, it might look as if they were doing well. But the same students might fail the district's criterion referenced tests, do poorly on achievement tests, and be recommended for retention at the end of the year.

9 See Rutter (1983) and Goodlad (1984) on the relationship between school norms and school effectiveness, defined in terms of student achievement.

Chapter 4

The Classroom Within the School

In Chapter 3, we indicated the ways in which school district and school policies affect the daily lives of students, particularly those students in Escalante School who were diagnosed as requiring special attention. These policies also affect what happens in classrooms, but there are many other influences on the classroom that contribute to the creation of a particular social organization in which students must learn to operate. It is these social organizations and a child's adaptation to them that largely determines whether a child is identified as at-risk. If the child adapts well, s/he will be associated in the teachers' minds with other 'normal' children. If the child has difficulty adapting, the teacher and possibly the other students will view the child as a problem, or as being at-risk.

In this study, we observed three classrooms in two schools that were located in two different school districts. We soon realized that the classroom in Escalante that was taught in the morning by Ms. Osgood and in the afternoon by Ms. Wilson should be considered as two classrooms bringing the total to four. By looking across these classrooms, we were able to observe some common elements as well as many aspects that varied. The combination of common and varying elements created four unique classrooms. Further, even in the Plaza classroom that was team taught, expectations of, interactions with and activities created by one teacher were quite different from those of the other. By observing the organizations and activities in each classroom, and having determined the beliefs of the teachers toward learning, teaching and appropriate behavior, it was possible to see how and why many of the sample students were seen as at-risk by their teachers.

Further, it was possible to speculate that at least some of these students would not be 'at-risk' in another sample classroom.

Our focus, in this chapter, concerns the factors that made the sample classrooms places in which certain students were labelled as at-risk. In addressing this, we will draw on descriptions of the classrooms, and of the ways in which the identified at-risk students operated within them. We identified the following factors as influencing the commonalities and variations in classroom features: the ecology of classrooms, school district and school influences, and teacher beliefs and expectations.[1] But first, we will provide a brief description of the classrooms.

The Classrooms

The three classrooms used in this study were quite different. The Plaza classroom could be described as 'informal', with movable tables and many learning centers and activity areas. Ms. Osgood's classroom at Escalante resembled the Plaza classroom, although there were not as many activity spaces; and Ms. Santana's classroom was quite traditional. The appearance of each classroom predicted the instructional program of the rooms.

Plaza Classroom

The Plaza School classroom was a team-taught, combination second and third-grade classroom. It consisted of two large rooms connected by two doors that were usually open. The first door led into the room where there were tables and chairs for the entire group of students. This area resembled a traditional classroom. The second room was similarly constructed but had a more informal appearance. The teachers' desks were in this room as well as a davenport, a reading rug and a large wooden frame 'house' with an upstairs and downstairs. This was considered a special place and was used by students for reading, playing and socializing.

Housed in these rooms was a group of seventeen second graders and all thirty-three third-graders in the school. Eighteen of these students were new to the school/classroom this year while the others had been with Ms. Jones or Ms. Green since first grade. As with the school population, children in this classroom represented a culturally diverse group including Black, Anglo, Hispanic, Indian and Chinese students.

The majority of the students came from lower-income families and thirty-five of them received free or reduced-fee lunches. The second and third graders were not separated by grade.

Instruction in this classroom was provided by two experienced teachers who were in their second year of team teaching. They were supported within the classroom by an aide and a music teacher, as well as by a part-time LD teacher and part-time speech therapist who worked with students outside the classroom. Although the two teachers had different personalities and backgrounds, they were able to work well together and there was consistency in their approaches. Several times, one would share an insight, thought or concern with us that the other had also expressed but which they had not yet discussed between themselves. These observations were supported by others as well. In an interview with one at-risk student (Ann), she said, 'I think it's really good to be with a class with teachers that can cooperate like that.'

The social organization of this room was informal. Children talked as they worked at tasks, moved around the room without asking permission and often worked together. The students were free to sit wherever they wished as long as they were responsible for their behavior and did not bother others. The children often sat by their friends and would move as these friendships changed. They were responsible for helping one another. At the beginning of the year, the 'old' students were expected to help the 'new' students become aware of classroom rules which were few but applied consistently. Individual differences were dealt with through assignments and with the help of other students. On one occasion the researcher commented to Ms. Jones that Jerry, an at-risk student, appeared to have had difficulty with the reading lesson. Ms. Jones responded, 'Was he working alone? He should have had a partner.' The teachers felt that they were all a family and expected the children to 'get along'.[2]

In contrast to this informal social organization, the academic organization was more structured and formal. Students were assigned to groups and the teachers usually developed the activities/task in which they were to participate. They were expected to accomplish a certain amount of work or complete a task. At other times, when working in a large group, they were often given a designated amount of time in which to complete an activity. The teachers had high expectations for the students and the students knew this. Ann, one of the students in the study, said, 'I think they're really nice and good because they help you learn a lot, and instead of taking so long on teaching you just one particular thing, they go on and force you to go on with it.'

These teachers provided encouragement as needed and verbal reinforcement to motivate and encourage them. Neither teacher appeared to pay special attention to the at-risk students identified in this study. Both stated in their interviews that they did not like the idea of singling out a student because such attention might label the child in the eyes of his/her peers.

The day began and ended with whole group activities, described by Ms. Jones as 'a coming together and a renewal of our bond'. Students seldom required reminders to be quiet during the initial activities; and the teachers did not use harsh or loud words. The time in between these activities was quite flexible except for lunch and computer lab time. Activities at the centers spanned the academic program, including handwriting, reading, creative writing, social studies, science and mathematics. The teachers attempted to gear time to the activity rather than vice versa. Thus, math might be scheduled one day and not the next, depending on the length of the activity.

The teachers' developmental philosophy was reflected in their assignment of students to centers. Assignment to the reading center, for example, was not based on ability but was instead chosen for the theme or topic. Direct instruction was minimal and students were encouraged to read together, help each other with unknown words, and complete work assignments.

Escalante Classrooms

Shortly after the study began, the second grade teacher, Ms. Osgood, initiated her afternoon duties as 'team leader' for the nine second and third-grade teachers. Another teacher, Ms. Wilson, took over her classroom from 11.00 a.m. to 2.00 p.m. each day. As a consequence, we had three classroom teachers in our sample at this school, each representing a different style of teaching and different views of at-risk students.

Ms. Osgood's second-grade classroom gave the impression of being a busy and crowded place. Just inside the door was a rug in front of a large chalkboard, where the class or smaller groups often met. The teacher's desk was at the back, crowded into a corner. In between, the students' desks were grouped into four areas named by colors: red, green, etc. There were five to seven children per group (the total enrollment hovered around twenty-three). The groups remained basically the same for the four months of observation, but shortly after our observations ended, Ms. Osgood reported a major reshuffling and rearrangement.

In the morning, after opening activities which included the Pledge of Allegiance in English and Spanish on the PA, Ms. Osgood began her own opening routines. These included: choosing the 'special person', describing the day's centers, time for reporting individual important news and sometimes time for children to begin working at centers or doing a brief activity before the reading group 'switch'. Reading time lasted from 8.30 to 9.40 a.m. Shortly after the study began, Ms. Osgood made the special arrangement where as an alternative to the usual pull-out routine the LD teacher came into her classroom during this time to work with the LD reading group. As a consequence, Ms. Osgood had both a fairly large English reading group and the Spanish LD group of seven children working in her classroom four mornings per week.

After reading, there was recess, followed at 10.00 a.m. by more centers time and sometimes a writing activity until 11.00 a.m. when Ms. Wilson came on duty. There were approximately seven centers each week, with activities loosely tied to math, listening, reading, art, visual-motor skills, etc.

At 11.00 a.m. each day, Ms. Osgood and Ms. Wilson had a brief meeting to exchange messages and directions, and then **Ms. Wilson** was in charge. She supervised the rest of the center time, and encouraged children to complete the math assignments posted on the chalkboard, until lunchtime. After lunch, there was silent reading and math workbooks until it was time to switch with Ms. Bernard, the teacher across the hall, for science. Ms. Bernard taught the Spanish science lesson, and Ms. Wilson, English. All of the target children were in the Spanish science group. Ms. Osgood seemed to specialize in teaching reading and language arts, while Ms. Wilson covered math and science. Both shared responsibilities for seeing that children completed all the centers for the week.

Ms. Osgood and Ms. Wilson's teaching styles were very different. Ms. Osgood had set up the original group plan in the classroom and the organization of centers. She seemed to have a preference for activities which reinforced *social* skills and attitudes in the classroom, in the context of academic work. Much more often than Ms. Wilson, she assigned children to work in groups or pairs on projects. Times when children had opportunities for self-expression, such as Share and Speak, the morning sharing time, and the 'special person' program, were also initiated by her. Each day the class selected a special person of the day through a name drawing, and this person's name was posted on the door. The special person was for the most part a helper, with the privilege of fulfilling certain classroom duties such as taking the attendance register to the office and handing out papers. Ms. Osgood encouraged children to participate actively in discussions, which at times became multiple, excited conversations among the students. She had a very high tolerance for noise and activity in the classroom. She had a voice which carried over the sound in the room and always caught the group's attention, if that became necessary. She had no control problems in the classroom, though she might overlook some off-task behaviors in the general buzz of activity. She was an enthusiastic person with a very keen sense of humor and could make any activity entertaining.

Ms. Wilson's relationships with students were less personal and focused on their completion of academic work. She appeared to have a lower tolerance for noise and was very serious about keeping students on task and promoting an orderly classroom climate. The children for the most seemed eager to please her, or at least cooperative. For most of the children, receiving Ms. Wilson's approval seemed truly rewarding; with these children Ms. Wilson forged warm relationships. Children who did not comply, on the other hand, seemed to frustrate her. She emphasized quiet, orderliness, concentration on assigned tasks, cooperation and effort.

Neither teacher singled out the at-risk children for any special treatment. Ms. Osgood purposely placed students in heterogeneous groups, and she encouraged the at-risk students to interact with higher achieving children.[3] She did not draw classwide attention to the failings of the at-risk children.

The environment of **Ms. Santana's** classroom presented yet another contrast. Her room was arranged more traditionally than Ms. Osgood's, with individual desks or pairs of desks in rows. She placed a table for herself at the front and a desk at the rear. Bulletin boards reflected current classroom themes, including mostly 'academic' topics such as the writing process, parts of a letter, telling time, math and science concepts.

Ms. Santana's instructional methods were also somewhat traditional. She alternated whole-group presentations and question-answer sequences with seatwork in a steady, rapid pace throughout the day. Ms. Santana was almost always instructing, either presenting lessons, explaining task directions, or asking or answering questions. Group participation consisted mainly of raising one's hand to be called on for a short answer. Some children became particularly tense about being chosen, holding their hands high and calling 'Pick me!'. In this classroom, communication with students focused almost exclusively on class work or school business. She also assigned homework every night, generally copying words for handwriting practice or spelling and math problems.

Ms. Santana was very business-like, though her tone and interactions with the children were warm and friendly, and the children seemed to like her very much. Like Ms. Wilson, she emphasized work completion, but unlike Ms. Wilson her classroom schedule did not allow for long periods of extended task time. After the morning PA ceremonies and announcements, Ms. Santana took care of classroom or school business. Then she assigned a task for the short time until the reading switch at 8.30 a.m. None of the target children were in her reading group, so that we did not observe her instructional methods in this subject. After recess, Ms. Santana's class went to either physical education, art or music, subjects which rotated every three weeks. About twenty minutes into these classes, the Spanish-dominant students, more than half of the class, left for the English as a Second Lanaguage (ESL) class. Following this, the class had an early lunch.

After lunch, Ms. Santana presented math, science, writing and social studies lessons. These were generally short presentations with participation followed by seatwork assignments. She used lots of worksheets and other brief activities in quick succession. The students worked at three activities individually rather than in pairs or cooperative learning groups. The sheer volume of work expected was large, but there was not much depth in any single assignment, reflecting her emphasis on basic skills.[4] Ms. Santana used slate and marker activities, with a pattern of listen, write, lift, erase. She especially emphasized *quiet* and simultaneous lifting of slates. She also praised children who used neat formats for their papers and 'beautiful' handwriting. The students received frequent feedback and she was able to track her students' performance from day-to-day.

Most of the children had adopted the same business-like attitude which Ms. Santana demonstrated, completing work and piling it up with little fanfare or fooling around. Some of the high achievers seemed to eke out a little bit of free time by getting ahead on their assignments, even finishing their homework if they had a chance. The slower workers, among them the at-risk children, were usually running behind the pace.

Ms. Santana spent much more time than any of the other teachers with the at-risk children in her classroom, helping them complete their assigned tasks. This was not easy, because in the meantime the other children would crowd around with their questions and papers to be checked. During these times Ms. Santana displayed great patience and the ability to simultaneously juggle many demands.

These four classrooms[5] presented interesting contrasts that allowed us to look at the bases for the differences and their effects on the at-risk students. The next sections of this chapter examine classes of factors in the environment that seemed to affect the classrooms and the students within them.

Influences on the Classrooms

The Ecology of Classrooms

Doyle (1980) described six aspects of all classrooms that affect teachers and students in common ways, regardless of the curriculum, instructional program, or teachers' philosophy. These elements are: multidimensionality, or the large quantity of tasks and events in the classroom; simultaneity, or the fact that many of these tasks and events happen at the same time; immediacy, or the rapid pace of events; unpredictability; publicness, the fact that the teachers' actions are witnessed by a large number of students; and history, the fact that classes meet five days per week over nine months, thereby establishing their own cultures and understandings. These conditions create the need for a classroom management system that allows the teacher to monitor and regulate student activities, and motivate the students to participate in the joint production of the activities.

In this view of schooling, the systems of social and instructional organization in classrooms are jointly constructed and learned by the students. This process is orchestrated by the teachers, and because the systems are more or less jointly constructed, most students understand and operate within them. As in all groups of students, some students will accept and operate within these rules more than others. The students who do not conform create management and instructional problems for their teachers since classroom management is an overriding concern of teachers, particularly in elementary schools.[6] In this study, those students who did not conform were labelled at-risk.

While the systems in the four classrooms in this study were different — and these differences will be discussed below — it was clear that there were several common features that related to the identification of at-risk students. For example, as discussed in Chapter 2, all five teachers mentioned a certain percentage of students in their classroom as at-risk, and the number remained quite stable. This behavior may relate to limitations of human information processing. While teachers are able to consider and plan for groups of students[7], they may, at a particular point in time only be able to pay attention to a limited number of the students *as individuals*. Thus, as expressed in the interviews, each teacher focused on a certain percentage of their students as at-risk,[8] and this percentage was maintained throughout the year, even though the particular students on the list did not remain stable. When other students' needs become more severe, as pointed out by Ms. Osgood, other students with less severe problems previously thought of as at-risk are no longer considered to be problems.

This process of identifying a subset of students for particular attention is reminiscent of the work on steering groups.[9] This work suggested that teachers select a small group of students to use as a reference group in making decisions about pacing a lesson. If this group seems to be doing well, the teacher moves on; if not, the teacher slows the pace. The use of steering groups could also be related to the information processing difficulty of paying attention to all students in the classroom as individuals.

A second common feature related to at-risk identification concerned the particular students selected as at-risk. It was clear that new students walking into any of the sample classrooms in the middle of the year were particularly vulnerable to being at-risk, unless they were very adaptable and/or had learned to participate in a similarly organized classroom. This makes sense within Doyle's (1980) ecological framework. A new student would have to learn a new system that s/he had not helped to construct. For a while, therefore, such a student would be operating quite differently from the majority of other students in the class.

In all of the sample classrooms, the at-risk lists were altered in the spring to include new students (see Table 3). In the highly mobile Plaza classroom, Ms. Jones added five of the new students, and Ms. Green added two. Between the two interviews, one new student, Joseph, had been considered at-risk by both Ms. Jones and Ms. Green, but had been taken off their lists at the time of the second interview. The teachers described the new students' problems in terms of their difficulty in adapting to the classroom. Bill, a new student in Ms. Santana's class, from El Salvador, was described as 'trying to make adjustments to the class and to the personalities of the children'. In the Plaza classroom, new students who had difficulty working with other students in groups were thought of as at-risk. Both Sam and June, new students to the Plaza classroom, were described as aggressive and antisocial, as had Joseph. However, Joseph had finally adapted and was no longer seen as at-risk.

The findings from these four classrooms suggest that teachers and students construct management systems in classrooms because of the ecologically-created need for control, and because the teacher perceives that a certain percentage of students are not operating within the system in a manner similar to the rest. The percentage selected may be more related to the information-processing capabilities of the teachers than to absolute problem behavior on the part of the student.

However, although teachers create management systems and identify students who are adapting to the system in a manner different from the majority of the students as a function of the ecology of classrooms, the particular systems they create may be affected by what is going on in the school and the teachers' own beliefs about students and teaching. The next two sections will address those aspects.

School and School District Effects

As described in Chapter 3, Escalante School was located in a school district that was instituting reforms aimed at 'technical schooling'. The anxiety over grades, testing and possible failure that was a feature of such reform was also evident in the interviews of teachers, students and parents. The teachers described the problems of their at-risk students in academic and clinical terms, often peppered with the jargon of LD. Juan, for example, was described by Ms. Santana as 'bilingual learning disabled', Gilberto as 'dyspraxic'. The teachers also had great concerns about covering content. Since the mandated content consisted of the micro skills and tiny bits of knowledge contained in the competency-based curriculum, coverage of content seemed to become a higher priority than coherence in the curriculum and deep understanding.

Ms. Santana's performance came closest to the expectations of the school district. Direct instruction and time on task were extremely high, and her instructional system matched the system proposed by the district.[10] The consequences of this were that the curriculum was broken up into tiny chunks, with the emphasis on basic skills rather than on in-depth understandings of concepts. Children worked individually, and there was an emphasis on speed and accuracy. This was particularly problematic for highly anxious children such as Carmín. Carmín seemed to have mastered the form of being a student, but not the substance. Ms. Santana's daily 'mad minute' math exercise, a timed math problem, was particularly difficult for Carmín, who was observed crying when she could not finish her problem in the time allocated. The emphasis on speed did not help Carmín master the skills, and perhaps prevented her from gaining much at all from the exercise because of her anxiety.

As evidenced in her interview and in classroom observations, Ms. Wilson equated completion of task with learning the mandated curriculum. There was great emphasis, in her classroom, on working hard and completing the many worksheets that, for her, apparently conveyed and provided practice in the curriculum. For those students for whom the work did not make much sense and who were not willing to participate in the system, Ms. Wilson was stern and demanding. Further, they were labelled as at-risk. For example, Mateo was a very able student who could easily have completed his assignments. But during seatwork time, he watched other children or devised games with his classmates. Ms. Wilson tried both persuasion ('couldn't you do just one?') and punishment (keeping him after school), but Mateo remained uninspired.

Ms. Osgood, the teacher seemingly least affected by the Raintree mandated systems,[11] was able to create a more relaxed environment in her classroom that emphasized the development of social skills and experiential learning. Nonetheless, there was still a press to cover content, and the content consisted of the micro skills and competencies that were mandated by the school district. In order to work with small groups of students in a personal manner and provide experiences for the many skills required in the curriculum, Ms. Osgood organized her classroom such that many of these skills would be covered in a center organization. Each week, the students had to complete seven of these centers. They ranged from a listening center with books and tapes to small group games, to a center with pegboards and blocks. After completing a center, the student marked it off on a chart. Students were expected to work independently or with small groups of students and to plan their time such that all seven centers were completed during the week. While the students were working at the centers, Ms. Osgood checked papers with small groups of children. She was seldom observed circulating around the centers to provide assistance to the students.

Most of the students in the class were able to move independently through the centers and accomplish their requirements. In fact, the type of system developed by Ms. Osgood allowing the students to regulate their own task activities, has been associated with the development of student beliefs about themselves as task performers that positively affect student achievement.[12] Nonetheless, several of the at-risk students had great difficulty accomplishing the work at the centers. This task required the student to hold in mind the procedures for accomplishing the tasks and/or be able to read the directions at each center, and/or ask other students for help. It also required that students be able to plan their time and work for a whole week without much guidance or rewards.

Victor had great difficulty doing this. He wandered from center to center, often misusing the equipment and then being told to leave the center. For example, he made 'karate sticks' from a set of plastic blocks in the math center and started an impromptu karate match. Victor seemed to work best in a structured situation with considerable adult feedback. In his interview, he evidenced complete lack of understanding of the purpose of the centers. Both Ms. Osgood and Ms. Wilson were extremely frustrated with Victor's inability to complete the tasks. Finally, towards the end of the year, Ms. Osgood and Ms. Wilson reduced the number of centers required for Victor. He was asked to complete at least two. This tactic seemed to work for Victor.

In contrast to the teachers at Escalante, Ms. Green and Ms. Jones were not driven by concern about test scores. As described in Chapter 3, Plaza was allowed to be 'constructivist' in part because it was located in a school district that was certainly concerned about grades, but was more loosely coupled than Raintree. Plaza had considerable autonomy within the system to choose their own philosophy. The philosophy chosen was developmental, reflected in the Principal's, counsellor's and teachers' interviews.[13]

The developmental philosophy was played out in various ways in the Plaza classroom. The teachers' selection of at-risk students included those who had social and emotional problems. In fact, two of the sample at-risk students were doing extremely well, academically. Greg had a perceptual problem that apparently affected his handwriting, but not his grades, and Ann's problems were seen as social and emotional. The classroom encompassed two grades, and had included three the previous year. The teachers, therefore, felt that they could work with the students over a two or three-year period of time. By de-emphasizing tests and grades, Ms. Jones felt that she could prepare the students for grade 4 without destroying their self-concept: 'We found that by giving them time and not putting pressure on them that our failure rate was much less . . .' Materials and tasks could be assigned to students on the basis of their skills and needs rather than their grade level, and content coverage was clearly not a critical component driving the curriculum in the Plaza school.

The concern about testing did, however, creep into the Plaza classroom. Each morning, the teachers worked on language activities with the whole group. These activities resembled the activities at Escalante in their choppiness and emphasis on speed. Most of the at-risk students at Plaza seemed uninvolved in these activities. In fact, Ann was uncharacteristically late many mornings from the school breakfast room because, as she stated in her interview, she disliked these activities.

The developmental philosophy and concern for self-concept were the rationale used by both teachers for not working individually with the at-risk students. As Ms. Green stated, 'We don't single them out, or isolate them'. However, this decision left several of the at-risk students in the lurch. Students having difficulty were expected to seek help from other students. This, however, required social skills that Jerry didn't have. Thus, Jerry was often observed daydreaming, turning pages back and forth, and otherwise not engaging in the activities. Travis, also, could have used individual help and guidance in learning the multiplication tables; help he received neither at home nor at school. Thus the humanistic concern for not singling students out may have left some students without the skills necessary to push on in the curriculum.

Another contrast between the two schools that was reflected in the classroom concerned the school level organization of instruction. As pointed out in Chaper 3, Escalante had recently moved toward a team approach in which different subjects were taught to the same group of students by different teachers. The effects of this were not only to increase complexity at the school level, it provided each teacher with little flexibility in scheduling. The reading lesson would have to take place at a particular time every day, and a particular lesson would have to fit within the allocated time period. Therefore, the activities were developed on the basis of available time.

On the other hand, the team teachers at Plaza had much more freedom to allocate time on the basis of the activity. As Ms. Green pointed out in her interview, 'a student may not have math everyday. He may not have social studies, he may not have reading everyday but he will have a block of time where he will participate in those activities. We feel we can give more of ourselves by blocking off a large amount of time for a subject. There is no time pressure.' The two teachers planned their weekly activities around units and the schedule changed frequently.

Thus, school district and school policies did appear to affect classroom organization and instruction. However, within the constraints created by school and school district policies and the particular student populations, the teachers had considerable leeway to impose upon their classrooms their own unique approaches to teaching.

Individual Teacher Beliefs and Expectations

By far the greatest variation in the classrooms seemed to be related to the individual teachers' beliefs and expectations. As described above, even though there are common features of classrooms that may be traced to ecological features, and common features that relate to school and school district policies, the three teachers in Escalante created quite different environments for their students.

The two pairs of team teachers provided good examples of the ways in which individual teachers' expectations and emphases differentially affect individual at-risk students, even though the school policies, physical setting of the classrooms and the groups of peer students were the same. Lina, for example, an at-risk Escalante student who was mentioned by both Ms. Osgood and Ms. Wilson as having social and academic problems, did not seem to be an active participant in the recitation sessions. With her head often down on her desk, and her leg dangling over the edge of her seat, she often appeared to have tuned out. However, when Ms. Osgood became animated and excited about a particular topic, which she often did, Lina became actively involved. Lina also had difficulty working independently at a table with other children because she was easily distracted. Much of Ms. Osgood's morning instruction required Lina to work in centers with other students, and Lina was not particularly efficient at those tasks. When assigned to work cooperatively with other students, Lina seemed to be able to focus on the task. However, Ms. Wilson's tasks involved the type of seatwork that could be accomplished independently. She often isolated Lina from the many distractions around her, such as placing her at her own desk, facing the wall. During these moments, Lina was able to finish her work in an acceptable manner.

Even in a true team teaching situation such as that at Plaza, with teachers who taught together and held similar developmental philosophies, their beliefs about the important functions of schools and students affected their approach to individual students. Travis, for example, was an LD student who was named by Ms. Green but not by Ms. Jones at the beginning of the year as at-risk. At the end of the year, Ms. Green was convinced that Travis would always be at-risk because of low self-concept, but again he was not considered by Ms. Jones to be at-risk. Travis was rarely observed participating in recitation activities. He did not look at the teacher, nor raise his hand; nor was he asked questions by the teachers. This was clearly a problem for Ms. Green. She mentioned several times in her inteview that she 'didn't know him'; that he was 'hard to figure out'. Ms. Green explained her failure to get Travis to respond to her by suggesting that Travis' self-concept was low. On the other hand, Travis was seen by Ms. Jones as not at-risk because of her emphasis on social skills and relationships. Travis worked well with, and was liked by, other students. Two of the other at-risk students favorably mentioned Travis in their interviews. He was observed as a responsible group member, and one student mentioned that Travis sometimes reminded others at the table to 'be quiet'. Thus, because Ms. Green and Ms. Jones focus on different aspects of classroom participation, they held very different understandings of Travis' potential. Unfortunately, neither provided for Travis the attention he felt he needed:

> Like they don't pay attention to me. Like they're not wanting to teach me. It seems like the worst ones get the most attention. I've never got an award all the time I've been here and I think I never will. Most of the time I'm nice to people.[14]

Conclusions

The purpose of the descriptions of mismatches between the instructional organization in these classrooms and the behavior and needs of individual at-risk students has not been to suggest that these teachers were ineffective. In fact, these teachers were effective for the majority of their students. All students in all observed classrooms benefited from elements of the instructional system, and most students benefited enormously. These descriptions of mismatches were meant to demonstrate how at-risk status is jointly constructed within a classroom.

This construction does not rely solely on characteristics of the at-risk students, but on a combination of these characteristics and the particular social and instructional organization of the classroom. To a certain degree, classrooms are affected by common features of classrooms in Western societies. These features include placing twenty to thirty students of approximately the same age who are required by law to be there, in a room with one or several adults who are expected to pass on to the students certain skills, knowledge and understandings. As we saw above, classroom ecology sets up imperatives for teachers and schools to establish management systems to which students more or less adapt. In addition, school districts and schools adopt policies that add additional imperatives for classroom operations. And teachers, themselves, have goals and expectations for what they want their students to be and what is important in their students' behavior. Those students who do not adapt are seen as disrupting the system of the classroom, or of not living up to their potential, and may be considered, therefore, at-risk of eventually dropping out, failing, committing suicide, becoming pregnant or being recipients of some other socially unacceptable outcome. The students' own characteristics are thus only one element in their condition of being at-risk.

This analysis suggests that more students will be considered at-risk in school systems with top-down mandates for prescribed behavior and outcomes than in systems with tolerance for a wider latitude of behavior. Demands for higher test scores on one standardized text, for coverage of common content, for using a common lesson delivery system all place pressure on school personnel to notice and become concerned with students (and teachers) who do not quite conform. As Erickson pointed out in responding to this study: 'As you narrow the range of acceptable behavior for teachers and students, you put more people at-risk for not acting right'.[15]

Notes

1 The nature of our inquiry, of at-risk students as identified by teachers, led, logically, to a discovery of mismatches between the organization of classrooms and the behaviors and needs of the students. A different focus would describe the way in which these aspects and other students' meshed. Thus, the following descriptions should not mislead the reader into the understanding that these were ineffective teachers.

2 The following comment from Ms. Jones gives a good overview of the social organization in the classroom: 'We do all the academics but we do it from a social angle. If we're doing multiplication worksheets . . . then we ask them to check each others' answers. . . . It makes them work together and depend on each other and cooperate with each other. . . . I don't think we have much competition either'.

3 However, the children, themselves, imposed language and gender barriers among themselves. See also Lampert (1985).

4 For example, when the children wrote stories in one lesson, they were required to use a certain fixed method of connecting six sentences with transition words indicating chronological order. This was to emphasize the concept of *sequence*. For example: 'The little girl got up. Then she got dressed. After that, she ate breakfast . . .' When the class wrote letters

to their pen pals in another school, Ms. Santana assigned them topics, for example, 'My New Year's Resolution'.

5   That is, the Jones/Green classroom at Plaza and the classrooms of Osgood, Wilson and Santana at Escalante.

6   See, for example, Doyle (1986), Duke (1979) and Duffy (1981).

7   The literature on teacher planning has been summarized by Shavelson and Stern (1981), Clark and Peterson (1979), Borko and Niles (1987) and Borko and Shavelson (in press).

8   Ten students, or 18 per cent, for both Ms. Jones and Ms. Green; eight students, or 38 per cent of her class, for Ms. Santana; six or 26 per cent for Ms. Osgood; and seven or 35 per cent for Ms. Wilson.

9   This work was conducted by Dahllof and Lundgren (1970, as reported in Clark and Peterson (1986).

10   As mentioned in Chapter 3, teachers and other personnel in the district had received training in the Essential Elements of Instruction (EEI), and system of lesson presentation developed by Madeleine Hunter (1976). In addition, many principals used an observation checklist instrument based on EEI for teacher evaluation. See an evaluation of the Hunter program in Stallings and Krasavage (1986).

11   This is curious given that Ms. Osgood had been elevated a step in the district's career ladder program on the basis of, among other things, a number of classroom observations.

12   See Marshall and Weinstein (1984), Anderson, Stevens, Prawat and Nickerson (1988), and Harter and Connell (1984).

13   Both the Principal and counselor held social constructivist views of at-riskness. The Principal, for example, stated that the definition is dependent on a classroom environment. The counselor, who felt that all students have the potential of becoming at-risk, liked to observe the referred students' behavior in the classroom. She felt that the at-risk student's behavior 'could be related to the specific setting'.

14   Irvine (1988) points out that: 'Children who feel unliked by their teachers frequently do not like themselves or school. They feel alienated and discouraged, and they eventually fail. This effect is exaggerated for low-income and minority students because they are more likely than middle-class students to hold teachers in high esteem . . .' (p. 507). See also Kash and Borich (1978).

15   ERICKSON, F. (1988) Response to at-risk symposium at the annual meeting of the American Educational Research Association, New Orleans, April.

Chapter 5

Home and School

This chapter is about perceptions and expectations: perceptions expressed by the school personnel in this study about their students' lives at home, with their parents; perceptions expressed by the children's parents about their children, at home and in school; and the expectations held by each of those sets of concerned adults about each other. We also include here our own perceptions as researchers, of the home environment of the twelve children included in this study.

Our analysis suggests that each of the children is the object of a set of perceptions that differ according to the *role* of the perceiver. Each is primarily a student to the teacher and a child to the parent. That is, the teacher has an opinion of the student as a participant in the school and classroom, while the parent has an opinion of the child within the family history and home environment. The differences that result from those contrasting perspectives have been noted by Mercer (1973). She found that parents may rate their children high in the practical and social knowledge needed to function as a family member or neighborhood playmate, while teachers may rate the same children low on the academic or social skills needed to function in the classroom.

In addition, and not unexpectedly, we also found that teachers hold perceptions of the student as his/her parent's child and about what life is like at home for the student. Similarly, parents hold perceptions of their child as a student in the school and classroom. Finally, both parents and teachers hold perceptions and expectations about and for each other.

Thus our data has been analyzed with the following questions in mind: How do teachers view their students? How do parents view their children? What are the teachers' perceptions of the home? What are the parents' perceptions of the school? What do teachers expect from parents? What do parents expect from teachers?

From the beginning of the study we were struck by the frequency with which parents, and the home in general, were mentioned as major contributors to a child's condition of 'at-riskness' by school personnel. This theme was strongly present in all but one of the teachers' interviews, as well as in the responses of school specialists such as the nurse, counselor and school psychologist. In addition, children whose families were considered to be dysfunctional were often also considered least likely to recover from being 'at-risk'.

The tendency to emphasize the influence of family and home on their students' school success was not unusual. Many of the official definitions of children 'at-risk' refer to students whose family characteristics may place them at risk. The family's economic status, the language spoken at home, age and marital status of the mother, and other characteristics, have all been considered by various educational agencies as indicators of future school failure (McCann and Austin, 1988). These characteristics, often in aggregation with behavioral indicators such as frequent absences and lack of achievement, are sometimes used as check lists to predict school failure. Children thus identified are then targeted to receive special services (Phoenix High School District, n.d.).[1]

We believed it important, therefore, to incorporate data on the family into our understanding of the at-risk status of the child. This was done in four ways. First we gained knowledge about the teachers' perceptions of the children and their home environments through our teacher interviews. The teachers were not asked directly about their students' home environments, but in speaking about their students they often added spontaneous comments about the general contribution of the home to school success, and specific references to the homes of individual children. Sometimes they also expressed their own expectations for the parents. These comments, as well as their comments about the children themselves, were recorded and analyzed. Similar information about the home was also forthcoming from other school personnel, and sometimes was also found in the school records. Thus, through a variety of sources, we were able to gain a school's view of each of the children and their respective home environments.

The second, and more direct, source of information about the home environment and perceptions about the children was obtained from the children's parents, in all but two cases, their mothers. Parents also expressed their perceptions and expectations about the teachers and about the schools. Parents were interviewed twice at their homes. At the beginning of the data gathering phase we explained the purpose of the study and asked for their permission to include their child. None of the parents denied their permission. Later, after we had had the opportunity to observe the children in the classroom, examine their school records, and interview their teachers, we visited and interviewed the parents for a second time.

The parent interviews were lengthy, usually of one-hour or more, and took place in their homes. In only two cases were the families unavailable for the second interview: Ann's foster mother was unreachable, and in any case would have been unable to provide the historical information we were seeking; and Jerry's family moved out of the neighborhood before the end of the school year. Efforts to locate the family were unsuccessful.

The interviews were guided by a semi-structured instrument (see Appendix 1) designed to obtain information about each child's infancy and school career. We also sought the parents' perceptions about their child's competence in and out of school, their perceptions about the school, the teachers, and education in general, and their expectations for their children's future. A third source of information about the home was the students themselves. The children were not asked directly for this information since that would have violated our agreement with their parents. But children, unlike adults, do not always draw clear boundaries between their home and their school environments. In the process of discussing their school experience some, like Ann, appeared to be so overwhelmed by their problems that their comments about their home life dominated the interview. Others, like Mateo, kept their personal distance. But most interjected brief comments which helped us to understand their relationships at home, with their families.

The fourth and last perspective on the home and of the students was our own. In our two visits to the students' homes, and through our interactions with the parents, we were able to draw our own inferences about this part of the children's lives. We do not claim infallibility for these views. We understand that our perceptions are as prone to subjectivity as those of the parents or school personnel. Two visits and accompanying interviews do not give us authority. Instead we present our own perceptions in contrast to or support of those expressed by teachers. We were particularly intrigued by discrepancies that surfaced in the perceptions of parents and teachers about the students, and between ourselves and the teachers in regard to the home environment. We take responsibility for our own views and present them to you clearly labeled and supported by the evidence that led us to these conclusions.

In the next few pages we will review the demographic characteristics of the families in the sample. Then we will discuss the home environment from two points of view, the school's and our own view as gleaned from our visits to the homes and our interviews with the parents and students. In a final section we will highlight areas of agreement and disagreement between these two points of view.

Demographics.

As mentioned above, many studies of children 'at-risk' have attempted to identify family characteristics that might increase a student's risk for failure in school-related activities. The families of the children in this study varied widely in such characteristics (see Table 5). Most families at both schools were in the low to middle end of the socio-economic scale, as defined by their eligibility for free or reduced price lunch and our own observations. Only one family among the twelve in the sample could qualify as 'middle-class'.

Families varied in their ethnic characteristics. All the sample children at Desert View School were of Mexican-American descent, but then, so was 85 per cent of the student population at that school. The six students at Plaza School reflected the greater ethnic diversity of the students at that school. Three of the six students were Anglo, two Black and there was one case where the mother was Vietnamese while the father was Anglo.

The families also varied across education and employment. Where the fathers were present (in four of the twelve homes), they were most commonly employed in blue-collar jobs. Gary's father, a university professor, was the one exception. Most of the mothers at Escalante were not employed outside the home, perhaps reflecting their lack of fluency in English. The one exception, Carmín's mother, was a bank teller and fully bilingual. She was also the only one among these six mothers to have completed high school. All but one of the mothers of the Plaza School children were employed and most had completed high school, one had a college degree. The one exception was Jerry's mother, who similar to the mothers of the Escalante School children, also lacked fluency in English.

Family size also varied. The number of children ranged from one in the smallest household to seven in the largest, but the average was

Table 5: Characteristics of Parents of At-Risk Students

	Family status	Family size*	Home language	Qualify for free/reduced lunch?	Parent employment**
Plaza					
Jerry	Married	5	Vietnamese and English	Yes	F: Sales, construction M: Home
Ann	Foster parents – married	3	English	Yes	No record
Gary	Married	3	English	No	F: Professor M: Counselor
Travis	Single mother	3+	English	No record	M: Secretary
Andy	Single mother	3	English	Yes	M: Store clerk
Brad	Single mother	4	English	Yes	M: Waitress
Escalante					
Juan	Single mother	4+	Spanish	Yes	M: Home
Carmín	Single mother	3	Spanish	Yes	M: Bank teller
Gilberto	Single mother	8	Spanish	Yes	M: Home
Victor	Single mother	4+	Spanish	No Record	M: Home
Lina	Married	6	Spanish	No Record	F: Mechanic M: Home
Mateo	Married	4	Spanish	Yes	F: Construction M: Home

*　+ indicates extended family
** F = Father
　　M = Mother

three children per family. Most of the children (seven) lived with single mothers but in four of these homes living arrangements included extended family members. These often included adult males such as uncles, grandfathers, older cousins, or their mothers' male friends. One student (Ann), lived with a foster family.

Another area of comparison was the degree of stability and mobility of these families as reflected in the students' school attendance. Recent research (Ingersoll, Scamman and Eckerling, 1988) suggests that geographic mobility is an aversive influence on student achievement, even after controlling for economic status, thus we were interested in this aspect of the children's lives and found it to vary widely. Only three of the children had remained at the same school since kindergarten while seven had attended at least three or four different schools during that brief period.[2] Two children had changed schools once; that is, they had been enrolled at two different schools.

These then were the demographic characteristics of the children included in the sample, and their families. In the next section we will use data from the interviews and from our own field notes to discuss teacher and parent perceptions of students.

Teachers' and Parents' Perceptions

As suggested by Mercer (1973), we found discrepancies between teachers' and parents' perceptions of the children. These perceptions stood in contrast to each other in terms of the child's home life as well as in terms of the child's competence.

Contrasting Perceptions of the Child at Home

We sometimes found that teachers' perceptions of the home situation were inaccurate and often based on what we have called 'school folklore', that is, beliefs that arise among school personnel, based on scant evidence, perhaps hearsay, and which though never officially recognized, follow the child from classroom to classroom and teacher to teacher. The 'snake story' was one such example of 'school folklore'.

We first heard the 'snake story' from one of Andy's teachers. She noted that he was 'a real interesting kid . . . the one who never gets out of bed at night because his mother tells him that there are snakes on the floor'. The school counselor also mentioned the story adding that although kids always have an imagination 'some things stem from (Andy's) home that are almost cult in thinking'. Andy's mother was asked about the snakes. She noted that both she, her mother, and Andy were afraid of snakes. Andy himself admitted being afraid of snakes because 'they bite. They're poison' but never mentioned the bedtime situation recalled by the teachers. As far as we were able to tell, the story was originally told by Andy and later retold and embellished by school personnel.

Sometimes teachers' beliefs belied their tendency to rely on middle-class values to judge children's home situations. For example, both

Victor's teacher and his mother agreed on some of his home circum-stances but they attached different values to his activities at home. The teacher referred to 'home problems. He is the caretaker for himself and his younger brother and sister'. Victor's mother described her son as 'very industrious, he likes to help me around the house but fights a lot with his brother and sister . . . because he talks to them as though he were their father . . .'.

Andy's teacher also noted how he 'pretty much gets himself up and gets himself to school' in relation to lack of support at home. But Andy's mother expressed pride in his responsible behavior which allowed her to work various shifts at the convenience store: 'I always tell him to watch out for his sister when I'm gone and try to protect her . . . I tell him to straighten out his room or find some of his work to do for school before he goes out to play.' She was regretful that extra responsibilities fell on Andy because he was the oldest and because she had to provide for her children, but these were the realities of life for her and her family. But the teachers tended to assume parental neglect when the children were given responsibilities at home.

In another case the school nurse described Carmín's family as 'very weird', and noted there was 'not really a nuclear family left'. Carmín's mother, on the other hand, explained that she had always been the child's primary caretaker though she had relied on her mother and sister to care for her children while she worked. At the time of the study Carmín's mother would drop her off at her sister's every morning so she could attend school with her cousin. Carmín would return to her aunt's home after school. Carmín's mother called her daughter every day after school to ask her about school and remind her to finish her homework before going out to play. She would pick up Carmín after work and get home in time to prepare dinner.

Andy's mother also relied on extended family members to help with child care. Her sister's family, including husband and two children, lived with her and shared babysitting. She worked long hours at a convenience store and felt she had done 'pretty well' in 'keeping a roof over (the children's) heads and feeding them'. However, the school counselor, after one visit to the home, commented how, 'The mom will meet you at the door in a bathrobe, regardless of the time of day and just sort of pass the time of day without really giving answers.' This was not our experience. We found Andy's mother to be tired but cooperative and interested in her child's education.

School records, and teacher information about the home were some-times at odds with the facts as we uncovered them. Gilberto, for example, was said to be a 'foster child' and the youngest of ten children in the family. But a visit to his home revealed that Gilberto had always lived with his mother, and he was the middle child in a family of seven.

Gilberto's teachers had also commented that his family 'sometimes takes care of him, sometimes they don't'. We found a very poor, crowded home but an orderly environment. Several of the children came through during our visits and always demonstrated a respectful attitude toward their mother and her guests.

Carmín also was said to be a 'relative foster child'. Her aunt had even been questioned about the child's birth and infancy, although we found the mother to be available. Carmín's stay with her aunt, as we have noted, was for purposes of caretaking, and also motivated by her mother's decision to move her child from another school to Escalante School in an effort to improve Carmín's educational experience.

Brad and his family were also well known to the staff at Plaza School. All those interviewed had known the boy since he was in the second grade and some since the first grade. The school counselor had been working with the family since that time in order to help the children cope with their father's drunkenness and abuse. Brad's mother was very grateful for the support her children had received from school personnel during that difficult period. At the time of the study Brad's father was no longer living at home and the boy commented there were no more fights.

Information about Juan's home situation was mainly available through the language therapist. She had been working with Juan for several years and had in fact been instrumental in his transfer to Escalante School where she could work with him on a daily basis. She had also successfully advocated for mainstreaming the boy and saw him as intellectually competent in spite of his severe linguistic handicap. The language therapist also implied that Juan's brain injury was due not to an accidental fall but to child abuse. She noted that other children in the family had been seen for suspicious fractures. We had some inkling of a family cover-up when we noticed the mother's signals to the daughter as we were discussing Juan's infancy during the interview. Through the language therapist, then, the teachers were privy to accurate and helpful information about the boy.

We found teachers' comments to be most congruent with our own perceptions of family situations in cases which had received official recognition, such as that of the Child Protective Services. Ann's, Brad's, and Juan's were examples of such families, they had all come under the supervision of the CPS. In addition, in each of these cases support staff such as the counselor and language therapist were also available to provide an informed liaison between the teachers and the home. As a result, these children appeared to be receiving more carefully targeted instructional and social help from the school staff.

Parents and teachers also differed in how they judged the competence of the children at home and at school. Carmín, for example, was described as a case of 'learned helplessness' by the learning disabilities (LD) teacher. She found Carmín moody and noted that 'something isn't registering there'. Her classroom teacher said Carmín had a 'lot of difficulty retaining things' and would often 'drift away' during discussions. She thought language problems were Carmín's primary obstacle to achievement.

According to her mother, Carmín was a healthy, active, sociable baby who walked and talked early, and became the center of attention at family gatherings. She explained how Carmín's social skills and understandings made her seem wise beyond her years. She found Carmín to be a capable helper, taking care of her younger sister on week-ends so her mother could sleep in, and cleaning the house. Carmín's mother was puzzled by the contrast between her daughter's cleverness at home, and her failure at school. She told a story to illustrate Carmín's behavior. When Carmín was about 3, her natural father after a long silence, offered to take her shopping for some clothes. Her mother acceded but only if she could come along as well. As they left the store with the new purchases, Carmín's father carried her on his shoulders. From there she said to him: 'Gracias Chino', using the nickname by which he was known in the neighborhood. Her father responded with displeasure 'Who did you say?' At that, Carmín turned to wink at her mother as she said: 'Gracias *papá*', correcting herself.

Gilberto's mother was similarly intrigued by the discrepancies between the boy she knew at home and what she was told about him in school. She described her son as friendly, enterprising, daring and clever — as well as lazy. He was always very sure of himself, she said, and willing to start a conversation with anyone, 'whether rich or poor'. Gilberto's mother could not understand his difficulties in school, since he was so clever and quick at home. She speculated that perhaps he was getting distracted in the classroom or that maybe his teacher was not hard enough on him. She had been told of his difficulty in being able to articulate his thoughts but could not understand the problem since he learned quickly from TV and was very good at telling stories.

In school Gilberto had been diagnosed as being learning disabled and 'dyspraxic', that is, 'he had the thought but cannot physically move the muscles of his mouth to communicate and get his messages right'. And he had been assigned to receive both learning disabilites instruction (for intensive work in visual processing, memory, discrimination, and tracking, auditory memory and attention, and perceptual motor skills) and language therapy (to improve his coarticulation skills for 'maximally intelligible speech'). However, the boy we saw in school was particularly adept at manoeuvering a complicated schedule and relationships with many different adults. Our view of him was closer to that of his mother than to the boy described in the school records.

Gary's teachers and parents also differed in their assessments of the boy. But in this case, it was the parents who saw problems where the teachers did not. A psychologist friend of the family had 'diagnosed' Gary as 'learning disabled' when he was in kindergarten. Gary had also been prescribed glasses. Gary's teachers described him as a 'marvelous student'. They agreed that his penmanship lagged behind his academic skills but expressed no concern about this. They also believed that he did 'almost as well without [as with] his glasses'. Gary himself expressed confidence in his academic skills and in teachers' favorable opinions about him, but he was unhappy about wearing glasses. In spite of his strong self-concept and his academic achievement, and contrary to teachers' opinions, Gary's parents, intent on having him achieve, had succeeded in securing a placement in the learning disabilities class for their son. It was interesting that in spite of these basic differences, we heard no criticism regarding the behavior of Gary's parents.

Teachers' and Parent's Expectations for Each Other

Interviews with parents and teachers revealed not only their perceptions about each other, but also the expectations they held for each other. We were interested in this aspect of home-school communication because Epstein (1986) found that differences in teacher and parent expectations toward parent involvement accounted for differences in parent and teacher behaviors. Parents, she found, tended to wait for school initiated contacts, while teachers often judged parents' interest in their child's education on the basis of frequency of parent initiated contacts. These assumptions on both sides often led to a stalemate that resulted in lack of contact between the teachers and the parents. Epstein also found a significant relationship between teacher leadership in establishing communication with parents and higher student achievement.

School personnel opinions about Andy's mother are a good example of misplaced expectations for parents. We have noted earlier the innuendo in the school counselor's comment regarding his mother's appearance during her one visit to the home. Both of Andy's teachers also seemed to believe that his main problem was his home situation. His mother was judged to be 'not real supportive of the school' because she did not come to the school: 'if he had more support from the home he would be doing better'. Andy's mother, on the other hand, believed school personnel had 'done real good with him'. She was unable to attend parent conferences because she lacked transportation. She knew there were problems and wished she could help him more but indicated she had little time to spend with the children because of work.

Teachers' perceptions of parent involvement in their children's education seemed to be affected by superficial impressions of the parents. For example, one teacher commented that Travis was 'very well cared for at home and there seems to be real interest in school'. She mentioned one call from the mother as evidence. However, as noted above, Andy was supposed to lack support at home, although the teacher had also spoken to his mother on the telephone. We speculate that differences in surface characteristics such as speech patterns and social skills might contribute to these differences in perception. Travis' mother had a white-collar job where she was used to dealing with the public. Andy's mother did shift work at a convenience store.

Victor's case provided another example of lack of communication between home and school. As far as we could tell, there had been only one visit to Victor's home by any member of the school staff. According to the nurse, when she visited the home the mother mentioned that she had been reported to Child Protective Services the year before because she had slapped Victor and he had gone to school with a bruise. Based on this visit, and on Victor's stories, the teachers had concluded that Victor was the 'caretaker' for his brother and sister, and that his mother did not seem to think it was 'her job' to send him to school. His mother, according to school personnel, 'rarely rose before noon' and Victor had taken 'quite a few blows to the head'. As a result of these perceptions, Victor's mother was not contacted when he misbehaved because his teachers did not expect her to be helpful and feared he would be mistreated. One of his teachers noted receiving monthly phone calls from Victor's mother to enquire about his progress, but she continued to doubt the mother's sincerity.

We found no evidence to support teachers' perceptions of Victor's destructive home situation during our visits. We were however impressed with his mother's ability to describe Victor's reading behavior in precise terms, demonstrating that she was indeed in touch with his school work. Victor's mother complained about missing parent meetings because her son would not bring notes or homework home from school. She felt that Victor's biggest problem in school was his 'feistiness' and she counseled him against fighting. She also mentioned that he frequently brought home good grades and 'presents' from his teacher and she understood these to be signs that he was doing well, especially since she had not been told otherwise. Victor's mother was confident that as he matured and developed more understanding, he would improve. With time, she said, 'he will gradually learn all those things'.

Consequences of Parent-teacher Miscommunication.

Lack of communication, or distorted communication between parents and teachers is only important insofar as it affects the behavior of either towards the children. We found this to happen in various ways. One was in the lack of information given to parents about their children's placement in special classes. Carmín's mother, for instance, was not informed about the Child Study conference until after it had taken place. She was then told that Carmín would need special help in 'reading' and she agreed to her daughter's participation in this activity. Ironically, Carmín's mother was very grateful to the staff of Escalante School for their willingness to communicate with her. She contrasted this school with the previous one attended by Carmín where the psychological report had never been made available to her.

Andy's mother had also been visited by 'a man' the previous year who had told her that her son was going to be placed in a special class. She had not heard anymore about this and did not seem to be aware of his classification as 'learning disabled'. And Gilberto's mother had been told about his 'memory' problems but again did not seem to be aware of the label attached to her son.

These situations recall a recent study by Brantlinger (1987) which suggests that low income parents may not have the information they need to offer a truly informed consent to special education placement. And a study of the referral and assessment process by Mehan, Herwick and Meihls (1986) also concludes that parents may be given such information but may not comprehend the special language in which it is couched. Instead parents tend to be used more as sources of information on the home and health histories of children than as equal participants in decision-making. The parents in this study seemed to fit these descriptions. In fact, only Gary's parents seemed to have the background knowledge and information necessary to be equal participants in this educational decision. They were also the only ones to have college degrees, and their decision occurred outside of the school and was not fully supported by school personnel. Thus we found that important educational decisions which were bound to affect the future of the children, were often made in the absence of effective parental participation.

Another situation where lack of communication with parents resulted in serious misplacement of children occurred in the cases of Lina and Carmín. Both of these girls were placed in English language classes in the first grade on the basis of school perceptions of language dominance. In both cases their mothers had assumed that they were receiving instruction in Spanish, and in both cases it was the threat of retention in grade that caught the mothers' attention and brought them to the school to pursue what Atkin, Bastiani and Goode (1988) have called a 'full frontal' strategy. This strategy contrasts with parents' usual willingness to take the school's advice on trust and show restraint when things are not going well. It is assumed only when parents are sure of their convictions, whether or not they conflict with official judgments.[3]

Lack of communication between parents and teachers also resulted in Victor's case. The teachers' well-intentioned attempts to protect the child from what was perceived to be an unfortunate family situation, led them to misrepresent the students' progress to the mother, and perhaps encouraged Victor to resort to the manipulation of concerned adults in order to avoid the unpleasantness of his academic failure. It is not our intention to defend the mother's behavior. We do not have enough information to determine her sincerity or to judge her as a parent. It did appear to us, however, that isolating the mother from the school was not contributing to positive changes for Victor.

Finally, misperceptions may be encouraged by the school's well-intentioned attempts to give students, especially low-achieving ones, credit for effort. Travis' mother, for example, pointed to her son's report cards as evidence that his academic work was above average. She had asked the teachers to be sure to call her if there was anything she could do to help him but she had not been called, instead she had been told that he was doing well. However, one of Travis' teachers considered him to be 'at-risk' and below grade level, 'though not tremendously so'.

Conclusions

Family Characteristics

The home life of most of the children in these case studies, with the exceptions of Ann and Jerry about whom we have only scant information, was markedly unexceptional. All the children had been healthy at birth and, except for Juan who had suffered a severe head injury about age 1, all had normal infancies and childhoods. Most of the mothers said their children had walked and talked early, and several described the children as 'restless' or 'mischievous'. Only one child, Andy, was described as 'hyper' by his mother, while Mateo was described as 'quiet and shy', and Travis was called 'the lonely one' by his mother who remembered his unwillingness to play by himself. Many of the mothers had been employed and left the children with babysitters, who were, in many cases, relatives of the child.

Most of the children had responsibilities at home; for some this included taking care of younger siblings. Two of the children, Victor and Carmín, were credited by their mothers as being very helpful. And two mothers complained about their children's behavior at home. Lina was said to be irresponsible at home because she did not pick up after herself. Juan just refused to do anything around the house because he said he was 'the man' and did not have to do housework.

The entertainment of the children in these families also appeared to be rather typical of their age group. They all liked to watch cartoons on TV, ride bikes, and play with friends. Juan was somewhat different in that he preferred being with adults, especially an older male cousin. The cousin and Juan's father had taught him how to drive. One day he had moved the car from the front to the back of the house all by himself. Most of the mothers at Escalante School also said their children liked music and dancing and quiet Mateo liked to do jigsaw puzzles. Carmín liked sandlot baseball and would have been on a Little League Team, but there were too few children to organize one in the neighborhood. She had become the unofficial cheerleader for her favorite adult sandlot team.

In general, the parent's descriptions of their children suggested that they saw them as competent and capable with some of the common flaws of children everywhere. With the exceptions of Travis and Brad, the children were also reported to like school. All but Juan, the one child with a serious physical impairment, had begun school with high hopes of success. As a consequence, several mothers expressed puzzlement at their children's unexpected difficulties in school. However, most parents also seemed to believe that current problems would pass as soon as their son/daughter became a little more mature. In only two cases, Carmín's and Gary's, were the parents seriously concerned about their child's progress in school. Carmín's mother said she was 'demoralized' by her lack of success. Interestingly, these were also the parents within the sample who themselves had the highest levels of education at their respective schools.

Parent satisfaction was generally high for parents at both schools. One mother said Plaza was 'the best school in town', while Gary's parents qualified their praise for the same school with complaints about deficits in the district's program. In spite of their children's problems, most of the parents appeared to have faith in the teachers and schools. Lina's mother said she was not knowledgeable about teaching, she felt that was the teachers' job and she expected them to know what to do. Her trust had been shaken somewhat by Lina's misplacement in English rather than bilingual classes but she remained supportive of the school. The trust placed in the teachers was particularly apparent in the tendency of the mothers at Escalante School to compare teachers' concerns with motherhood. Four of the six mothers used this comparison to describe the way a teacher disciplined their child. Within the Spanish culture comparisons with a mother's care is considered high praise indeed.

Communication and Miscommunication

All but two of the parents interviewed had limited school involvement, and both of these were at Plaza School. The two black mothers, both of whom worked full-time, reported they had little contact with the school. On the other hand, the Anglo mothers of Brad and Gary reported that they were quite involved with the school. Brad's mother said she visited the school often, and was involved with the PTA. Gary's college-educated mother was the most involved, and also said she often initiated contacts with the teachers. Gary's mother and father were also personal friends of the Principal and said they visited often.

At Escalante School the daily homework policy was reflected in the mother's comments. They repeatedly said they were willing to help their children at home. The veracity of these statements was supported by their accurate descriptions of the work their children were doing at school, as mentioned earlier in the case of Victor. Two of the mothers were involved in dialogue journals with one of the teachers and both seemed to enjoy this opportunity, they liked the consistency of the communication and the chance to verify their children's understanding of assigned homework. None of the parents in this school mentioned involvement in PTA or being volunteers in school activities but we heard from the teachers that in at least two cases parents had attended school-sponsored activities.

The problem of miscommunication between parents and teachers loomed large in these case studies, in spite of the fact that the teachers were all caring and concerned individuals who worked very hard. At Escalante School, where all our sample students were Mexican-American, the teachers were also members of this ethnic group. All of them had the linguistic skills and cultural sensitivity to work effectively with that population. And at Plaza School the teachers put a great deal of emphasis on their students affective development. Nonetheless, at both schools we found instances of parent-teacher miscommunication.

Not surprisingly, we also found that parents had their own problems in maintaining communication with the school. Some had younger children to care for, others, like Andy's mother, lacked transportation and/or worked long and uneven hours which made attendance at school functions difficult. In addition, most expected teachers to initiate communications with them in case of problems. In the absence of the teachers' initiative, parents tended to assume that all was going well in school. While teachers, in the absence of parental initiative, tended to judge the parents' silence as evidence of their lack of support.

In addition, we have some concern about the form parental involvement should take. Some forms of parental involvement, such as the requirement for informed consent in the case of special education assignment, are prescribed by law but as we have seen, the law was sometimes bent. In most cases, the preferred, and most common way used by schools to involve parents, consisted of school-initiated activities which tended to retain the status of the professional as educational expert and the parent as valued assistant. Both schools sponsored volunteer programs, parent-teacher organizations, parent-teacher conferences, and encouraged parent attendance at school sponsored activities. In addition, at Plaza School, special effort was being made to involve the community at large in the school.

Several researchers have argued that limiting parent participation to these activities may reflect a narrow view of parents' contribution to the school. They maintain that parents are more than sources of support for the school values, or volunteers to provide service, or extensions of the teacher in the home. Parents are also privy to essential and valuable information about children.[4] Most frequently they remain an untapped resource even when critical decisions are made about their children's future.[5] We tried to tap this knowledge and compare it with that of school personnel in the belief that congruency in the beliefs held by parents and school personnel would facilitate educational planning for the child.

We must be cautious not to romanticize parents, and remain cognizant of the reality of pathological family relationships such as those exemplified by Ann's and Jerry's families. It is likely, however, that from the educator's perspective, what we would call the 'instrumental' view of parents is currently so pervasive, that a conscious effort would be required to modify that general assumption.[6] It was clear in several of these case studies, that the parents could offer school personnel important and useful information about their children which might have, if accepted, changed school personnel perceptions about their children. This is what we might expect, given a social-constructivist orientation since the home and the school represent different contexts. However, this information was neither sought, nor, we suspect, would it have been valued if offered.

We agree with Comer (1980), that parental participation is probably most needed in low-income, minority communities or 'wherever parents feel a sense of exclusion, low self-esteem and/or hopelessness' (p 127) because parents in these situations are likely to transmit these attitudes to their children. If the school teacher and the parents stand in opposition to each other, he adds, then the child may be forced to rebel by rejecting the learning situation. He argues, instead, that schools must build on the knowledge parents have of their children, and the relationship they have established.

The position taken here is not that parental involvement as usually conceived is detrimental. In fact, there is a lot of evidence to support the value of parent participation predicated on the school's initiative.[7] We argue instead for extending that limited view to a 'parent-centred' philosophy, as advocated by Atkin, Bastiani and Goode (1988). Such a philosophy differs from most current advocacy positions in its recognition of the 'crucially important knowledge and experiences' (p. 13) possessed by parents and which can constitute an essential resource to the school.

In accomplishing this, the schools must take the initiative. As we have seen, this is what most parents expect. Their expectation has been supported by the National Education Association in their (1982) report on this issue. They concluded: 'it is therefore the responsibility of schools to contact parents as needed and to minimize barriers that tend to overwhelm parents'.

Notes

1 Phoenix High School District (n.d.). *At-risk Factors*. unpublished district document, Phoenix, Arizona.
2 In the case of two of the children, Ann and Jerry, school records were either unclear or unavailable. At least three changes can be documented in the case of Ann, and at least four in the case of Jerry.
3 Atkin, Bastiani and Goode (1988).
4 See, for example, Lightfoot (1978) and Sinclair and Ghory (1981), also, Atkin, Bastiani and Good (1988), and Kugelmass (1987).
5 In their angry and personal account of their family's battle against a school-imposed label of 'mental retardation' on their son, the Granger's cite Glenn Donan, whom they say has worked with children with demonstrable brain injuries for years, as saying that: '. . . almost no professional people talk to mothers, and god knows that nobody listens to them. What makes this so especially sad is that mothers know more about their own child than anyone else in the world.' (Granger and Granger, 1986).
6 An instrumental view suggests parental involvement on the school's own terms. This position is not usually openly acknowledged but it is subtly suggested in policies that 'involve' parents through invitations to become volunteers, to participate in school activities, and to support the school's instruction through home activities. Writers such as Rich (1987a and 1987b) and Berger (1987) all emphasize that view of parental involvement.
7 Epstein, (1986) Goldenberg, (1984) and Clark, (1983).

Chapter 6

Special Populations of Students: At-Risk, LD and Language

As reported in Chapter 2, there was substantial overlap between the categories 'at risk' and 'learning disabled' (LD) among the students identified by teachers for our study. At Escalante School, this fulfilled a prediction made by the Principal that teachers would name LD children as at-risk, rather than children whose needs were not being met by the school. At Plaza School the teachers mentioned 'LD' almost automatically as they described their at-risk students. When teachers were asked explicitly about this in their final interviews, they generally said that most or all LD students were at-risk. The exceptions were children who had learned to overcome or gracefully accept their disabilities. The overlap was intriguing, since one might assume that children who had been tested and placed in special education programs would be *less* at-risk — if those programs were really helping them to succeed in school.

Further, a number of LD students in the Escalante sample were also labelled Limited English Proficient (LEP); all came from homes where Spanish was the primary language. This second area of overlap in student classifications brought up further questions, regarding the relationship between learning disabilities and bilingualism. Thus, we decided to investigate student labelling procedures, and how being labelled LD might shape a students school experiences. We asked teachers in both schools about these procedures, and at Escalante we were able to interview the LD teacher, the school psychologist and the nurse and to observe students in their LD classes. At Plaza, however, the LD teacher declined to be interviewed or observed.

Learning Disabilities: A Controversial Field

Theories and practices regarding learning disabilities have been subjected to considerable scrutiny in recent educational literature, much of it critical of the use of this diagnosis with minority children.[1] Originally welcomed by white middle-class parents as an alternative to labelling their children 'mentally retarded', the LD category has more recently been called a 'dumping ground for minority students who are failing academically' (Cummins, 1986). Since eight of the ten LD students in our study were also minority students, their LD labelling raised some genuine concerns.

Even broader criticisms have been levelled at the LD label. Cummins (1984a) argues that learning disabilities are not coherently defined, that there are no valid measures of these conditions, that estimates of their incidence inexplicably vary from 2–20 per cent, and that remedial pedagogy is often inconsistent with current learning theory. Learning disability as a diagnostic category is over represented among the special education population in the US (General Accounting Office, 1981). In addition, two recent qualitative studies examined the referral and diagnosis process in LD cases and found it quite lacking in objectivity (Mehan, Hertwick and Meihls, 1986; Smith, 1983). As Meighan (1986) has described, 'spurious objectivity and precision' are attributed to the measures and classification decisions of school psychologists, while the actual basis of labelling is often 'rumor, gossip, instant decisions, guesswork, conversations, discrepant information and imperfect biographical stock-taking from memory' (p. 341), i.e., in the opinions of some educational researchers, a student's LD classification is socially constructed, rather than scientifically determined.

Despite doubts about the meanings of the LD label and the efficacy of treatment for these conditions, teachers are likely to refer children for testing and labelling if classroom solutions have not worked and the child is in danger of failing (Willig, 1986). Referral for expert assessment is a way for teachers to share responsibility for at-risk students with other school staff. Special education placement is a readily available solution to the perennial problems of too many students and too little time to devote to those with extraordinary needs. From an administrative perspective, special education programs serve to draw additional resources, especially federal funding into districts and schools. (Mehan, Hertwick and Meihls, 1986)

Labelling Procedures

Nevertheless, the referral and placement processes were not taken lightly at either of our schools. Both principals had concerns about the proportion of children placed in special education at their schools. Both had taken steps to ensure that labelling students, minority students in particular, would not be as easy as it had been in the past. In both schools there was tension inherent in the different roles and powers of classroom teachers, administrators and specialists in the labelling process.

At Plaza School, the Principal had been convinced by teachers Ms. Jones and Ms. Green that 'you can take an at-risk child, without giving them LD help, and that child will succeed'. As mentioned in Chapter 4, she had adopted a Teacher Assistance Team (TAT), a group of teachers whose purpose was to explore in-class alternatives to special education referral (Chalfont and Pysh 1981). The three-member TAT met weekly to hear reports from teachers on students who were having either academic or social difficulties. The teacher and the TAT would generate a list of ideas from which the teacher would choose five ideas to try in the classroom. After two weeks, the teacher would report back on the success or failure of the TAT plan. Only if this plan had failed to work would the child's case be referred to the Child Study Team. This team was made up of the Principal, counselor, school psychologist, social worker, LD teacher and regional LD representative. Even the Child Study Team considered alternatives to testing. For instance, they may have decided that the child's situation called for counseling or social work intervention rather than psychological assessment. The Principal, counselor and social worker may have balanced the clinical perspective of the psychologist and special education personnel with a social/emotional perspective. For instance, the counselor expressed the opinion that schools 'label kids many times too soon and place them in environments that maybe are not the right placement, and I think we really need to be careful to look at that'. Perhaps because of this caution, and an emphasis on alternatives, proportionally fewer students at the Plaza School were labelled LD than at Escalante.

Still, the elaborate process at Plaza caused some teachers concern. As Ms. Green commented, 'You have to go through a lot of meetings . . . and it takes a tremendous amount of time. If you want to get somebody placed, you're talking about four months.' According to Ms. Jones, labelling processes were difficult to fathom. 'I've never understood exactly how you get into LD Lots of times over the years, we have put a child up and they scored too low to go into LD. Or ones that have scored too high . . . I think LD has become so riddled with rules and a hierarchy and forms that it's no longer meeting its function.'

This ambivalence and confusion was reflected in several of our student cases. Even though Brad was doing very well by the end of the year, Ms. Green had decided not to try to remove him from the LD rolls, because, 'it's very difficult to have them removed and then have them put back on'. On the other hand, she also remarked on the 'stigma' attached to the LD label. The Plaza teachers thought that Jerry needed extra services, but he had not qualified because he was considered to be working up to his potential! In Gary's case, the teachers would not have chosen to label him LD, but the decision was out of their hands since a physician consulted directly by his parents had made the recommendation.

Escalante School provided bilingual special education services for students from throughout Raintree District, and as a consequence of this and its much larger size, housed a larger number of special programs and specialists than Plaza. The Escalante staff prided them-selves on performing this function fairly, on providing non-biased procedures for placement in special education. For example, bilingual and non-verbal testing of children referred for special education scre-ening were a standard practice. In fact, despite drawing its special education population from across the entire district, Escalante had a lower-than-allowed percentage of special education students. This was a source of contention between the school psychologist, who wanted to screen more children, and the Principal, who was protective of her minority students.

Until just two years before our study, Escalante had relied on a computerized learning lab, rather than special education programs, to meet the needs of students who were failing to progress academically. As the school psychologist described it, teachers 'arbitrarily' sent chil-dren who 'needed additional help' to the lab. This system had been haphazard and, in his view, ineffective. He said that since the switch to a special education model, there had been a huge increase in referrals for testing, 'probably because there were many kids that were not diagnosed earlier and should have been. Definitely.'

Escalante School did not have the interim teacher-controlled step of the TAT preceding referral of children to the Child Study Team. We did observe teachers exchanging information about children, especially children they shared through their teaming system. We also observed teacher efforts to enlist parent assistance; however, they did not always receive the hoped for response from parents. The next step was to recommend for referral students who were failing to progress to the Child Study Team. This group included the Principal, the school nurse, the school psychologist, and a special education teacher. According to the psychologist, less than a third of the children who were 'child studied' were eventually placed in special education. The number of child study meetings was very high, he explained, since teachers saw them as a good way to get some extra help with their problem students.

We heard that ideally the Child Study Team was a resource for the classroom teacher, offering fresh ideas for instructing and motivating a low-achieving student — rather like the TAT at Plaza School. At their first meeting the team generated ideas for the teacher to try with the students for the following thirty days. However, if the child continued to fail, he or she was very likely to be tested, labelled and pulled out for special services. Once the student's problem was firmly in the hands of the Child Study Team, the medical and psychometric expertise of the school nurse and school psychologist became much more influential. In fact, the school psychologist referred to himself as 'pretty much chairperson' of the team. The nurse completed health and home histories of referred children through interviews with parents, usually on home visits.

Since according to the school psychologist the vast majority of parents did not come to the final decision-making meetings of the team, the nurse's view of the home and parents might be the only one presented.[2] The absence of a parental point of view meant that the decision was based almost entirely on the student's behaviour in the environment of the school, rather than on what Kugelmass (1987) has termed a genuinely 'ecological' assessment of the child.[3]

The Roles of Classroom Teachers and Specialists

Teacher referrals of students to special education are based on a complex interrelationship among teachers expectations, observations and judgments, and student behaviors — a decision process which varies widely across teachers (General Accounting Office, 1981; Mehan, Hertwick and Meihls, 1986). Teacher referrals to special education and teacher efficacy may be negatively related, according to a recent study by Miller (1988). Ms. Jones at Plaza seemed to feel so efficacious, so confident in her abilities to devise classroom-based strategies for almost any student, that she rarely saw a need for referral.

Ms. Santana at Escalante, a third-year non-tenured teacher who seemed much less sure of her efficacy and the security of her position, referred at least three of her twenty third-grade students during the months of our study.[4]

On the other hand, Ms. Santana did exercise her discretion to defer referral in one case. She waited until the end of the year before referring one of her at-risk students, because she did not want him to follow in a family pattern of special education placement. However, even if they resist or postpone referring students, teachers each year receive students who have already been placed in special education categories. Though student classifications are reviewed yearly, students are rarely removed from the special education rolls on the basis of a classroom teacher's recommendation.

Once classroom teachers have made special education referrals, their roles in decision-making about student labelling may become limited, in comparison with those of specialists. Mehan, Hertwick and Meihls (1986) found that teacher participation in classification and placement decisions is limited to providing their 'non-expert' observations of the student's classroom behaviors, which are interpreted and redefined in technical terms by the 'experts'. In the files of our at-risk LD students we found some evidence of this in a contrast between the mundane, commonsensical language in which teachers framed their reasons for referral, as opposed to the technical language of the final diagnosis and individual education plan (IEP). Teachers also said that they did not fully understand the basis of the LD diagnosis.

Therefore there was a sense in both schools that once an at-risk student was officially labelled learning disabled, that student's educational fate was somewhat removed from the classroom teacher's control and placed in the hands of specialists. At Plaza School, relationships between the classroom teachers and the LD specialist seemed distant. The teachers complained that 'we never get any kind of report from the LD teacher'. The LD teacher declined to be interviewed for our study, and seemed to become quite defensive about the possibility that we might scrutinize her practices or reveal her student's test scores. She appeared to answer to her supervisor in the central office rather than to the school Principal.

At Escalante, in contrast, the bilingual LD teacher we observed and interviewed was very warm and communicative, and definitely part of the school team. The teacher expressed a great deal of trust in her abilities. The fact that she had previously been a bilingual classroom teacher may have helped her stay on close working terms with these teachers. For example, she was happy to cooperate with Ms. Osgood in devising an alternative 'pull-in' plan for Osgood's LD students. She also participated actively in the staff retreat we attended, where she quite candidly admitted that she sometimes felt fallible in her abilities to solve the problems of LD students. Nevertheless, she said that she considered LD students to be at-risk if they were not referred for services as soon as possible in their school careers.

The teachers in our study also had great faith in the nurse at Escalante, a bilingual Anglo woman who had become enthusiastically involved in reform efforts at the school. The nurse discussed these reforms in 'popular psychology' terms, explaining that teachers were moving toward a 'non-neurotic and centred' approach to children, and that many families in the neighbourhood needed a 'real nurturing environment'. The importance of the nurse resided in the part she played in the Child Study process, and in her follow-up of children's medical problems. Because of her home visits, she was a primary source of information on families at Escalante, many of whom in her opinion were caught in a 'vicious cycle' of poverty and abuse. Unlike the nurse at Plaza School, who seemed to share the teacher's developmental perspective, the nurse at Escalante employed an epidemiological model. That is, she referred to characteristics of the home environment to explain the at-risk status of students.

The teachers expressed some doubts about the role of the school psychologist. The psychologist assigned to Escalante was also the District Director of Psychological Services. His perspective as a district administrator and his large case load may have contributed to his more objectified, impersonal view of the students at Escalante. He also outlined a very linear, epidemiological definition of at-risk children and their families, and expressed a sense of hopelessness about students with family backgrounds characterized by poverty, illiterate parents, large families, and what he considered poor language use in the home.

When we asked the teachers whether having the psychologist in a key role in the referral process might have presented additional risks for low-income, bilingual children, Ms. Osgood adamantly contended that there were many instances in which teachers had resisted his labelling decisions. For example, children who had recently immigrated from Mexico, or Spanish dominant children who had mistakenly been educated in English at other schools, were given every chance to succeed before they were retained or referred for testing. The Principal, Ms. Bolivar, was known for stepping in to save Spanish-speaking children on the brink of retention or labelling.

LD Programs and the Schooling of At-Risk Students

In both schools, LD and other special services were provided through pull-out programs. At Plaza School, LD students were in the regular classroom except for the brief time when they left to meet with their LD teacher. In fact, Ms. Green remarked that she did not know what the benefits of twenty minutes per day could be. An additional problem was that some of the LD students in this classroom did not *want* to be pulled out of the classroom, and balked when it came time to leave.

At Escalante School, LD-labelled children's schedules and their exposures to the general curriculum were more fragmented. As described in Chapter 4, the school's system of 'switching' reading groups and rotating art/music/PE classes meant that even unlabelled children regularly left their home classroom. In addition, children labelled LD, EMH, LEP, language impaired, or speech/hearing disordered, traveled around the school to attend their pull-out programs. Two of the at-risk children, Gilberto and Juan, were in three special categories, and between reading lessons and pull-out programs spent most of their time away from their homeroom.

Gilberto and Juan attended pull-out sessions with the LD teacher, the language therapist and the ESL teachers. Most mornings they also attended a reading group in a classroom other than their homeroom. Therefore, they each had to adapt to as many as six changes in classroom organization and teacher expectations in a single day. Ms. Santana had devised little paper clocks for their desks to remind them of their complicated schedules.

Gilberto and Juan's relative levels of at-riskness also seemed to be related to their relative success at the social skills required by their school program. Gilberto was skilled at social adaptation. Until he became tired at the end of the day, he closely attended to each teacher's expectations, and cheerfully complied. During lessons he kept up a joking banter with his teachers, and asked interesting questions. If he needed help, he sought it with a smile. Because he had been diagnosed as 'dyspraxic', and was below grade level in reading, Gilberto was considered to be academically 'at-risk'. However, his homeroom teacher, Ms. Santana, thought that his 'noble' and 'sparkling' personality would pull him through his school career successfully. He was also becoming increasingly fluent in English, and in another year would lose his 'LEP' classification. His teachers considered him to be becoming less and less at-risk.

On the other hand, Juan seemed to be at ease in only one of the settings in his schedule, his one-to-one sessions with the language therapist. She had worked with Juan for years and seemed to have found the key to drawing out his playful, creative side. In other settings, Juan was serious and quiet. His impaired speech took some effort to understand, and he never seemed to spend enough time with any teacher, or any group of students, for them to get to know him well. He spoke only Spanish, after four years of school. As a consequence, Juan was considered to be a long-term case of being at-risk.

Pull-out students had special difficulties with work completion at Escalante because they often entered or left the regular classroom in the middle of lessons. We observed both Gilberto and Juan 'killing time' by postponing a task when they knew they would leave the classroom shortly. When they returned, they had to depend on individual teacher attention in order to catch up. Under such arrangements, they could fall further and further behind.

This was much more acute in Ms. Santana's room than in Ms. Osgood's, since Osgood and the LD teacher worked together on their alternative 'pull-in' program. The LD teacher came to the regular classroom three mornings per week during the regular reading time and conducted a group lesson with seven LD children, while Ms. Osgood conducted her English reading group. Though the room was noisy and ccrowded, and Victor seemed more interested in the English group's discussions than his repetitive LD lessons, this was a case in which a classroom teacher was willing to intervene in the special education program for the benefit of her students. Meanwhile, in Ms. Santana's room the 'special' children came and went according to their own individual schedules, out of sync with homeroom tasks, routines and social events.

Interestingly, we also found that the supposedly specialized nature of LD services was actually rather generic. For example, in both schools LD instruction was delivered to groups, not to individuals, as might be expected given the 'Individual Education Plan' (IEP) required for each student. In addition, the psychologist at Escalante admitted that there was no administrative relationship between the psychological and learning disabilities services provided by the district. Therefore, there was no necessary relationship between the psychologists' diagnosis and the instruction provided, presumably in reponse to those diagnoses.

Why Do LD Children Remain At-Risk?

We can propose two reasons why LD-labelled children seem to remain at-risk in their teacher's views. First, these were children for whom ordinary instructional methods had apparently failed. The unresponsiveness of these children might be disturbing to teachers, perhaps as a reminder of their limited efficacy, or their failure to find solutions. Referral was a way to share responsibility for a student's low achievement with others in the school. However, the trade-off was that classroom teachers lost some control over the scheduling and curriculum exposure of special students, and no longer sensed that they had complete knowledge of what was happening with such children at school. The technical knowledge and methods of the school specialists took precedence over the classroom teacher's practical wisdom and experience in the education of these children.

Secondly, the remedial interventions of the LD teachers seemed to have little relationship to tasks in the regular classroom. At Plaza School, the LD teacher was so aloof from the regular teachers that they had no idea what the purpose or format of her lessons might be. The LD lessons we observed at Escalante School were repetitious, standardized activities unintegrated with the mainstream curriculum. For the most part they consisted of drills with isolated syllables or words. Back in their homerooms, the LD children continued to do poorly on the curriculum-based criterion-referenced tests given by the district.

The Plaza teachers both said that a more effective LD program would involve closer teaming between classroom and LD teachers. The two groups could share their expertise and knowledge of students and the specialist could be pulled into the classroom for tutoring and support of the LD students. Such an arrangement seemed highly unlikely, given a lack of communication between regular and special programs at this school. At Escalante, Ms. Wilson felt that at least one LD student, Victor, could benefit most from one-to-one tutoring on 'regular' classroom materials, so that he would begin to experience some success among his peers at his own grade level. But the Raintree school psychologist defended the disconnection of the special education program from the classroom curriculum, saying that he did not want the special education teachers to be 'tutors' for the classroom teachers. He wanted them to 'remediate'.

In short, the classroom teachers knew that by 'regular' education standards LD children were not progressing, at least not very quickly. The children still participated in regular classroom tasks as much as possible, but there were inevitably different expectations for their performance because of their handicaps. And there were also expectations that at least part of the LD students' academic needs were being fulfilled by specialists who had the expertise to 'really' help them.

Discussion

Classroom teachers acknowledge that they need extra help with children who are not progressing as expected. Referral for special education screening is one way to get this extra help and to share responsibility for at-risk children. Often this seems to result in the child being labelled LD and pulled out for special services. However, because of the technical nature of the diagnosis and treatment of learning disabilities, and the delegation of these functions to specialists who may be only loosely connected to the school, classroom teachers may feel somewhat shut off from making substantial contributions to the child's school progress. They may wonder about the relationship between 'remediation' and regular classroom tasks. It is hardly surprising, then, that they see a connection between being labelled LD and being at-risk for difficulties in the regular classroom.

The teacher-controlled TAT at Plaza School may have played a significant role in promoting in-class alternatives for academically troubled students, reducing the number of special education referrals at this school. In praise of such programs, Willig (1986) notes that a sincere effort to develop in-class solutions 'places the onus for academic failure on the instruction rather than the child' (p. 194). However, teamwork between regular and special teachers was absent at this school. Any approach to the education of LD children must seriously consider both in-class solutions and closer teamwork between regular classroom teachers and the special education program. Until then, they remain at-risk in the eyes of classroom teachers.

LD and Language

When compared to Plaza School, Escalante School was a much more complex environment in terms of instructional programming. The school's role as the center for bilingual special education services, and its linguistically diverse student population, offered a natural laboratory where the interaction between these two school characteristics could be observed.

The overlap between LD and limited English proficiency (LEP) is a common theme in the literature (see, for example, Cummins, 1984a; Willig and Greenberg, 1986). The overrepresentation of Hispanics within this category of special education has also been documented. In Texas, for example, the overrepresentation of Hispanics in this classification has been estimated at 300 per cent (Ortiz and Yates, 1983). Several researchers have argued that one of the reasons for the misidentification of LEP students as LD is the lack of understanding, on the part of the educators, of the process of second language learning.[5] The normal processes of second language learning, according to these researchers, becomes confused with language problems in general. These problems are then seen not as transitional, but as permanent characteristics of the child.

Three of the target students at Escalante School were officially labeled as LD and two others had been referred to the Child Study Team for a diagnostic workup which, in their cases, failed to result in a recommendation for LD placement. Another target child was classified as EMH (Educable Mentally Handicapped); he was the only one who had a documented brain injury. All of these children had also been described as Limited English Proficient (LEP), although two of them, Mateo and Lina, were no longer considered to need English as a Second Language (ESL) services. In addition, three of the remaining five students originally nominated by the teachers for the study had also been diagnosed as LD, and all but two of these were also considered to be LEP.

Among the at-risk students many of the specific conditions officially cited to support their LD diagnosis appeared to be language-related. The psychologist stated, for example, that Tom (not one of our target students, but one who was originally nominated for the study) was confused and did not know which language he was speaking at a given time. Carmín, according to her kindergarten teacher, had failed to develop oral language. Gilberto was described as suffering from 'dyspraxia' or the inability to express his thoughts in speech. Though Victor had been officially classified as Spanish dominant, and placed in a bilingual first grade classroom, his teacher had instructed him primarily in English, and his academic and social difficulties in this classroom had resulted in the teacher's referral for assessment.

All of these children came from homes where Spanish was the first language. When interviewed by a bilingual interviewer they all chose Spanish as the preferred language for that purpose, although they sometimes would use English words or phrases as well. This 'code-switching' behavior has been found to be a normal occurrence in the speech of bilinguals (Genishi, 1979; Gumperz and Hernandez-Chavez, 1972). Code-switching by bilinguals has been found to retain the grammatical integrity of the sentence, thereby demonstrating the speaker's control over the oral expression. The children in this study demonstrated this characteristic in their oral language when they switched between Spanish and English. Carmín, for example, described one of her books: 'Tenia un libro que era segundo, first second, es un tiger, y ya lo termine porque ya yo supe cursive bien.' combining the two languages in a grammatically correct sentence. Among all the children, she was the one who exhibited the most extreme case of code-switching, perhaps suggesting some degree of language interference. However, as can be noted, her statements maintained their linguistic integrity. And although she would spontaneously lapse into code-mixing during conversation, she was also able to shift from one language to the other upon request.

The Case of Carmín

We will use Carmín as an example of the special problems faced by children who enter school as speakers of other languages (LEPs). Her school history reflects not only the problems of language placement, but also the overlap between learning disability and the treatment of LEPs.

Carmín grew up in a Spanish-speaking home, but she attended an all-English kindergarten when she spent some time in Arkansas with her aunt. Upon her return to the South-west she was placed in an all-English first grade. Her kindergarten experience in English probably led to her development of a superficial knowledge of classroom English which, in turn, led teachers to assume English language dominance.[6] Carmín's problems in school shortly began.

When her mother became aware of her difficulties, she requested that Carmín be changed to a bilingual classroom. This request was denied on the basis that the child would 'get confused'. Carmín's mother accepted that decision, but not the next one. When she was told that Carmín would have to be retained in first grade, she demanded bilingual placement for her daughter. By the time Carmín was finally placed in a bilingual second grade classroom, she was already trailing those students who had started out in Spanish reading. Since she had received no previous instruction in Spanish, the teacher isolated her from the rest of the class and left her to fend for herself with individual skill sheets.

Carmín's mother continued to be dissatisfied with the treatment her daughter was receiving, and she was frustrated in her dealings with school personnel who, she says, never gave her the information she requested about her daughter. As a result, she decided to transfer Carmín to Escalante School late during her second-grade year.

At Escalante, Carmín was placed in a bilingual third-grade class, while still unable to read in either Spanish or English. She was instructed in Spanish reading and given much individual attention in this classroom, but the teacher, Ms. Santana, felt she was making little progress. As a result, Ms. Santana referred Carmín to the Child Study Team early in the spring. After examination by the school psychologist, Carmín was diagnosed as LD and assigned to receive instruction from the bilingual LD specialist.

According to the psychologist, Carmín had average intellectual potential, but difficulty in processing information. He diagnosed her as 'especially weak' in perceptual motor skills, visual sequencing, tracking, organization, and auditory skills. The diagnosis appeared particularly puzzling to us, given Carmín's ability to copy. Her best work in school, in fact, was penmanship, and she copied words and sentences with great accuracy. Carmín's records included a note in the psychologists report providing assurances that language or cultural problems could be ruled out in Carmín's case. This is a required caveat for LD placement in the case of students whose first language is not English. Yet, as we have seen, such a statement ignored her school history and the changes she had experienced in the language of instruction.

Carmín's LD instruction was in Spanish and consisted of intensive word-attack skills. The group was given a list of words having phonological characteristics in common, for example, the 'ch' sound. They would then go through these words, pronouncing them by syllables, and then writing them. This 'remediation' did not appear to contribute to Carmín's reading development. When asked what she was learning in reading, for example, Carmín responded that she was learning 'che y cha', that is, Spanish syllables. She did not seem to understand the process of reading: that syllables combine to form words, and these combine to form sentences. She did not try to make sense out of what she read. When she was asked to read from a primer during the interview, Carmín 'read' letters and sometimes sounds, seldom words, and never sentences. And when asked to read a whole sentence she combined words that did not match the sense of what she had already read. Yet her conversation in Spanish was coherent, prim, adult-like, and often wise beyond her years.

In her home classroom, Carmín's bilingual teacher used both languages concurrently. She alternated the languages through continuous translations of almost everything she said, including directions and instructional content. She had to instruct in this manner because the students in her classroom could be placed on a continuum extending from English monolinguals to Spanish monolinguals. The decision to combine students with a variety of language competencies in the classrooms had been made by the school's faculty in an effort to avoid the social stigma that had plagued the former separation of English and non-English speakers.[7] However, although this organizational change was seen by the faculty as an important step in changing the climate of the school, it placed extraordinary demands on the teacher and limited her choice of language of instruction.

The continuous amalgamation of the languages required by concurrent translation during instruction has been found to be less effective in bilingual classrooms than separating the languages into monolingual instructional blocks (Dutcher, 1982). The problems it created were clear in the case of Carmín, who needed to clarify her use of the two languages. In addition, concurrent translation limited the possibilities for elaborated language. Teacher talk in the classroom tended to be limited to short sentences or phrases, and to questions requiring only brief answers from the students. Wells (1987) argues that the lack of elaborated language in the classroom limits the opportunity for language development among children whose home languages differ from the school language.

Carmín's school history is a vivid, instructive example of a prevalent problem of mismanagement in language placement in schools. There was no denying that Carmín had severe reading problems, but it was more difficult to determine whether those problems arose from an inherent deficiency, as her LD diagnosis presumed, or whether they were the result of mismanagement by school personnel. Carmín's school history suggested the latter. In addition, her mother's description of Carmín's childhood and of her behavior at home suggested that given appropriate instruction, Carmín could be successful in school.

The problem was how to provide such instruction within current school organization and practices. For Carmín the need appeared not to be for 'remediation', that is, for 'remedies' for her proposed affliction, but for 're-mediation'. Re-mediation, in the Vygotskyan sense, entails the use of different strategies for 'mediating' instructional content (Vygotsky, 1978).

Discussion

Carmín's is not an isolated case. As cited earlier, much has been written about this topic. The problems children like Carmín experience appear to be due to several factors: (a) lack of adequate assessment (Cummins, 1986); (b) school personnel's limited understanding of language learning (Ortiz and Maldonado-Colon, 1986); and (c) the institutional press to develop English language competency before students are ready and without regard to the consequences this transition may have on their cognitive development and on other academic areas (Wong-Filmore with Valdez, 1986).

For language minority children, school placement is usually dependent on an assessment of language dominance. Several instruments have been developed for this purpose and yet, none of them is considered to be reliable in the prediction of achievement in English reading. In fact, several of the most commonly used tests have been found to be less able to predict future achievement than teachers' ratings of students. In one study the teachers' predictions accounted for 40 per cent of the variance in reading achievement scores, while none of the tests accounted for more than 4 per cent of the variance (Ulibarri, Spencer and Rivas, 1981).

Assessments can also be confounded by reliance on reading proficiency in the second language. Miramonte (1987), for example, found that possibly 50 per cent of the Hispanic students in her study who had been diagnosed as LD due to reading problems did not demonstrate the same reading problems in their first language. In fact, they resembled 'good readers' in Spanish. Their supposed 'reading disabilities' only surfaced in their English reading. She argues that assessment strategies that concentrate on reading skills in the second language are likely to underestimate and wrongly assess a student's ability.

The inadequacy of assessment is compounded by the inadequacy of the knowledge most educators have of second language learning. Many, for example, assume that a child who can use English in the playground or in formal environments such as the classroom, knows enough English to participate in a monolingual English classroom (Cummins, 1984b). Educators also tend to frown on code-switching and to interpret this tendency as an indication of deficient language development (Genishi, 1979). They may also ignore the steps through which a second language learner must progress on the way to linguistic competence and discourage a student's use of English with demands that the language be used *correctly* (Ortiz and Maldonado-Colon, 1986).

Or they may not understand that in the process of second language learning receptive knowledge precedes productive knowledge. They may, as a result, underestimate their students' comprehension by judging their capacity to understand a given text on the basis of their ability to speak the language (Diaz, Moll and Mehan, 1986).

Teachers in bilingual classrooms may also not provide enough opportunities for unstructured conversation, limiting the classroom interaction instead, to one word or one sentence responses (Wells, 1987). Lastly, many educators underestimate the time necessary for language development, and the important cognitive support the native language provides the second language learner (Wong-Fillmore with Valdez, 1986).

In addition, a portion of the difficulties faced by language minority students in the school is directly related to the institutional press for learning English. Bilingual education policies are based on the premise that language minority students in general are at-risk, that their home languages are quasi-handicapping conditions which must be 'cured' through linguistic assimilation.[9] These pressures and stigmas are felt by language minority parents. For example, one at-risk student's mother had been convinced by his kindergarten teacher to place him in English-only instruction. The student's second-grade teacher, Ms. Osgood, felt that this had set his progress back considerably. It is very likely that Carmín's mother's decision to send her to live with a relative in a South-eastern state during her kindergarten year was influenced by her desire that she learn English quickly in order to succeed in school.

Teachers' comments often suggested that they also felt the pressure for their students to learn English. One commented that her LEP students needed to learn English in order to improve their social relationships. One teacher observed that children tended to group according to language preferences, but we saw no signs of problems in social relations among Spanish-speaking children or between them and their monolingual English-speaking classmates. Although bilingual themselves, these teachers had been shaped by an educational environment that tends to judge students' success in school by their ability to learn English as soon as possible.[10]

From the institutional perspective, for our bilingual at-risk students, the goal of schooling was to learn English. The possibility that they could also learn in their own language, and that indeed, learning in their own language may be a necessary pre-condition to learning in the second language (Dutcher, 1982), was discarded in favor of transitioning these children into English-only classrooms as quickly as possible. This practice is particularly reprehensible in light of recent research indicating that LEP children who become additive bilinguals enjoy cognitive advantages over monolingual children.[11]

In summary, in the identification of learning problems it appears that where language differences are involved, extreme caution is necessary. Language disorder specialists have described the characteristic patterns of children with true language disorders.[12] And others have pointed out ways to reduce the inappropriate referral of language minority students to special education (Cummins, 1984a; Ortiz and Maldonado-Colon, 1986). Thus, there is information to help teachers work in this direction. But additional information will do little to change an environment that belittles the place a student's home language may play in the school and ignores the advantages that might accrue to students through the development of their full bilingual potential. Changes in the larger society will be necessary if we are to stop seeing differences in language as cognitive inadequacies that must be remedied rather than skills to be preserved — and to stop seeing bilingual children as inherently at-risk.

Conclusions

In a study of the labelling of children as 'emotionally handicapped', Kugelmass (1987) concludes that appropriate classification of a child depends upon an

> ecologically-orientated assessment that would place the child's functioning within the context of his or her experience. In the case of understanding the behavior of children in schools, the culture of the community and the school system's place within it must also be understood. For an individual child, his or her behavior must be seen in the context of the school building he or she attends, as well as the culture of the classroom. (p. 148)

That is, from an ecological position, judgments about a child's handicapped classification are to be withheld until a well-rounded, contextualized assessment, including multiple points of view, can be constructed. In this study we found that the points of view of teachers and parents both were somewhat excluded from the labelling process. The teacher's prerogative is to defer referral of at-risk children to specialists, but there are institutional pressures to share responsibility for students who are not progressing. The teacher's subsequent influence over the schooling of classified children is constrained. However, once the referral is initiated the parent's point of view, other than as interpreted through school personnel, may be excluded altogether.

We did find labelling processes to be context-dependent. Different teachers varied in their referral practices, and policies and practices regarding learning disabilities varied across two schools in the same city. This local variation can serve to either decrease or increase the number of children referred, and either to fragment or integrate their remedial services in relation to their regular program. Some might deplore this situation, and argue instead for decontextualized, totally 'objective' criteria for LD classification and treatment. There are many, however, who doubt that such criteria can be developed.

In the case of Escalante School, one could clearly argue that *more*, not less, local adaption of labelling procedures might be of benefit to language minority students. If LD-labelled children are considered to be at-risk, language minority LD children are considered to be doubly so. Not because of conditions inherent in such children, but because of the institutional cultures that surround them.

Notes

1 See Cummins (1986) and Willig (1986). Recent literature on special education includes a considerable body of work from a critical theory or Neo Marxist point of view, which argues that the fundamental, historical purposes of special education are to legitimize social inequality (see Carrier, 1986; Coles, 1987; and Sigmon, 1987.) Our study presents a view from inside the institution rather than a macro perspective.

2 This view was not always confirmed by our own observations — see chapter 5.

3 As early as 1973, Mercer argued that special education classifications must be based both on a child's school behavior and an assessment of his/her 'adaptive behavior' outside of school. The nurse's interview with the parent was designed to elicit such an assessment by asking about a wide range of home behaviors of the child. However, only the nurse's *interpretation* of the parent's assessment was presented at the meeting and recorded in the child's files. With regard to 'emotionally handicapped' children, Kugelmass (1987) has argued that such interpretations are likely to be based on class and ethnic biases, and that the classification process is disempowering to poor, minority parents in particular.

4 Miller (1988) found that high efficacy teachers refer fewer students to special education than low efficacy teachers.

5 See Ortiz and Maldonado-Colon (1986), Cummins (1984a) and Willig (1986).

6 This phenomenon has also been described in Cummins (1982).

7 See Chapter 3 for additional information about Escalante School's history and organization.

8 This pattern was similar to that found in other bilingual classrooms studied by Wells (1987) and by Ramirez and Marino (1988).

9 Kjolseth (1982) notes that linguistic assimilation is the goal of most 'bilingual' education programs across the country. Ruiz (1984) argues that this is due to a predominant 'problem orientation' in language policy. Knowledge of non English languages is not considered a resource to be developed, but a problem to be solved. To be fair, we were likely to have found a similar situation in Suroeste District, which had a high percentage of Spanish-speaking students and, except in certain bilingual magnet schools, a policy of early transition from Spanish to English in the classroom. Because of political and economic constraints, few districts nationwide have made a commitment to maintenance of students' first language skills.

10 See, for example, the US Department of Education's response to a Congressional report on research favoring bilingual education (General Accounting Office 1987).

11 See Hakuta (in press); Hakuta and Diaz (1985); and Kessler and Quinn (1987).

12 See Cummins (1984a) for a summary of the research in the area of language proficiency assessment.

Chapter 7

The Social Construction Of The Identification Of At-Risk Students And The Dilemmas Of Schooling

The identification of at-risk students as practiced in schools is an interesting and complex process. The epidemiological model of prediction based on background and personal characteristics of the students did not seem to operate in the schools we studied, although most of the students identified by their teachers in this study were low SES and minority. We found instead, that the social constructivist framework better explained school practices related to the identification of at-risk students. Further, we were able to identify four types of at-risk students within the social contexts of the two schools that we studied.

The social constructivist model suggests that at-risk status is constructed through interactions between the teacher's expectations, and the nature of the child and his/her actions within the context of the classroom. And yet, there were constraints on the operation of the model that caused similarities across classrooms not only in the processes of construction, but also in the outcomes we were examining. Clearly, these constaints may be explained by the social, political and economic culture surrounding schooling in the US. However, a discussion of such aspects is well beyond the scope of this book.[1] Our approach in this chapter is to focus somewhere between what Sigmon (1987) described as the micro-system, or the 'actual social interactional patterns', and the macro-system level, the 'superstructure . . . (or the socio-political system)' (p. 81). Thus our view concerns the operation of school districts, schools and classrooms, rather than the broader forces that create the ecological conditions within which these entities operate.

One way to explore the constraints that does not violate the assumptions inherent in the social constructivist model is through the language of dilemmas. Used by Berlak and Berlak (1981) in a study of schooling, the dilemmas notion is useful because it is framed within George Herbert Mead's philosophy which suggests that individuals are a product of social forces while at the same time contributing to the production of those forces (Mead, 1934). Thus, it is compatible with the interactive, nested model that was employed in this study.

This chapter is divided into three parts. The first summarizes our understanding, thus far, of the social construction of at-risk status in schools. The second describes the constraints on the operation of the social construction of at-risk status as experienced by administrators and teachers as they confront the dilemmas of schooling; these dilemmas having been imposed upon the system by broader social, political and economic forces. And the third discusses our particular resolution to the ultimte dilemma arising from this enquiry: If at risk is socially constructed, are there 'true' at-risk students? And if so, how are they to be identified?

Social Construction of At-Risk Status

In a study that traced teachers' decisions to refer students to special education child studies, Mehan, Hertwick and Meihls (1986) suggested that the referral process appeared to fit within a 'social constructivist' perspective. This perspective suggests that the perceptions of a student's classroom performance is a function of the norms, expectations and values of the perceiver interacting with the essential nature of the student. Thus, 'the teacher's decision to refer students is only partially grounded in the students' behavior. It is grounded also in the categories that the teacher brings to the interaction, including expectations for academic performance and norms for appropriate classroom conduct' (p. 87). An additional aspect of the theory is that what the teachers bring to the interaction can affect the students' behavior.

In Chapter 2, we noted that the two sets of team teachers agreed on the status of about two-thirds of the students they identified as at-risk. We recounted a situation in which two team teachers did not agree on the at-risk status of one student, and suggested that differences between the two teachers' expectations for appropriate classroom behavior affected their identification of at-risk students. These different judgments by the team teachers were made within the same classroom and school context and with the same set of students.

This study suggests that Mehan, Hertwick and Meihl's (1986)

concept of the social construction of teachers' labelling of at-risk students could be extended in two directions. First, the teacher's views of appropriate behaviors are, themselves, situation specific. That is, while the teachers' decisions about which students are at-risk are affected by their expectations for academic performance and norms for appropriate classroom conduct, they also appear to be affected by the particular set of students in the classroom. Therefore, as Ms. Osgood stated, a teacher can only pay special attention to a small number of students. These are the students who stand out, negatively, in the class. As these students begin to act like the majority of the students in the room, or if a new student with more abnormal behavior patterns enters, the initial at-risk student will no longer be considered as such.

The second extension of the theory is that the teachers were intuitively aware, in part, of the situation-specific nature of the identification of at-risk students. All of the practitioners interviewed, except the nurse and psychologist in Escalante, stated that students who are at-risk in one classroom may not be considered at-risk in another.[2] This finding is similar to that of Erickson (1985) who concluded that teachers, because they consider what one student is doing in relation to what others are doing, are 'intuitive social constructivists' (p. 7). At the same time, the teachers did not appear to be conscious of their *own* role in the creation of social conditions that contribute to a child's at-risk behavior. Thus, when they began to talk about one of their at-risk students, they described the problem as a stable trait, inherent in the child or, more often, the child's family.

Context Effects on the Identification Process

The context clearly played a part in shaping the teachers' understanding of appropriate and aberrant behavior. Schooling requires that students exhibit a certain set of competencies that are not necessarily appropriate in other contexts such as the home. On the other hand, parents may view their children as competent because the context of the home and family sets up different expectations. Such seemed to be the case for a number of the identified at-risk students. For Gilberto, for example, the teachers and parents did not agree on his competence. His teachers said that Gilberto's problems in school are due to 'dyspraxia', but his mother considered him to be 'very enterprising, knows a lot, he learns words quickly'. The teachers' narrow concerns for Gilberto's competence in academic tasks may have masked other types of competencies that were more apparent in the home context where participation in a broader set of tasks is valued.

In part, as we learned in Chapter 3, the teachers' expectations for appropriate behavior were also shaped by school and school district factors. At Escalante, the approach was highly diagnostic and learning disabled-oriented. Thus, all of the students selected were described in terms of their academic performance. At Plaza, which had a developmental philsophy, there were concerns about the social and emotional well-being of students. Ann was an excellent student; but both teachers and the counsellor were worried about her emotional problems. Further, a higher percentage of students were named at Escalante as at-risk than at Plaza. This difference could reflect the pressures for academic performance exerted on Escalante School by the Raintree School District.

Placing the 'Blame' for At-Risk Behavior

The pressure for student performance, and the teachers' lack of understanding of how the identification process was operating in their classrooms, seemed to lead the teachers to focus on the home as the cause of at-risk behavior in students. As was pointed out in Chapter 5, teachers seemed pressed to blame the family for a child's at-risk condition rather than either the school or the child. Thus, we saw a reverse of the commonly adhered-to notion in the teacher expectation literature that teachers label the student on the basis of knowledge of the non-mainstream nature of the family (Cooper and Good, 1983). In this study, teachers seemed, instead, to label the family, in large part, on the basis of the child's at-risk behavior.

In developing their views of the at-risk students' home, the teachers held beliefs about what a 'good' family is. While their models of the good family varied,[3] they did agree that 'good' parents were those who are seen often at school and who interacted with the teachers. However, it was also possible for parents to affect their children adversely by pushing too hard. The variety of complaints about the at-risk students' homes and parents and the comments about 'good families' lead us to conclude that the teachers could always find something wrong with the homelife of a student identified as at-risk.[4] Searching for the problem at home appeared to relieve them from the normatively inappropriate response of blaming the child, or the soul-searching attribution to their own classroom and school.

Both the social constructivist nature of the labelling of at-risk

students and the teachers' lack of understanding of it can have a profound effect on the nature of the attention students receive. Those students who comply with specific classroom norms of behavior may not be labelled at-risk, and thereby perhaps not receive the extra attention they need. Other students who do not adapt their behavior to the norms of the classroom may be labelled at-risk and placed in remedial programs that set the effects of low expectancies in motion.[5] The next section discusses the constraints that are operating around the social construction of at-risk status in schools that causes the process of construction and many of its outcomes to look similar across the schools.

Dilemmas in the Organization and Management of Schools and Classrooms

The language of dilemmas, as described by Berlak and Berlak (1981) 'captures contradictions that are simultaneously in consciousness and in society' (p. 124). Formulated in each act are:

> the forces which shapes teachers' actions (those forces that press toward particular resolutions to a dilemma) and the capacity of teachers not only to select from alternatives, but to create alternatives. Each of the dilemmas thus represents contradictions in the society that reside also in the situation, in the individual, and in the larger society — as they are played out in one form of institutional life, schooling. (p. 125)

Lampert (1985) used the notion of dilemma management to describe teaching. She suggested that teachers have multiple goals that often compete, making a 'solution' to one problem the cause of another. She pointed out that the typical resolution does not eliminate the conflict, but rather avoids additional conflict. 'This way of submerging the conflict below an improvised, workable, but superficial resolution is, of course, quite different from what many cognitive psychologists or curriculum experts would advocate' (p. 189).

In this study, we noted that the dilemmas faced by both school districts were similar, as were those at the school and classroom levels. Given the different contexts of the schools and school districts, however, each of these dilemmas was managed in different ways. Rather than reflecting one extreme or another, the actions were located on a continuum between the opposite poles of a dilemma. The location of these actions had profound effects on the at-risk students.

School District

Although Suroeste and Raintree School Districts were in close proximity to each other, Suroeste had almost five times as many students at Raintree. This difference in size may have been responsible for the ways in which they responded to a major dilemma in schooling: *Control versus Autonomy*. This dilemma has been exacerbated recently by calls for accountability and increased test scores. These calls have pushed state and local officials in the US toward top-down controlling mandates of standardized instructional methods and outcome measures[6] at the expense of provididng a professional and autonomous environment for principals and teachers.

At the time of study, Suroeste had not adopted a specific instructional model. Direct district influence was limited to the imposition of a computer-assisted instructional system (CAI) and a requirement that teachers use a plan book that was to be examined weekly by the Principal. There were also other less obvious district influences, for example, on the textbooks available for use. But, in general, the school district appeared to provide a considerable amount of autonomy to individual schools.

In contrast, as pointed out in Chapter 3, Raintree District, with the lowest test scores in the area, was under pressure to improve student achievement. This position also contributed to actions designed to improve teacher performance and accountability. Thus Escalante enjoyed considerably less autonomy than plaza, and, in turn, its teachers were more closely monitored and their behavior more prescribed than that at Plaza.

Interestingly, Suroeste had not deliberately adopted its loosely-coupled structure out of a desire to provide conditions of autonomy for its individual schools. This structural outcome was more related to the sheer size and politicization of the school district that created conditions within which decisions that would lead to tight control could not be made. Forces are constantly at work at the national, state and school district levels that could push Suroeste into a more controlling stance. For Plaza, the result of the autonomy was an effective school, a positive outcome of the loosely coupled system. What about those schools that are not effective? Strategies for standardization of methods and outcomes are designed to 'fix' the less effective schools, without concern for their effects on schools like Plaza. Thus, Plaza's relative autonomy was fragile; a condition that could change quickly in this social and political environment. Unfortunately, Escalante's tightly coupled condition is less fragile.

The Schools

A major dilemma faced by the principals of the two schools in this study was planned *change versus stability*. While schools and classrooms change constantly, there is sometimes a call for major structural changes designed to alter important aspects of a school such as climate, social relations, and the instructional program. At the same time, change is discombobulating and painful,[7] and could be detrimental to student learning.

Both principals had been recruited to 'fix' their respective schools. And both had sought to do so with major structural changes. The difference between the two was that Ms. McGuffey was now in her sixth year at Plaza, and Ms. Bolivar in her second at Escalante. Ms. McGuffey had spent most of those years improving the school climate after a desegregation order drastically changed the school population. The school seemed finally stable, and she was turning her attention toward improving the academic climate. Ms. Bolivar was in her second year at Escalante School. She also was concentrating on the school climate which, in the case of Escalante School, was affected not by a recent court order but by the generalized sense of powerlessness that often afflicts minority communities (Ogbu, 1982). However, while Ms. Bolivar was attempting to improve school climate, the school district was simultaneously pressuring her to make changes in instructional program and the structure of the teaching staff.

The planned changes on many fronts in Escalante School created a stressful situation for both teachers and students. It could be seen in the teachers' hectic pace, and in the often incoherent curriculum offered to the students. Such a situation probably impacts more severely on at-risk students since they appear to be more sensitive to school and classroom climate than other students.

There was an additional, if only implicit, pressure on the staff at Escalante: pressure to develop, as quickly as possible, the English language competence of their students. The source of this pressure was well beyond the school. It is, in part, a national press that, in the face of contrary evidence,[8] insists that children who are linguistically different are a problem.

Thus, Escalante and its students and teachers were suffering from too much planned change. The slow, deliberate pace of change at Plaza School allowed its school people the luxury of time to reflect together on what was effective about the school and what changes were needed.

The Classrooms

All of the teachers in this study were considered to be effective. And after considerable observation in their classrooms, the researchers agreed that they were, indeed, effective teachers. Nonetheless, we saw teachers in both schools struggling with three dilemmas that significantly involved the at-risk students while developing strategies that affected their lives.

The first dilemma — teachers' attention: *the individual versus the group* — is created, ecologically, by the social organization of the classroom. Classrooms are unique examples of asymmetrical organization here groups of twenty-five to thirty children are under the direct supervision of one adult. The unavoidable range of individual characteristics present in such groups requires the teacher to accommodate instruction to individual needs continually while simultaneously attending to the total group.

The second dilemma — *form versus substance* — emanates directly from personally-held values concerning the outcomes of instruction. Educational goals often combine two worthwhile goals: the development of cognitive skills and the inculcation of good working habits. Effective teachers must strike a balanced approach in the pursuit of these goals. But teachers, as all individuals, differ in their beliefs about what is important. Their beliefs slant their choices of classroom activities, and their evaluation of student performance towards one of those goals.

The third dilemma — *teaching to the test versus teaching for deep understanding* — has been created by society's interest in ensuring educational accountability through the use of standardized tests. Although the tests are supposed to measure student learning of the curricular content, they are not always compatible with the required curriculum. Teachers must continually choose between teaching the prescribed curriculum and teaching to the test. They must also choose between providing a relaxed, comfortable atmosphere where competition is minimized, and preparing students for test-taking through competitive, timed activities.

In the following sections we will describe each of these dilemmas within the contexts of Plaza and Escalante Schools, as well as strategies used by teachers in their attempts to resolve them.

Dilemma One — Teachers' Attention: Toward the Individual or Group

This is the most enduring, crucial and prevalent dilemma confronted by teachers in classrooms as they are organized today. Fraatz (1987) refers to this dilemma as the 'paradox of collective instruction' (p. 24). The enhancement of cognitive skills and understandings for some students requires extended individual attention from a teacher — whether it is a regular teacher, a special teacher, an aide, another student, or, as some propose, a learning device such as a computer. If this attention is provided by the regular teacher while the students are in a group, it could demean the student, and/or create a situation in which other students withdraw their involvement in the lesson. If the attention is provided to the individual student outside the group, management problems ensue unless the group is well disciplined and engaged in another activity. While most students require such individual attention some of the time, at-risk students are particularly in need. Thus, this dilemma, and the strategies developed in response are particularly crucial for at-risk students.

Various attempts to individualize the curriculum respond to this dilemma; however, there are a variety of other alternatives as well. The following were used by some or all of the teachers in this sample.

Pull-out Programs

These programs were developed as a response to the apparent need of some students for specialized and individualized attention. Such pull-out programs reduce the range ,of individual differences in the classroom and thereby allow the teachers to work with the whole group, while allowing the students-in-need to receive more individual attention.

However, as shown in Chapter 3, such programs have unintended consequences.[9] The teachers in Escalante all mentioned that a team approach taught the students to be adaptable as they moved from one teacher to the next. While adaptability may be considered a virtue, such learning may become more important to students subjected to six teachers a day than other kinds of learning such as cognitive skills. This outcome may be particularly detrimental to low achieving students. Good (1986) pointed out that low achieving students have a particularly difficult time moving from one teacher to another. These students were also observed to lose an excessive amount of time in transitions from classroom to classroom.

Specialists in the Classroom

In part, as a response to the problems inherent in the pull-out programs, teachers in both schools thought that team teaching situations in which a regular teacher would team up with a specialist to deal with the students with learning problems would be a possible solution. One teacher in Escalante had already arranged for the LD teacher to work within the regular classroom.

While this strategy provided stability for children, and encouraged closer coordination between the classroom teacher and the specialist, it also presented its own set of problems. First, the limited space available forced the special teacher and her group of students to work under very cramped conditions; second, the classroom setting offered many distractions to children who tend to be susceptible to distraction and third, the group of children receiving the special instruction could be unequivocally identified as slow learners by their peers.

Grouping

Cooperative learning activities with extensive amounts of peer instruction were used heavily in the Plaza classroom and in one of the Escalante classrooms. These groups served a variety of purposes such as (i) accommodating individual needs; (ii) allowing students to work cooperatively; (iii) developing social skills; and (iv) reducing competition among students. While neither classroom employed any of the classic models described by Slavin (1983), they did, variously, employ individual elements, particularly peer instruction. These group activities also allowed the teachers to work on other tasks such as direct instruction with another group, individual counselling, planning or marking papers. Ms. Jones explained that this organization of instruction provided an alternative to individual instruction: 'In each group the motivation and skills emphasis would be the same and then each child works according to their own level.' She also encouraged the students to work together and cooperate, and she built in some group scoring techniques.

In most instances these group activities appeared to serve the functions mentioned above. Students did work together, progress at their own pace, and help each other with the tasks. But there were times when the at-risk students spent too much time on a task that was too difficult for them and gained little from the task. They needed more help than could be provided from peers who had not been trained in peer tutoring.[10] On these occasions they needed, and would have benefited from, more direct instruction.

Centers

Centers were designed to provide students with hands-on experience to solidify concepts learned in other forms of instruction. They also provide activities to engage students while the teachers are working on other tasks. But in order to reduce management problems in the classroom, these centers also need to be engaging and to capture students in an activity of intrinsic value to them for a period of time. In managing the dilemma of individual attention in the classroom, teachers often appear to focus on the latter goal rather than the former. That is, centers are created to provide a capturing activity for students rather than to develop concepts and understandings. Both observers noted that some center activities at Escalante seemed unimaginative, for example, coloring preprinted pictures of 'care bears'; or so unstructured and unsupervised as to lose any connection with their presumed instructional purpose. For the children, centers were a place where 'we play games'.

Homework

Homework is sometimes mandated in school districts, and is seen by some elementary teachers as an extension of school activities, and an opportunity for students to receive individual help from their parents. Homework was an element of the instructional program in both schools. In Plaza, students were only to receive homework on Tuesdays, Wednesdays and Thursdays. No homework was assigned over the weekend, the counselor stated, so that students could spend time with their families and 'get away from school kinds of things'. The counselor also stressed the fact that homework had to be related to a concept already introduced in the classroom and could not be 'busy work'. The Principal and counselor worked with the teachers to reinforce this approach.

One teacher in Escalante used the concept of homework to promote communication between herself and the parents of at-risk students. She used 'dialogue journals' with both Mateo's and Lina's parents. This project involved sending homework and notes between home and school via the child each day. The parents could thus track their children's daily performance and receive frequent feedback and direction from the teacher. The parents reported in their interviews that they liked this method of becoming more involved in their children's instruction.

In other instances, however, homework appeared to be a set-up for the at-risk students. In both schools it was recognized that parent involvement was essential to the child's completion of homework. In Plaza, for example, the students were assigned to take home the 9, 10, 11 and 12 multiplication facts and learn them. Ms. Green said, 'I'm not going to take time to help you memorize them here.' Three weeks later, Andy and Travis still had not learned them and their instruction required this knowledge.

Except for the dialogue journals, there was no consistent effort to provide specific direction to parents about how to help. Further, some students did not appear to have the environment and support system conducive to doing homework in the evening. This may be particularly the case for some at-risk students. Thus, if important work is to be learned at home, certain students who may need it the most do not receive this help and fall further and further behind.

Language choice

Linguistic competence is one of the many dimensions across which groups of children may differ. These differences are magnified in schools such as Escalante which include many children whose home languages differ from the school language. Faced with such a diverse population educators may choose to segregate children by home language competence, thus Spanish-speakers might be isolated from speakers of Chinese, and English monolinguals from both. This type of organization had been used in the past at Escalante and was discarded by Ms. Bolivar who found that the student's home language was used as a tracking device and served to isolate Spanish-speakers. Low expectations on the part of teachers and minimal academic challenge had characterized the treatment received by those students. As a reaction to the situation she found upon arrival as Escalante, Ms. Bolivar chose to combine students in linguistically heterogeneous classes. This choice led to a better integration of all students while also presenting teachers with a major challenge: which language to use during instruction.

Teachers responded differently to this challenge. Some minimized the use of Spanish, although Spanish was the only language spoken by some students. One consistently translated all instruction, a task that seemed to consume a lot of her energy and was perhaps counter-productive for students such as Carmín who was in need of intensive language development. The use of this strategy also tended to impose limits on the potential for elaborating either language into complex statements. Thus teachers were faced with a choice between using the children's native language to enhance their pupils cognitive development while they learn English, or to accelerate their pupil's rapid acquisition of English by disregarding the home language.

Dilemma 2 — Form versus Substance

Most teachers feel that the tasks they provide are meaningful and important. Further, they use the tasks to teach both substantive skills and working habits. In this study, the latter — good working habits — sometimes became more important than the substance. Ms. Wilson, for example, seldom mentioned in her interviews problems with students who failed to learn skills. Her at-risk students were those who did not complete their work, or did not bring in their homework in the morning. If students are 'working', they are not causing management problems; further, they are learning to be responsible — a major student goal for all three teachers at Escalante, and one that was also mentioned by the two teachers at Plaza. Thus a dilemma in these classrooms concerned the development of tasks that met two very different types of goals: the learning of a cognitive skill and the development of a trait of character — responsibility. Further, these goals had to be met in a way that preserve a classroom environment of quiet and hard-working students. In managing this dilemma, the ways in which students approached a task often became more important than what they were learning from it.

While this seldom happened at Plaza, the instances of such an approach were very hard on the at-risk students. Handwriting activities were busy work more often than a cognitive learning activity, yet the at-risk students missed other instructional activities to finish a handwriting task. This was the case when Andy spent over an hour writing seven lines, starting over when he was half-done because he had forgotton to 'skip a line' and never getting to the extended activity that was provided for that group. The lack of finished work also excluded the at-risk students from being chosen to do special things. Travis wished that he was chosen more often like some others in the classroom. When asked why he thought other students were chosen, he said: 'Cause they get done with their work'.

At Escalante, Ms. Santana and Ms. Wilson both emphasized completion of work as well. This emphasis was not accompanied by explanations of the meaning or importance of the work or its relationship to other activities. The basis of non-completion of work seemed to vary for different at-risk students, even though all of them faced the same challenge. For Mateo, for example, tasks seemed uninspiring; for Victor, many tasks seemed impossible given his present skills. Ms. Santana also emphasized 'beautiful' or 'neat' work, and assigned frequent copying tasks for spelling, handwriting and writing. For Carmín, who could neither read nor write at even the first grade level, neat copying and handwriting had become sources of pride and ends in themselves. However, for high achievers, neatness and completion of the tasks were just the icing on the cake of successful performance.

For the high achievers in both schools, neatness and completion were a part of the 'school game'. Brad, the high achieving at-risk student from Plaza, was observed erasing two lines of already written print. When asked why, he responded that he had forgotten to skip a line. He was asked why he thought this was important. He said, 'So it fills up more room and I get done faster'. Many of the at-risk students in the study had not figured out the school game, and seemed to understand school as the form of tasks rather than the substance.

Dilemma Three — Teaching to the Test versus Teaching for Deep Understanding

One example of a dilemma in Lampert's (1985) study of an elementary school math classroom was provided by her description of a teacher who was ambivalent about knowledge as portrayed in standard curriculum tests and fundamental understanding of a phenomenon that may not be measured accurately in a standardized test. She felt, however, that students should be prepared to take these tests because they so strongly affected their futures. Lampert indicated how this ambivalence was managed in working with students on correcting their tests.

This dilemma was also salient to all teachers in this study. Standardized tests were important aspects of school accountability; and scores on tests by grade level were published each year by school in the local newspapers.

The teachers in Plaza attempted to deemphasize the testing program as much as possible. They felt that if they could work for three years with the students without potential negative experiences such as tests to destroy a student's self-confidence, most of their students would be more than satisfactorily prepared for grade 4 by the end of that time. They did, however, work with students on some test taking skills in the mornings. They had also developed a number of timed activities. Most of these activities had content expectations as well, but for the at-risk students the timed aspect seemed more important to them than what was to be learned from the activity. The teachers unconsciously fostered this attitude by usually stressing the time and not discussing the value that was to be gained from the lesson. For the students who worked slowly, this put an additional burden on them and either caused them to lose interest or not attempt the task. It also affected their attitude. Travis said: '. . . sometimes I just don't know what to think of and I sometimes I just think that there's . . . it's not too fun in the classroom'. It seemed to foster the notion that getting the task done was more important than how it was done.

As mentioned in Chapters 3 and 4, the tests were more salient to the teachers in Escalante. In fact the curriculum was adjusted to provide experiences for students that would permit them to score higher on tests. Since all of the students in Escalante had been identified as at-risk on the basis of academic problems, most were receiving remediation of one sort or another. The focus in Escalante was on revisiting the same curriculum as covered but not grasped before. The lessons, then, were aimed at teaching simple 'decoding' and computational skills, at a level often far below the children's interest and comprehension. In their 'regular' reading groups, some third graders were still working in first grade basal readers. Attention and motivation problems and 'off-task' behaviors were observed.

Both teachers and students in Escalante were anxious about grades and tests. The teachers, who wanted to provide grades on the basis of effort felt that giving low grades to students on the basis of achievement was not fair and would lower motivation. They also felt that the concept of outcomes-based education conflicted with the use of standardized tests. An additional concern was that the tests were given in English to their LEP students.

The teachers admitted that this dilemma was not being managed well in Escalante, and they hoped that the school district would begin to understand the extreme contradiction of the two approaches to education such that they would be able to provide a coherent message to their students and the parents of their students.

The Identification of At-Risk Students

Ultimately, the question concerning the identification of students at-risk must be addressed. If at-risk status is socially constructed, is the label totally relative, even ultimately meaningless, or are there students who really do require extra help? And can we come to some consensus as to who they are? These questions represent the paramount dilemma we had to face in this study. If we conclude that there are students who require extra help, and we have a sense of who they are, we either have violated the social constructivist framework or become, ourselves, an element in the construction of at-risk status. This dilemma has undoubtedly confronted those who have approached, critically, the identification of students as learning disabled or special education students. For example, in his *Radical Analysis of Special Education*, Sigmon (1987) reiterated several times that he does believe in learning disabilities. True LD students, he stated, exist: 'i.e., those with obvious average intellect who have learning problems which were traced to some medical-related problem — prenatal illness; birth problem; postnatal disease, injury, illness; or a genetic disorder (p. 101). However, he did not tackle the problem of the identification of those he would label as 'true LD students'.

As educationists, our sense of the resolution of this dilemma lies in the interaction of the context with the identification process. Within the environment of schooling as we know it today, there are students who, as Sigmon (1987) suggested are true L.D., or in our classification system, 'readily identifiable'. These students do need extra help within schools as they are organized today and within our society with its particular set of values. Others, however, are only at-risk in some schools, or classrooms; but not in others. It is our feeling that students who are identified as 'problems' are, in fact, at-risk because the set of understandings, expectations and beliefs that surround these students are liable to propel them in adverse directions. However, we also feel that the immediate environment of the school classroom or home is creating those conditions; and it is those environments that we can work toward changing.

At-Risk Students

The four types of at-risk students that emerged in this study differ in terms of the nature and severity or obviousness of a student's condition as the student interacts with school and classroom structures. The four types may be arrayed along a 'context dependency' dimension.

Readily identifiable	Severe	Context dependent	Masked
I	II	III	IV

While, as we said above, the status of all at-risk students is socially constructed, the first two types of at-risk students would be considered at-risk in most classroom settings in the US. Thus, their identification is somewhat independent of the school context, at least within the US. The designation of other students, however, less stable. That is, the third type of at-risk student would remain labelled as at-risk in some contexts but not in others, and the fourth would be masked in many school contexts. Descriptions of the four types are as follows:

I Readily identifiable: Students with identifiable physical/ cognitive/emotional conditions that lead to academic problems in the regular classroom

This category includes children with sight, hearing or speech problems, and/or severe emotional or cognitive processing problems that obviously interfere with the students' attempts at gaining academically from the regular classroom environment. These students require help in developing strategies that allow them to benefit from the regular school program. While a large number of the at-risk students in this study were designated as learning disabled, and thus were receiving such special help, it was not clear that all of them belonged in this category.[11] In fact, only Juan, at Escalante School, appeared to demonstrate an unequivocal, identifiable physical condition likely to result in academic problems. Thus treatments for this category of students are being used to deal with students in the first three categories of at-risk students, including the less severe.

II Severe: Students whose background and family circumstances lead to problems that make it extremely difficult for the school to provide an adequate instructional program from which the students benefit

Jerry, whose family moved at least three times during the year, is an example of this type of at-risk student. The school may attempt to respond in extraordinary ways to Jerry, but the abuse in the home and the family mobility patterns prevent the school from carrying through its program of intervention. Some of these students may be only temporarily at-risk because family circumstances such as divorce cause momentary disabling conditions in the child's life. Others, like Jerry and Ann, appear to live in conditions that could lead to more permanent problems.

III   Context dependent: Students who are sensitive to classroom and school settings, and are seen as at-risk in some, but not in others

Most students' behavior varies from one classroom to the next. The students in this category, however, are considered at-risk in some settings but not in others. Approximately one-third of the students in this study who were in the classes with more than one teacher were considered at-risk by one teacher but not by the other. Further, a number of others were taken off the at-risk list during the course of the study. This is one indication of the degree of instability of the at-risk designation. Limited English Proficient students may also fall within this category. Within a school and classroom context that welcomes the richness of a dual language approach, LEP students are not at-risk. In schools that view LEP students as problems to be remediated, such students would be considered at-risk. Thus, the values attached to particular characteristics, and/or the school or teacher's willingness to adjust instruction to meet the students' needs, are important determinants of at-risk status within this category.

IV   Masked: Students, who because they adapt well to the class-room are not diagnosed for learning problems, and thus are not provided with the help they need to eventually succeed.

Students in this category may be very similar to those described in category I, but they mask their academic difficulties by learning how to 'pass'.[12] These are students who respond well to the social organization of the classroom and participate adequately at a surface level in classroom tasks. This responsive behavior, however, masks some basic learning problems that may go unnoticed by their teachers for some time. One of the students followed by Goldenberg (1986) was of this type; and a study of students who were and were not referred to special education uncovered such a group.[13] In that study, it was primarily girls who had not been diagnosed by the regular classroom teachers as needing special attention, but with in-depth diagnostic tests were identified as special education students.

These four categories provide a useful scheme for organizing the various conditions that led the teachers in this study to identify students as at-risk. They also highlight the degree to which individual student characteristics interact with school factors and the ways in which the term at-risk may be used inappropriately. For example, minority students, as well as Speakers of Other Languages (SOLs) are often automatically labeled at-risk solely as a consequence of their ethnic, racial or linguistic status. Within our conceptualization, those students would fall within category three, suggesting that the designation may be more a function of school factors than of student characteristics.

Summary

We accept the nature of the social construction of at-risk status. However, as educationists, we reject the position assumed by Marxist sociologists who, after a critical analysis that places the blame for all ills within the educational system on the macro social, political and economic culture, may suggest that the only solution is massive restructuring of society. Instead, we feel that it is possible, indeed critical, to work within the system to improve the lives of children through schooling. We are encouraged by the differences between the two schools in this study. Not everything related to at-risk status is determined by macro forces. The next chapter will describe our vision of what schools may do to reduce the chances of students being at-risk in those environments.

Notes

1 See, for example, Sigmon (1987) and Carrier (1986) for more Marxist sociological analyses, and Coles (1987) and Kugelmas (1987) for critical analyses of learning disabilities and special education.

2 The psychologist and nurse expressed views that more accurately fit the epidemiological model: students at-risk were those with certain background characteristics that they considered to be negative, such as ethnicity in the case of the nurse, or family characteristics such as low SES, illiterate parents, or poor language usage in the home in the case of the psychologist. The psychologist's outlook was that: 'They're not kids who are ever going to benefit from whatever we do with them'. The size of the school (750 students), the role definition of these two positions (the psychologist saw many students in the school district in trouble but only saw them again if they remained in trouble) within the school, and their own conceptions of their role seemed to contribute to their adoption of the epidemiological model.

3 Ms. Green, for example, felt that not at-risk students come from

traditional families that provide extensive background information experiences such as trips to museums, and lots of books in the house. Ms. Jones described not at-risk students as 'serene, confident and other kids never tease them'. She attributed this state to an open atmosphere in the home in which children are always told what is going on, and are brought into decision making.

4 Several of the homes were, in fact, psychologically and physically detrimental to their children in school, and several others were marginal. However, the blanket of blame was also laid on families that provided physical and psychological care for their children, and were highly supportive of the schools.

5 In addition, as Erickson (1985) pointed out, the teacher's lack of understanding of the social constructivist nature of identifying problem students 'restricts the teacher's capacity to learn from experience' (p. 9).

6 See, for example, Elmore (1983), Metz (1987), and Richardson-Koehler (1988).

7 See, for example, Fullan (1985) and Huberman and Miles (1984).

8 There is consistent psychological (Laboratory of Comparative Human Cognition, 1981), social (Cummins, 1986) and linguistic (Hakuta, 1986) evidence that SOL students should not be rushed into an English-only instructional program, and that bilingual students have cognitive advantages over their monolingual peers.

9 See also Mehan, Hertwick and Miehls (1986() and Smith (1983).

10 See Mergendollar and Marchman (1987) for a discussion of this issue.

11 The survey responses of a sample of big city special education coordinators and research directors indicated that they also feel that too many students are mislabelled as LD (Buttran, Kershaw and Rioux, 1987).

12 See Rueda and Mehan (1986).

13 Described in Chalfont and Pysh (1981).

Chapter 8

At-Risk Status: An Interactive View

This study of at-risk students began with the sense that at-risk status is derived on the basis of an interaction between the characteristics of the child and the nature of the classroom and school. The focus of the study was on that interaction. As the study unfolded, the importance of this approach in describing the forces that lead to the identification and treatment of at-risk students became more clear and meaningful.

This interactional approach to the study of at-risk status contrasts with the commonly accepted model prevalent in the at-risk literature. The latter, called the epidemiological model in Chapter 1 (Figure 1), suggests a linear relationship between certain student characteristics and undesirable outcomes. Schools and social agencies mediate – negatively or positively — between the students' characteristics and the outcomes. The focus in this approach, however, is on the child rather than the interaction: the child's problem characteristics, behaviours and eventual unacceptable outcomes.

An Interactive Model of At-Risk Status

Our intial interaction model (Figure 2, Chapter 1) led us to investigate how the social and academic demands and characteristics of the classroom within a particular school interact with the family background and personal characteristics of the at-risk child. We were fortunate, however, to be able to study at-risk students in two different school districts. We found that school district policies, particularly those concerning curriculum and testing contributed to the way in which the individual classrooms functioned. Thus, our revised model (Figure

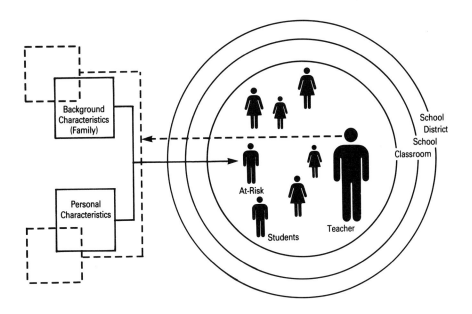

Figure 4: Interactive Model of At-Risk Status

4) includes a third concentric circle, the school district. We also found that the teachers' views of the child and of the child's family were strongly affected by the teachers' beliefs and expectations, the characteristics of the rest of the students in the classroom, and the school setting. Because of the power of these views, which seemed, at times, distorted, they have also been included in the model as dash lines.

The description of at-risk status, as derived from this study, and depicted in Figure 4, is as follows:

The Classroom

The *child* enters the social setting of a classroom that consists of other students, a teacher(s), a set of materials and equipment. The child initially behaves in certain ways because of a combination of family background, personal characteristics and previous school experiences. Within that same classroom, other students bring with them a set of personal and background characteristics. Together, the *student body* creates a set of behavioral norms which the child more or less adopts, and against which the individual child is compared. The norms are also shaped by the *teacher's* beliefs about learning, student work and how a classroom ought to operate. Thus the teachers' mindscape (Sergiovanni, 1985) interacts with the objective setting of the classroom (the characteristics and number of students, the materials, the school setting) to create a context to which certain students do not appear to respond. These are students considered at-risk. However, because individual teachers' mindscapes differ, as do the objective settings, some students may be at-risk in one classroom and not in another. And because the setting and circumstances that help to create the at-risk situation are in constant flux, a certain student may enter or exit the at-risk rolls at any time.

A student who does not respond appropriately to the classroom context as created by the teacher and the rest of the students provides a stressful situation for the teacher who then attempts to determine the causes for the maladaptive response. The teacher can select from among three causes: the individual child, the school or elements in the child's background that are external to the school. In this study, the teachers turned to the family as the cause of the at-risk students' problems. The children's personal characteristics and past school experiences were seldom mentioned as causing at-risk status. In blaming the family for the child's behaviour in class, the teacher may develop a distorted view of the family based on surface level observations of parents, stories told them by the child, and school folklore. For example, a parent's lack of attendance at school functions may be interpreted as lack of interest in school functions, and perhaps even in the child.

Further, the teachers' view of the child is unavoidably limited by the narrow range of competencies a child is called upon to display in the classroom. The teacher may generalize his/her perceptions and assume that the child's school behavior is representative of the child's totality. Thus the teacher's views of the at-risk student's competencies may also be distorted and at odds with the views of the student's parents.

The School

A number of aspects of the school, such as school size and nature of the student body and the faculty interact with the principals' and other administrators' beliefs, knowledge and skills to create a school context that, in turn, affects classroom contexts and the ways in which at-risk students are identified and managed. A school principal can help shape the ways in which students and learning are viewed by selecting like-minded teachers, creating atmospheres (including incentives)in which certain approaches prosper, or attempting to change teachers' views through formal staff development programs. The organization of the school — for example, the number of specialists and the ways in which they operate — also affects the classrooms and at-risk students. Further, the school's outreach program may help families create home situations that help at-risk students gain from the school context.

The School District

The school district's effects on a classroom are often felt indirectly, but as demonstrated in this study, may be quite powerful in the lives of at-risk students. The organization of the programs such as the special education and bilingual programs within school districts, for example, determines what is available to a school and whether the principal of a school supervises the program experts who work within that school. Thus, this organization may affect the degree to which the experts become members of the school community. The choice of curriculum and testing program, and more importantly, the ways in which the test scores are viewed and used affect school personnel's views, feelings and actions.

The concentric circle may be expanded further, by considering the local, state and national contexts; however, this study investigated only as far as the school district.

At-Risk Students

Within the model described above, we identified and described in Chapter 7 four types of at-risk students. These types differ in the nature, severity or obviousness of a student's conditions as the student interacts with school and classroom structures. The first type, readily identifiable, includes students with sight, hearing, speech, severe emotional or cognitive processing problems. These students would be considered at-risk in most classrooms in the US. The second type, severe, consists of students whose background circumstances make it difficult for the school to provide an adequate instructional program for them. Included in this category are students whose families are highly mobile, or who are victims of child abuse. The third type, context dependent students, includes those who may be seen as at-risk in one classroom context and not another. The fourth, masked, exhibit good social classroom skills such that the teacher may be misled into thinking that the student is progressing normally.

The recognition that at-risk status is not a blanket term, but rather an interactive and malleable one highlights the need to apply different resources to cope with the different conditions that may impede students from benefiting from instruction. The following section will therefore move from a descriptive analysis of at-risk status and students including the four types of at-risk students described above.

Change in Elementary Schools

A descriptive study of at-risk status in practice does not necessarily provide prescriptions for effective practice. In fact prescriptions from afar on how to organize a school and classroom and how to instruct students would be quite inappropriate, and, as has been indicated in recent literature, ineffective.[1]

One reason for the ineffectiveness of common prescriptions for the reform of elementary schools may be derived from this study. Both school districts and both schools confronted tensions that required their personnel to make decisions that were unique to their respective settings. For example, all school districts are faced with the tension between standardizing school and classroom practices and thereby raising the level of the least effective, and providing autonomy to principals and teachers in running their schools. The two school districts resolved this tension in quite different ways, and it is not clear that one resolution would be appropriate for both districts. Principals are also faced with the tension between creating a coherent curriculum and common approaches to teaching, and providing autonomy to the teachers as professionals to develop their instructional programs as they see fit. Some faculties, particularly those with inexperienced teachers, may require more top-down leadership than others. This tension must be resolved in a setting-specific fashion.

It is possible to conclude from our study and from current literature and practice that there is no standard blueprint for schools undergoing reform. Further, the changes that could be proposed on the basis of this study of at-risk students would not easily form a new 'program' that could be used in schools across the US. As is the case with all complex systems, solutions to problems often are located between extreme positions. The directions for individual school change must be chosen based on an intimate understanding of the context of the school and the abilities and views of its personnel. It is in this light that the following considerations the effective elementary schools for at-risk students are laid forth.

Effective Elementary Schools for At-Risk Students

While the following considerations are derived from a study that focused on at-risk students, it becomes clear that they may be appropriate for most children. Within our formulation of at-riskness, all students potentially may become at-risk for a variety of reasons. Thus, our particular focus on the schooling of at-risk students uncovered problems that, if alleviated, would benefit all students. Nonetheless, the problems in schools seem to affect the students who have been identified as at-risk more strongly and negatively than other types of students. A major goal for a school, therefore, is to create an environment in which students are not unnecessarily viewed as at-risk. The following discussion should help schools focus on that goal. Following the presentation of the considerations, there will be a discussion of those principles that are particularly appropriate for the four types of at-risk students described above and in Chapter 7.

The School District

Mandates

As pointed out in the effective schools' literature,[2] individual schools should be allowed to assess their own contexts and needs and shape their instructional programs for their students. One way for this to happen is for school districts to minimize mandates that attempt to control curriculum and instruction. While we were limited to examining only two school districts in this study, we did find major differences on this dimension. Raintree's mandates for instructional method, the structure of the teaching staff, the curriculum and the testing program, severely restricted Escalante's staff in responding to the needs of their student population. On the other hand, Plaza's relative autonomy allowed its teachers and staff to create a very special environment for its students.

Accountability requirements and testing programs

Some degree of accountability is both politically necessary and perhaps useful. We found, however, that standardized testing programs created far more damage than they engendered more effective education, particularly at Escalante School. The testing program should, therefore, be minimal, and be thought of as diagnostic for schools and classrooms.

We found a particular problem in the use of tests for special population students, particularly those who were speakers of other languages. Much has been written about the inappropriateness of the instruments used for diagnosing special education needs, and yet tests that have been found to be unreliable, and methods found to be inappropriate continue to be used.[3] As educators, we all bear an awesome responsibility when we contribute to the labelling of a student as 'handicapped'. In spite of our best intentions, the label is likely to affect the student's educational experiences negatively and therefore have conseqences on life chances. We should strive to expand the data-gathering net and increase its quality by using holistic strategies and the least invasive, most culturally sensitive procedures. Two such strategies are Feurestein's dynamic assessment and the use of ecological strategies as advocated by Mercer and Lewis.[4] School districts can and have used these alternatives to reduce the number of children in special education and to improve the diagnostic value of the assessment process.

The School

The school environment

Much of the effective schools and school reform literature has suggested that schools should provide a stable and coherent social-educational program for students. It suggests, for example, that school rules be consistent with classroom rules, and the curricula reasonably coherent among grade levels. However, we found a more subtle form of lack of coherence that could sidetrack at-risk students' academic learning; and this involved differences in teachers' expectations and communication rules — even if using the same curriculum and ostensibly reaching for the same goals. We found this in a very minor way in the team-taught classroom in Plaza School. However, it was very evident at Escalante, with its team approach to the organization of instruction that provided up to six teachers a day for its grade 2 students. This implies that the following two forms of organization of instruction could be beneficial: (i) An individual teacher working in his or her own classroom with the group of students, and possibly with the same group over several years; (ii) an organization in which groups of teachers work with groups of students. In the latter case, it would be important that the teachers agree on their approach to teaching the students, and that they be able to describe their approach as 'our's' rather than 'mine'. Most students may withstand minor conflicts in philosophy and approach between or among teachers and perhaps even benefit from them. However, more than minor conflicts could be detrimental to students, particularly those at-risk.

This principle also suggests that pull-out programs should be reconsidered. It appears to be very difficult in the present organization of schools for specialists and classroom teachers to meet and agree upon common approaches and coherent programs. One possible solution would be that the specialists become an integral element of the teaching team, and/or work within the regular classroom.

In our study, we found that schooling was particularly important for our severe at-risk students because it was a home away from home. The climate and organization of the two schools reflected a caring and warm environment and a place where children knew that their physical, personal and social needs were acknowledged and met, and it was a place where they wanted to be. In order to create this environment, some one person needs to care for the school life and personal growth of each student; and all adults in the school should feel responsibility for all students. Given this requirement, it is easy to see why a small school (less than 250 students) would more easily create this environment than a large one; but it may be possible to break a large school into minischools in order to provide this atmosphere for its students. This principle also implies that all adults, including the specialists, work together under the principal's leadership, to become a part of and help develop this climate.

It was also apparent in Plaza that the development philosophy that permeated the school helped to create this very special climate for its students. This philosophy honors individual differences in developmental growth, and creates a non–competitive atmosphere that mini-mizes anxiety for both teachers and children.

School faculty

The teachers in our study understood that the context of a particular classroom plays an important part in whether a child is considered at-risk. At the same time, they did not express an understanding of the ways in which their own classrooms affected the behavior and thus the indentification of the at-risk students they identified. Perhaps they did not have the time, nor the language to explore this issue. One way to approach the development of such understandings would be through staff development programs in which teachers reflect on their beliefs and expectations about students and learning, study cases of students, classrooms and schools, and talk with those who understand the culture of their students.

The presence in the school of adults who share the students' culture and ethnicity may contribute to better relations with the community and provide role models for the children, but does not guarantee it.[5] The teachers who have successfully navigated the academic world in which their students are floundering may find it difficult to deal with some students and families who they perceive to reflect badly on themselves or their ethnic group. These teachers may also face insti-tutional and social pressures that require them to behave in certain ways. Once again, these situations call for opportunities for reflection and analysis of deeply held beliefs and expectations.[6]

In addition, teachers need help in dealing with students they perceive as problems in their classrooms. Teachers indicated that it may take two or three months from the time they ask for a child study team to evaluation until the time help is received. The special education testing and referral process in most school districts is a long and difficult process that is designed to protect students from being needlessly labelled, and to provide information to parents about the process. As was concluded from a survey of special education and research directors in big city schools, however, many students are needlessly referred and accepted into such programs (Buttran, Kershner and Rioux, 1987), and teachers do not receive help in working with a student for several months.

Alternatives to this cumbersome referral process are programs designed to provide teachers with immediate support in handling students that they perceive as problems in the form of in-class alternatives with which the teachers can experiment. In schools with Teacher Assistance Teams (TAT) programs (Chalfont and Pysh, 1981), teams of teachers and a specialist meet once every week to provide guidance to teachers in working with problem students. Such a program allows teachers to respond quickly to students perceived as problems, and may reduce the numbers labelled as LD or handicapped.

Schools and parents

In this study, we saw the importance, at least in the teachers minds, of contact between parents and teachers. Other studies have also documented its importance in terms of student achievement.[7] At the same time, we also saw how difficult it is for many parents, particularly those who are single and working, to meet with the teachers before, during or shortly after school. The solution to this problem requires creative organizations and possibly additional funding. For we cannot place the burden of contacting parents at night and on weekends on the already overworked teaching force.

One possibility is to employ persons such as the counselor at Plaza whose functions include contact with parents. However, this means that the teacher's view of the family is one step removed from contact with the family. Creative organizations of teachers, however, may allow a teacher on a team to take a morning off to allow for home visits in the evening.

Schools and social agencies

In this study, we saw a number of incidents in which the schools were called upon to involve social agencies in the lives of their students' families. Unfortunately, the agency most often called upon was Child Protective Services. Families often respond to the CPS investigations by moving,[8] which may cancel the beneficial effects a school may be having on a child. While other agencies could be called upon by teachers, anyone who has tackled the maze of social agencies is aware of how difficult this is. Schools have not traditionally played this social services role, and thus there is no-one in the school for teachers to turn to for help.

Schools could develop or work with existing networks of social agencies to help families receive immediate assistance for problems affecting their students and to obtain feedback that would help teachers understand the individual circumstances of their at-risk students. This is a complex function, and may require an individual in the school who spends close to full-time on such activities.

Classrooms

The environment

Many at-risk students grow up in homes and neighbourhoods which are in constant flux, perhaps bordering on chaos. The classroom can provide for these students a safe, stable and predictable environment. The fewer contexts a student must negotiate each day, the easier it is for them to develop a coherent sense of their academic activities. This view of learning lends support to the notion of a student staying in a given classroom with one or a set of teachers for several years, as we saw at Plaza. Further, given the problems encountered by students who enter the school during the school year, careful procedures should be developed to socialize these new students and help them adapt more quickly to their new classrooms.

View of knowledge

One view of knowledge is that it is a commodity to be transferred to students. Socio-linguists have helped us see why minority at-risk students are particularly disadvantaged in a context in which knowledge is controlled by the teacher and conferred upon the students. All students bring to school a set of understandings and social learning processes that are reinforced in their homes and communities. Majority students' understandings are often similar to those of their teachers. Thus a majority student has a better chance of acquiring the teachers' meaning in a classroom in which the teacher functions as a conduit of knowledge. However, both majority and minority students would benefit from a system that allows the teacher to understand and value the meanings that their students bring into the classroom and those they develop while they are there. Knowledge, then, would be owned by all participants in the classroom and be manipulated in meaningful ways.

If knowledge is to be constructed in the classroom, the curriculum and its organization must be flexible such as it was at Plaza. It helps if the learning tasks are authentic and meaningful enough to allow students to connect and use knowledge and skills learned in different contexts in creative ways. A lock-step, hierarchical curriculum in which tiny chunks of information are fed to the students in a piecemeal manner does not allow for the construction of deep meaning. Further, it causes anxiety for teachers who feel they must cover the content of the curriculum, and this anxiety is passed on to the students.

Students requiring extra help

In Chapter 7, we discussed teachers' concerns about providing extra help for students while not seeming to single them out and thereby lower their self-esteem. We found, in the Plaza classroom, that students requiring extra received it in an atmosphere that was non-competitive and did not seem to demean the student having difficulty with a particular skill or concept. This is difficult to manage in crowded classrooms. However, there are some classroom organization alternatives to consider, depending upon the particular objective being pursued. For example, when certain cognitive skills are being learned and practiced by students, the teacher/pupil ratio should be low. One possibility is to bring specialists into the classroom to work with groups or individuals during times when the regular teacher is also working with groups. Another is to rely on peer tutors, and cooperative learning groups in which students work together to perform a task. Peer tutoring is an underused, undervalued and highly efficient strategy for classroom instruction. It is important, however, that student tutors receive direct instruction in how to tutor other students. Further, incentives based on 'not failing' a test or getting a low grade should be minimized. In fact, invoking the concept of failing is probably more detrimental that beneficial to at-risk students.

When students fall significantly behind, we often consider remediation approaches. However, as pointed out in Chapter 6, these strategies should re-mediate, or introduce new ways to mediate learning for the student (Vygotsky, 1978). When a student who has trouble learning how to make sense out of the written language s/he is unlikely to benefit from intensive and relentless repetition of the alphabet or syllables. Indeed, repetition may be a daily reminder of inadequacy and eventually cause a child to use avoidance techniques such as misbehavior and absenteeism. A different approach to the instruction of a subject may be required.

One possibility to consider for a child who has fallen behind is to *accelerate* rather than *decelerate* the pace of instruction. This counterintuitive notion suggests that the automatic slowing down of instruction for students who are not achieving at expected rates may be the wrong strategy. This is especially so when instructional activities are fragmented into smaller and smaller pieces that become meaningless and boring. These approaches may in fact ensure that a student will never catch up since they reduce expectations for students, slow down the pace of instruction so that the gap continues to widen, exphazize mechanics over substance, and contribute to loss of self-esteem without ever providing hope for students to advance (Levin, 1987). Students who have problems learning to read may respond to more interesting and challenging language activities such as story-telling or theatrical productions. Skillful use of these activities might provide the motivation to help bridge the student's skill gap. This may be particularly important for students with real cognitive deficiencies who may nevertheless be too mature for what they may deem to be 'baby' strategies. It has also been shown to be important for speakers of other languages (SOLs) whose comprehension level may be underestimated by teachers who assess student competency in reading on the basis of oral language development (Moll and Diaz, 1987).

Homework

We observed several situations in which the homework assignments required active parental involvement. These homework assignments seemed to disadvantage further the at-risk children whose parents could not, for whatever reason, provide support for the child's completion of homework. Thus, we should not count on homework as a mechanism for students to learn new knowledge and skills, particularly if its completion relies on parental involvement.

Effective Schools for Four Types of At-Risk Students

It is suggested that it would be useful for the above issues to be discussed in school districts, school and classrooms in considering the development of contexts that are desirable for all types of students, including at-risk students. However, some of the principles are more important than others in meeting the needs of the four different types of at-risk students described above.

Readily Identifiable

In recent years, federal funding has helped schools to establish programs for this category of at-risk student. This has led to pull-out programs and the use of specialists to work on the specific problems faced by these students. These programs, however, face several problems. First is the problem of the use of diagnostic procedures based on unreliable tests (Smith, 1983) with predetermined outcomes. Thus, a child who has problems with classroom tasks is tested with an instrument that mirrors classroom tasks and thereby is labelled deficient. The specialist may make an unjustified leap between failure to perform the tasks as measured and specific cognitive deficits. Further, the prescriptions are often based on a one-to-one tutorial model of instruction, and thus may be inappropriate for use in either a regular classroom, or a specialists' classroom with a small group of students.

In addition, specialists tend to ignore the social aspects of schooling. Thus they may work with a student on specific skills in a manner that often makes it difficult for these students to transfer those skills to the regular classroom tasks. In other cases, the sporadic nature of instruction by specialists contributes to a fragmentation of instruction that works against children who have difficulty integrating their learning activities.

Perhaps a more insidious problem is the potential these programs have to provide relief to a teacher in dealing with a problem student. At least part of this problem is due to the self-perpetuation of the bureaucracy that has grown up around special education (Smith, 1983). But for a teacher faced with a student who does not respond to instruction, even after considerable effort on his or her behalf, there are few alternatives. The most common is the referral process and the hope for instructional assistance from a specialist. It is particularly appropriate to consider two of the above issues: providing a stable and coherent social-educational program for students; and organizing the school to respond quickly to teachers' problems with individual children. The former would ask schools to consider alternatives to the standard pull-out programs, and the latter may reduce the number of students being referred.

Severe

If schools are to respond to at-risk students in this category they must accept roles that have not traditionally been performed by schools. That is, the school would operate in the areas of community and family social work. This presents a challenge to schools, organizationally, fiscally and politically. As was suggested above, the school could work more closely with other social agencies to ensure that the families of at-risk students receive the help that is available to them. Very often, this help must be provided quickly. Thus, the important function that the school could provide is knowledge and skills in 'pushing the right button' to ensure quick response from social agencies.

Context Dependent

What is required for these students is an understanding on the part of the school and its personnel that the school is part of any problem it identifies in this student. It therefore follows that the teachers are part of the solution. Thus the principle that suggests that school faculties be reflective about the social and cultural organization of their school in relation to the student's background would be extremely important for this type of student. Further, a quick response is essential in working with any school situation that places such a student in an at-risk category. The two-month referral process is too long. Students labelled at-risk for a period of time may become, as a result of low expectations from teachers and parents, and damaged self-concepts, more permanently disabled.

Masked

The principle that is important in working with these students is related to the development of reflective practitioners. Teachers should be helped to understand the difference between the performance of a task and learning; between the form of an assignment and its function. Most importantly, the school should enunciate the social goals for its students and help the teachers understand that while social and academic learning are related, they are not synonymous. Working closely with specialists, teachers should continue to assess and be concerned about the cognitive learning of all students in the class, whether or not they are also adept at social skills.

Conclusions

This study of at-risk students employed a methodology quite different from that used in quantitative, predictive at-risk studies. It also produced quite different findings and implications for schooling. The close examination of several specific student cases and a focus on the interaction between the characteristics of students and the context of schooling suggested a model that reflects the reality of existing structures and operations of classrooms and schools. More importantly, the focus on the lives of at-risk students provided fresh insights into the ways in which the dilemmas of schooling can be managed in ways that are more or less detrimental to these students.

Many of the highly touted reforms, particularly those that are designed to increase the status and prestige of the teaching profession, seem to ignore the individual learner; particularly the learner at-risk. As noted in this study, the reforms that combine the creation of hierarchies in both instructional objectives and in the teaching profession chop up the learner's day into minute particles of social and cognitive task demands that require the students themselves to pull them together into a coherent educational experience. At-risk students have great difficulty doing this. Thus, while the jury is out on whether these reforms increase the status and prestige of the teaching occupation, we are beginning to develop information that indicates that they are not necessarily good for students.

How can the schools change to meet the needs of the at-risk students? One finding of this study helps us think about an answer to this question. We found that the school people that we talked to felt an extraordinary amount of dedication, care and responsibility toward the at-risk students. Their motivations were strong, their knowledge about their students was sound and deep, and their skills in classroom practices were extremely high. The problem in the schools seemed to relate more to the culture of the school, and society's expectations for it. As Fraatz (1987) points out:

> In the culture of the school, as in any complicated social organization, the need for routine too easily becomes an end in itself and individual needs and differences go by the board. This tendency . . . is not a function of stupidity or callousness. [Teachers] are a dedicated, highly motivated group struggling to make a difference in the lives of disadvantaged youngsters. There are no villains here: there is a culture of the school that, when not

understood, works against outcomes consistent with stated goals. (p. *x*, Foreword)

School people should, therefore, be allowed to do what they do well, within a context that acknowledges and explores the culture of schooling writ large, and in each school. They need help in exploring that culture; but they do not need mandates concerning forms of instruction and the organization of teaching, nor pressure from testing programs that function as a control over teachers' behavior.

Notes

1   If a theme could be extracted from recent articles devoted to teaching policy, it is that the top-down, rational, prescriptive model of change does not work in elementary schooling (for example, Johnson and Nelson, 1987; McNeil, 1987; Metz, 1987). Further, it would appear that implementation of specific structural reforms as proposed in such reports as the Holmes Group (1986) and the Carnegie Task Force (1986) may have adverse effects on students (see Richardson-Koehler and Fenstermacher, in press).
2   For example, Purkey and Smith (1983).
3   See, for example, Smith (1983), Willig and Greenberg (1986), and Ulibarri, Spencer and Rivas (1981).
4   See a summary of these methods in Casanova and Howard (1987).
5   The three teachers in Escalante, for example, were Hispanic.
6   A recent study of 'second generation discrimination', reported in a recent *Education Week* (Snider, 1987) indicates that school districts with sizeable proportions of minority teachers refer a smaller proportion of their minority students to special education than school districts with smaller proportions of minority teachers. The researchers concluded that black teachers 'are probably less willing to decide that a black student is not teachable in the regular classroom' (p. 1).
7   See, for example, Tangri and Moles (1987).
8   There are no figures on this phenomenon, although it is folkwisdom among school people. It certainly seemed to be the case with Jerry's family who moved soon after the CPS started to investigate his home situation.

Appendix 1: Interview Guidelines

First Teacher Interview

The purpose of this interview is to understand the teacher's concept of at-risk, and to observe the use of the concept with reference to individual children. The interview will consist of three parts: background information — designed to create rapport between teacher and interviewer, and to develop a sense of the teacher's background experience and views of the school context; definitions of at-risk at a relatively abstract or generalized level; identification of at-risk students in the teacher's classroom, and reasons for the designation.

In addition, the interviewer will be able to explain the purpose of the study, and how it will impinge on the teacher's time.

Greetings, friendly 'situated' questions. (How has your day been, etc.)

Thanks for participating . . .

Purpose of the study (general): Review what was said on the phone — the purpose of the study is to gain a better understanding of 'at-risk' learners.

First of all, I wonder if you could tell me something about your experience as a teacher? (Probe for number of years, locations, grades, years in the school)

In general, what would you say is the approach to children that is practiced here at . . . ? Or goals. (Pick up on terms used, restate, clarify, ask for definitions)

What are some general things about your own approach that you think are special? (Do not go on too long with this, but get a fairly clear self-description)

How would you compare working at . . . with other schools you have worked in? Or how would you compare working with third grade with working in other grades?

If you were to make some broad generalizations, how would you describe the students here at . . . ? What kinds of students come to this school? Is there anything special about the kids who come here?

What could you say about the communities or neighborhoods the children come from?

Describe this year's classroom.

Now I would like to ask you about the idea of 'at-risk'.

You know, the term 'at-risk' seems to be used in many different ways. Our first task is to determine how the teachers in this school think about the term. Could you describe to me how you think about 'at-risk' learners?

(Try to move them away from descriptions of individual children — maybe you could say that we will be talking about individual children later on . . . but don't push too hard because they may only be able to think about the term in concrete ways)

Probes

　If they use a descriptive definition (for example, hyperactive kids), try to get at why they think kids act that way (without cuing them in on 'predisposing factors').

　If they start with a predictive definition, try to probe on how they know a kid is 'at-risk' (for example, if they don't read the kid's file).

　Try to get at their notions of why it is that two similar kids are different in terms of their 'at-riskness'.

Have you taught at different grade levels? If so, what was your notion of 'at-risk' there?

Would the other grade 2/3 teacher(s) in this school agree on the definition of 'at-risk'? If an 'at-risk' student in your class moved to a different school, would he/she automatically be an 'at-risk' student there?

Who do you talk to about your 'at-risk' students?

Can you think of some at-risk students in your class this year?

Can you tell me why you think that . . . may be considered 'at-risk'?

What had you heard about . . . ?

What do you think could help this child out of the 'at-risk' category? — Probe for resources.

Any other children?

(Let teacher talk about the students only prodding as appropriate to ask about those he/she might miss or to ask for explanations and additions if necessary.)

Are there any students who are on the verge of being 'at-risk'?

If so, how are they different from the 'at-risk' students?

Positioning Students for Success: Second Teacher Interview

The purpose of this interview is to probe more deeply into teachers' beliefs about at-risk students through general questions about the concept, and questions about specific students. The questions have been designed to be non-judgmental, and to sound as much as possible like we are interested in (but not concerned about) their thinking and expert practices — which we are.

This is a general guide. Certain questions have been placed after others (for example, about obtaining information about home life) so as to not provide indicators about what we want to hear. However, this is a very loose guide.

1   Were we to start this study all over again, right now, how would you define at-risk?

2   Given the new emphasis on at-risk — and maybe even this study — has your thinking about at-risk changed over the year?

3   At this point, who would you say are the at-risk children in your class? (Write down each name, quietly compare with names from first interview).

For each, why are they at-risk?

4   What about . . . (Names on the list who are not mentioned, or those you are particularly interested in.)

5   I wonder if we could go over each of the names and describe to me what the solutions may be — if you have tried anything special . . .

6   For each name, will he/she always be at-risk?

7   We are interested in how teachers obtain information about the home life of students because that appears to be an important element of at-riskness.

Allow for a general statement.

Then probe on individual names.

8   What does a 'non' at-risk student look like? Could you describe one?

9   Are there any LD students not labelled at-risk?

10   What makes the difference between an LD at-risk and an LD not at-risk?

Probe on at-risk, for example, are there any LD students you do not feel are really LD? Vice versa.

Or An open-ended provocative question at the end:

It has seemed to us, in looking at the data across two schools, that most of the at-risk identified students are LD. Does that surprise you? Will an LD student always be at-risk?

11   What about boys and girls — more boys than girls are named as at-risk. Why?

Principal Interview

Their background – years of experience

Philosophy at the school

This school and other schools?

Community/neighborhoods?

How would you describe the students here?

Feelings about kids at risk

Causes

How does your faculty view at-risk?

Marginals? Or gray area?

Does everybody have the same criteria (for example, would a kid be at-risk in another classroom)?

What do you hear about at-risk from the district?

What would you like to see at your school for at-risk kids?

How do you compare lower elementary and upper elementary at-risk kids?

Would you say that most of the students that you see are at-risk?

What about this designation learning disabled? Are all LD students at-risk?

Parent Interview

Introductions

In most cases you have already met once with at least one of the parents, probably the mother. Recall with the parent(s) the conversation you had then and what you discussed about the study. If this is the first opportunity to meet the parent(s) start out with a discussion of the study and its purposes, also why their child was selected as a participant. Take some time to explain the purpose of this interview and to reassure parent(s) that anonymity will be preserved, also remember to ask permission to record the conversation.

Questions

1   I'd like to know something about . . .'s family history. How long have you lived in Tucson, in this neighborhood? Where did you live before?

2   What is . . . position in the family? How many other members in the family? Who are they and how are they related to . . . ?

3   Can you remember the time just before and after . . . was born? (Probe: Was the child welcome, did any drastic changes result from the child's birth?)

4   What was . . . like as a baby? (Probe: Try to get at personal characteristics, for example, curious, happy, etc. as well as physical ones, for example, onset of walking, talking, frequency of illnesses, described as pretty, cute . . . ? You may suggest looking at family pictures together to get spontaneous descriptions).

5   Who took care of . . . most of the time during the day? (Probe: How did he/she get along with caretaker? Is it still the same caretaker?)

6   What are some of the important happenings in . . .'s life? (Probe: Are there any family stories about the child?)

7   When and where did . . . start school? Can you remember his/her first days of school? (Probe: Parent's own feelings about those days and about school and teachers.)

8   What is your opinion about . . .'s school experience? (Probe: What does the child say at home about school? How much has parent(s) learned first-hand?)

9   Of the three years . . . has been in school, which would you say

was his/her best/worst year? Why? (Probe: Was there a special [or especially disliked] teacher or activity?)

10 What would you say he/she most likes/dislikes about school? (Probe: Try to get at social as well as academic activities.)

11 What kinds of things do you or other family members do at home to help . . . in school? (Probe: Do they read at home, or take trips? How often does child get help with school-work? In what subjects? From whom?)

12 How do the teachers and principal at the school communicate with you? Is this communication helpful? (Probe: Does parent visit the school? How often? What are parent's perceptions about information shared by school people? Is communication two-way or only one-way?)

13 What is . . . like around the house, with family members? What are some of his/her favorite things to do? With whom does he/she do these things?

14 What are some of the fun things you do together as a family? (Probe: Check for child's participation in special activities such as Yaqui Pascua festivities or mariachi band.)

15 What does . . . do to help around the house? Does he/she do his/her work well and promptly? (Probe: Is child assigned *real* responsibilities? What happens when they don't get done?)

16 Do you ever worry about your child's education? If so, what is your biggest concern? Have you tried to do something about this problem? (Probe: Try to get at both social and academic concerns.)

17 What would you like . . . to be like as a grown-up? What kind of work would you like him/her to do?

18 What will you do to help . . . achieve that kind of person?

19 Are there any other things you'd like to tell me about your child and/or his/her school experience?

20 Do you have any questions to ask me?

Student Interview

It is time to start thinking about the kinds of questions we need to ask students. These will not necessarily constitute part of a structured instrument, rather they should serve as a guide to help frame our conversations with the students.

1   What is school like for you? (Let's try to get at their understanding of the schooling process and their feeling about their own partici-pation in this process.)

2   What would the ideal school be like? (Let's try to get at both physical and qualitative characteristics. We may want to provide materials and opportunity for drawing the 'ideal' school.)

3   What are teachers like? (The purpose here is to get at general characteristics these students identify with teachers. How they would fill the blank after the statement 'Teachers are . . .')

4   Are all teachers alike? How are they alike? How do they differ from each other? (Here we want to get at how they distinguish between teachers, do they see teachers as interchangeable? Do they differentiate between the classroom and 'special' teachers?)

5   What would the 'very best' teacher be like? (Does the student hold an image of the ideal?)

6   Tell me about your (classroom) teacher.

   (a)   How is he/she different from other teachers?

   (b)   What do you like best about your teacher?

   (c)   What do you like least about your teacher?

   (d)   What do you think your teacher thinks about you?

   (e)   How does he/she let you know?

7   Tell me about your school day. (This sub-set is meant to get at schedules)

   (a)   What happens first, and then . . . ? And what happens last?

    (b) What do you do in school (each day of the week and throughout the day)? (Although similar to the previous question, this should tell us something about how the student makes sense of the schedule.)

    (c) What do you like to do most?

    (d) What do you like to do least?

8 Tell me about your classroom. (In this case we're concerned with life in the classroom.)

    (a) What is it like in your classroom? (Again, we may want to use art to get at this.)

    (b) What happens there?

    (c) What do you do there?

    (d) What is your favorite thing to do in your classroom?

    (e) What do you dislike most to do in your classroom?

9 Tell me about your classmates. (Here we want to get at the student's relationships with his/her peers)

    (a) What are your classmates like?

    (b) Who is your favorite person in your classroom? Why?

    (c) Whom do you like least? Why?

    (d) What do you think your classmates think about you?

10 Tell me about the things you do in school. (The purpose here is to get at the content of schooling.)

    (a) What are some of the things you do while you are in school?

    (b) Who decides what you should do?

    (c) Who do you do these things with?

    (d) How do you know when you have finished?

    (e) What happens after you have finished?

    (f) What is your favorite activity?

(g)   What do you just hate to do?

(h)   What do you do best?

(i)   What is hardest for you?

11   Tell me about the things you use in school. (This is to try to get at student perceptions of textbooks and other instructional materials.)

(a)   What are some of the things you use while in school? (You may need to suggest some of these.)

(b)   What are they like?

(c)   What do you do with them?

(d)   Which of these do you like? Why?

(e)   Which of them do you dislike? Why?

12   Expectations for self.

13   What would your best teacher be like?

Appendix 2: At-Risk Student Case Studies

Carmín

Carmín was the second oldest of the six children at Escalante School; however, she appeared to be the youngest because she was exceptionally small for her age. Nevertheless, she seemed healthy and energetic. Carmín's face, with her large eyes and turned-up nose, was cute and expressive; and she seemed often to have feelings to express. There was a kind of tension about her physical being, as if she were a small bundle of nerves and emotion. She almost never seemed relaxed or content, and certain school tasks seemed to make her especially anxious.

Carmín had attended a preschool in Suroeste and then two different kindergartens, one in Suroeste and another in Arkansas. Though her kindergarten records were missing from her files, one could tell from a later report that she was instructed in English both in preschool and in kindergarten. A child study report at the end of her first grade year recommended that in lieu of retention, she be placed in a bilingual classroom in second grade, because she had not yet had an opportunity to learn in Spanish, her home language.

Second grade began on a positive note for Carmín, but her files indicated that things soon deteriorated. She was the subject of another child study, and again was recommended for retention. 'Language' in general, both English and Spanish, was implicated by her teacher as a 'contributing factor to her low achievement'. Faced with Carmín's probable retention in second grade, her mother transferred her to Escalante School in April of that year. Though her teacher there placed her at the 'pre-primer' reading level, she was promoted to third grade. At the beginning of third grade, Carmín was screened for language proficiency. The results indicated that she was more proficient in English than in Spanish. She therefore did not attend ESL classes at Escalante School. Her reading instruction was in Spanish, however, and she received bilingual instruction in other subjects.

Carmín's teacher, Ms. Santana, named her as at-risk because she felt that Carmín could not distinguish between Spanish and English, had a difficult time with reading and math facts, and could not concentrate for very long. According to the teacher, things did not 'come easily' for Carmín, and she was 'very frustrated' with school. Nevertheless, she 'tried hard' and had a 'lot of love in her heart'. The causes of Carmín's school problems seemed mysterious and perhaps linked to her complex school history. Ms. Osgood added her impression that Carmín's family life was irregular – that she had been 'fostered out' to her aunt and did not live with her mother. Because Carmín was making so little progress, Ms. Santana referred her for yet another child study shortly after our study began. The teacher noted on her referral form that Carmín's lack of reading skills held her back in all areas. She also had a tendency to 'get out of her seat whenever there's a chance'.

The child study team decided, after further assessment, that Carmín was Spanish dominant after all. The school nurse interviewed Carmín's aunt, her after-school caretaker, and the aunt said that Carmín 'got confused' about language. The school psychologist's assessment concluded that Carmín had average intellectual potential, but that she had difficulties with 'information processing' and was especially weak in perceptual-motor skills, visual sequencing, tracking and organization, and auditory skills. The team recommended LD placement, which entailed 30–60 minutes of Spanish remediation three times per week. Our observations captured the beginnings of Carmín's experiences as a 'special' student.

Parents and Home Experience

Carmín's mother was raised by her grandparents in a border town in Mexico. After she graduated from high school she married and moved to Suroeste. But she and her husband separated before Carmín was born, and they later divorced. Despite these marital difficulties, Carmín was a desired child. Her mother was happy and eager when expecting her, especially hoping for a girl. Carmín was a healthy, active, sociable baby who walked and talked early, and became the center of attention at family gatherings. Her mother proudly displayed a thick family album of pictures showing Carmín on special occasions, in mischievous situations, dancing or mimicking someone.

However, the period following Carmín's birth was also an unstable time for her mother. She had no permanent home, and temporary arrangements with her mother and sister did not work out well. When Carmín was two years old, her mother remarried; but that marriage also did not last. Carmín's sister was born soon after the mother separated from her second husband. The mother said that Carmín and her second husband had become close, and Carmín called him 'daddy.' He used to visit often, but came infrequently now that the mother was living with another man (her 'fiancé'), and he himself had remarried. The mother and her fiancé were planning to marry soon, and he had promised to adopt Carmín.

Carmím's mother had always been Carmín's primary caretaker, but she had relied on her mother and sister to care for the children while she worked. At the time of the study Carmín's mother worked as a bank cashier. In the morning she dropped the younger daughter off at a day care center and Carmín at her aunt's house near Escalante School. Carmín returned to her aunt's house after school and worked on her homework until her mother picked her up. Carmín's mother said she called her every day after school from the bank to remind her to do her homework. By the time the family returned home it was time for dinner, baths, and bedtime. Carmín's mother worried about these long days, and about the fact that little time was left for her to help Carmín with her schoolwork. Her fiancé appeared to be playing an important support role in Carmín's education. He was 'strict' with Carmín, and helped her with her homework. With her mother, he promised rewards for her school achievement.

Carmín's school problems also worried her mother. She could not understand the contrast between her daughter's cleverness at home and her failure at school. In her view, Carmín's social skills and understandings made her seem wise beyond her years. Carmín was a capable helper at home, taking care of her younger sister and cleaning the house. Ironically, her favorite game at home was playing school. For reasons which were unclear, Carmín had gone to live for a time with her aunt in Arkansas during her kindergarten year. The mother said that Carmín had done very well in the English language program there, and her sister had praised her for learning English quickly. However, it was extremely hard for the mother and daughter to be separated, and Carmín returned to Suroeste. Back in Suroeste, Carmín's school difficulties and her mother's worries began in earnest. Carmín's mother had intervened when the first grade teacher recommended retention. Instead, Carmín had been placed in a bilingual second grade classroom, where she would receive at least some instruction in Spanish. However, her school problems did not disappear, and Carmín's complaints about lack of help from the teacher brought her mother back to the school. The principal and the second grade teacher again insisted on retention for Carmín, and in April the mother decided to move her to Escalante School.

While continuing to be concerned about Carmín's slow progress, the mother did see improvement, and she credited the staff at Escalante for these gains. She was hesitant when they requested yet another child study, but eventually acceded, and was impressed by their thoroughness and promptness in reporting back to her. She was willing to help with Carmín's schoolwork, but skeptical about recommendations she had heard from the child study that she provide her daughter with dancing or gymnastics lessons. She considered these to be 'rewards' which should be reserved until Carmín progressed more in school. She held to the assumption that Carmín would succeed if she only stopped playing and paid attention. Though she said she became 'demoralized' worrying about Carmín's school difficulties, the mother still had high hopes for her future. She speculated that Carmín's interest in maths and in her own work with computers at the bank might lead Carmín in those career directions. But anything Carmín chose would be acceptable to her, and she would help in any way she could. She hoped that her daughter would retain her generous, cheerful and outgoing nature throughout her life.

School Personnel Perceptions of Carmín

According to her teacher, Ms. Santana, Carmín had 'a lot of difficulty retaining things' and trouble with spelling. For instance, she might 'know' a word but not know how to spell it. In discussions, Carmín would 'drift away' for some reason. If she did not like the results of her work she would cry. Because she was small, sometimes the other children gave her 'too much help'. The teacher was concentrating her efforts on language skills, which were Carmín's primary obstacle to achievement.

Through the child study process, Ms. Santana had learned more about Carmín's complex school history. It was unclear to her which language would be best for instructing Carmín. She believed that one language screening had shown English to be Carmín's best language, although the child study team had suggested that she was Spanish dominant. She had been instructing Carmín primarily in Spanish. Carmín was trying hard, and Ms. Santana was impressed by her efforts. The girl took homework home every night and on weekends. Her aunt (the teachers all seemed to think that Carmín lived with her) was helping her at home. Carmín needed this kind of one-on-one attention, a lot of reinforcement, and immediate feedback, according to Ms. Santana. She also needed to 'practice, practice, practice' on her basic skills. In case all this effort did not pay off, Ms. Santana was already thinking of retaining Carmín at the end of the year.

The LD teacher said that Carmín's referral to special education had been delayed so long because everyone thought from her history that she had a 'language of instruction' problem. According to her, Carmín was a 'typical example of a learning disabled child': low achievement but good reasoning skills. She was bright but her development was delayed. As she put it, pointing to her head, 'something isn't registering in there'. This teacher also had concerns about Carmín's psychological state, which she characterized as 'learned helplessness'. She 'fell apart' because she wanted to be 'perfect' and her failures frustrated her. In this teacher's opinion, Carmín would 'drown' in fourth grade; she needed more time to develop her skills, perhaps even a more restrictive environment until she could catch up.

The nurse, who was often a source of information about students' homes at Escalante, reported that Carmín lived in a 'very weird family', where there was 'not really a nuclear family left'. She stated that Carmín was being 'raised by an aunt' and was not clear about whether her cousins were her siblings – a kind of 'role confusion'. She described Carmín as unhealthy looking, underweight, and 'almost elflike'.

In Ms. Santana's April interview she summarized Carmín's year by saying that she had made a lot of progress. She now 'recognized letters' (a very basic skill indeed). In writing, she was dictating stories to the teacher and letting her 'ideas flow'. She seemed more confident. In reading, she was at the monosyllable level but adding some two-syllable words to her repertoire. These accomplishments, however, were far below those of the average third grader. Ms. Santana was recommending retention for Carmín, since she thought it would 'boost her confidence'. She did not know how Carmín's 'demanding' mother would take the idea of retention, though. For her part, Ms. Santana actually seemed positive about the prospect of teaching Carmín again, if Carmín were assigned to her class. 'If I have her again, I will work more at her level. This year I tried to introduce third grade things to her and it was a struggle'. She said they would start at Carmín's level and work slowly and carefully upward.

Carmín's Perceptions of School

Carmín chose to be interviewed in Spanish, although she was assured that she could switch languages whenever she wanted. She said she spoke both languages, but preferred Spanish. She also explained which language she used with different people in her life. She responded with stock phrases to many questions. For example: 'What is school like?' 'Esta bonita' (It is pretty); 'What do you do in school?' 'Hacemos muchas cosas.' (We do many things); 'What is your teacher like?' 'Buena.' (Good). Her favorite response was 'muchas cosas' (many things'. Carmín may have either been being evasive or trying to mimic adult responses. Her mother had said that she had a talent for imitation. Many of Carmín's responses, at any rate, provided little insight except for the few times when one could glean within the formulaic responses some idea of what school was like for her.

Carmín's descriptions of her school activities focused on her movements from one setting to another: 'Primero voy con Ms. Santana y le traigo todas las tareas y hago "cursive". Luego me voy con la otra maestra. Luego me vengo pa' atras a jugar. Luego comemos lunche y escribimos y me quedo con Ms. Santana'. (First I go with Ms. Santana and I bring her all the homework. Then I go with the other teacher. Then I come back to play. Then we eat lunch and write and I stay with Ms. Santana.)

Carmín's description of her LD teacher's instruction was illustrative: 'Ella nos enseña palabras, de "che", "cha", leemos, tenemos una prueba y la pase, me dio una A, y la hice bien . . .'(She teaches us words, of 'che', 'cha' [Spanish syllables], we read, we have a test and I passed it, she gave me an A, and I did it right . . .) The interviewer had observed Carmín during the LD lesson previous to this interview, which indeed consisted of syllables using the 'ch' sound, and words with the same sound. Carmín had become frustrated and cried during the lesson. I asked her why: 'Si, porque tenia miedo no iba a pasar. Mi mami quiere buenos gradod . . . y si no me dan . . . que you queria . . .' (Yes, because I was afraid I wasn't going to pass. My mother wants good grades and if not they won't give me . . . that I want.) What she wanted, learned the researcher after further questioning, was a Cabbage Patch Doll.

The interviewer asked Carmín what kind of student she was: 'A veces poquita mala'. (Sometimes a little bad.) To the question of what she meant by being bad, she answered: 'Porque lloro'. (Because I cry.) Why? 'Porque no lo puedo hacer.' (Because I can't do it.) Why? 'Porque no estudio.' (Because I don't study.) On the other hand, Carmín emphasized her strong points repeatedly. Her favorite topic for discussion was 'cursive'. She said she liked cursive because 'es bonito' (it is pretty). She also said she liked math because it is very easy and also 'porque mi mami me ayuda' (because my mommy helps me). During the second interview she displayed her books and her progress in cursive writing exercises. Her writing was neat and well-formed. However, she could not read the words she had written.

For her last interview the interviewer brought a set of primer level books and asked Carmín to read for her. She was able to read only the very first few words. After that she began to make up words, even when they made no sense at all. For example, she 'read': mother sings to the blouse. She was questioned about that but she did not correct her 'reading'. The interviewer decided to try to get an honest appraisal from Carmín and asked her directly if she had trouble reading. She did not answer directly, but eventually did admit to having problems. When asked how the interviewer could help, she demonstrated how to cover up portions of words so that only one syllable would be exposed at a time. She said Ms. Santana helped her that way, and that no one had helped her at her other school. And she added: 'me confundo cuando me dicen una palabra'. (I get confused when they tell me a word.)

Carmín also had problems with comprehension. After listening to a story she was not able to provide a good summary. Her responses were brief and seemed to focus on just a few items which were not of major importance to the portion of the story she had heard. The interviewer also asked her to tell the story in English and she recalled the same items she had mentioned in Spanish. A second story was used, with similar results. She indicated that she had picked up the rules of the interview process quickly by asking after she had provided a Spanish summary, 'ahora en ingles?' (now in English?).

Classroom Observations of Carmín

Carmín spoke both Spanish and English informally with other children, but she seemed more comfortable with Spanish. In English, she made little 'gaffs' which the teacher or other children would correct. Sometimes she mixed codes. Her English seemed immature, like the language of a much younger native English speaker (e.g., 'cotch' tape for 'scotch' tape), which would be perfectly normal for a second language learner. In contrast her Spanish expression seemed very grown-up and formal. Undeterred by her minor oral language difficulties, Carmín was very talkative and often volunteered to answer in whole group lessons. Excited and pleased when she knew an answer (or thought she did) she would practically rise up out of her seat, her hand held high, her whole body straining to catch the teacher's attention. About half the time, her answers were incorrect, but this did not seem to discourage her from participating.

Carmín also liked being in charge of tasks like passing out papers and monitoring lunchtime cleanup. She was very serious and officious about these duties, sometimes carrying this to the point where other children complained. On the observer's first visit to the classroom, two other girls volunteered that Carmín was a girl in their class who was 'very little and very mean' always fighting with people. On the other hand, Carmín seemed to have companions in the playground, and when she was caught off task it was usually because she was socializing with other children.

Carmín generally attended to the teacher. In fact, she was dependent on teachers for both motivation and assistance. She sustained her work the longest when the teacher was nearby to answer questions and keep her on task. If not, she might get up from her seat and had to be reminded to sit down. Her favorite and most successful activity was handwriting, which entailed mostly copying, a task at which she could excel. She was a very neat writer, and Ms. Santana often praised her for this. Carmín also consistently complied with schoolwork routines such as putting her name and date on the paper, copying her homework off the board, and packing her homework up at the end of the day. She reminded other students of rules and routines when they forgot.

However, though Carmín could have the air of a competent busy bee in the classroom, this masked some very real difficulties with completing most third grade level tasks. In fact, the observer came to think of Carmín as someone who had the form of being a student mastered, but not the substance, the achievement which really counted in school assessments. When her weaknesses were revealed, Carmín became very anxious. The harder she tried on difficult tasks, the more despairing she became.

Discussion

In summary, the year of our study was the year in which all of Carmín's school difficulties seemed to catch up with her. After her third child study she was labelled LD, and began receiving speech and language therapy. After being a regular student for so long, she became a special one. After being promoted for three years, she was retained. Carmín's case was a tragedy of errors for which she was bearing the consequences. The first error was her placement in an English language kindergarten far from home. Her subsequent placement in an English first grade program was probably related to this kindergarten experience. It was likely that with Carmín's skills at mimicking people and picking up school routines, she was able to parrot numbers, letters and other classroom language in English after her year in Arkansas. Her superficial knowledge was apparently assumed to indicate language dominance.

There was also a lack of school responsiveness in the other district, suggested not just by the mother's accounts but also by the school records themselves. Without the mother's intervention, Carmín would have been retained for another year of English first grade instruction. Assigning her to bilingual instruction for second grade was supposed to tilt the balance back in favor of her home language, Spanish – but her primary language of instruction was still English. Carmín's mother's decision to move her daughter to Escalante School appeared to have been a good one. At Escalante, there was a shared value of support for Spanish students among the primary grade bilingual teachers. Unfortunately, though, the psychological evaluation at this school had added to the confusion. While the evidence in the school files led to the conclusion that Carmín's problem was language-related, the school psychologist classified her as learning disabled.

The mother's assessment of Carmín cannot be dismissed. Carmín appeared to be bright and knowing. But she also appeared to have incomplete development in both languages. This appraisal is not based on her tendency to code-switch, which was minor and expected. It is based on some of the Spanish forms she used, which were direct translations from English and not of the type native speakers would be likely to use. Carmín's confusion of vowels also suggested that she would benefit from intensive oral language and reading instruction in Spanish, in isolation from English. The continuous code-switching in her bilingual classroom probably confused Carmín further. She also seemed to be missing the point of reading; how words create meaning together. Instead, she reduced words to meaningless syllables. Unlike one of the other LD children, Carmín did not invent a coherent story to cover for her lack of reading skills; she strung syllables together without regard to the meaning they might carry as words. This problem suggests that whole language instruction would be much more appropriate for her. The instruction she was receiving only seemed to contribute to further fragmentation of her reading process.

However, lest this sound like a 'blame the teacher' conclusion, it must be stressed that Ms. Santana, too, was a victim of the series of mistaken decisions that followed Carmín into third grade. By this time, Carmín's language and learning problems were very difficult to sort out, and the amount of attention she needed was hard for a classroom teacher to provide. Ms. Santana could not diverge from the school classroom language policies for Carmín's sake alone. She provided as much Spanish language instruction as possible, but also needed to 'transition' most of the children into English before fourth grade. She understandably relied on available school services to find extra support for working with Carmín.

Amazingly enough, Carmín still cared very much about school and wanted to be successful. Her enthusiasm, in spite of her failures, and her parents' love and assistance, were real assets. But it may have been only a matter of time. Carmín's fantasies were already beginning to dissolve, and her parents were becoming less patient with her lack of progress. By this point her emotional blocks to learning were threatening to become as debilitating as her academic ones. Carmín and her mother needed a different approach, one that would properly locate the problem not within Carmín, but in the schooling to which she had been subjected. One that would move toward recreating a meaningful educational experience for a very confused little girl.

Gilberto

A very sociable third grader, Gilberto seemed completely relaxed in all of the settings in his busy schedule. From early in the study he greeted the observer with a smile and asked unabashedly about her work in the classroom. He was the only child at Escalante whose appearance told of a home lacking in resources. His clothing was worn, especially his winter jacket, and unlike the other students he had no backpack for carrying his books and papers. But his surface appearance faded in importance in the light of his charming personality. Everyone we contacted at the school simply liked Gilberto very much.

Gilberto had a complex school history, because his family had moved frequently from town to town. Born in Suroeste, he entered kindergarten in a small town about fifty miles away. The kindergarten entry form said that Spanish was his primary language. In the middle of his kindergarten year, the family moved again, to a small border town. The withdrawal form from his first school said that he was an

'ESL student below grade level due to language barrier'. His first grade records showed that he attended bilingual classes at Escalante School for most of the year, except for one period in the border town. Again Gilberto was assessed as being more proficient in Spanish than English, but he was making steady progress in English. Although his grade reports were satisfactory, the teacher wrote, 'We're going to observe him in the coming year'.

Gilberto remained at Escalante School for second grade, but his attendance records did not account for forty days missing (out of 180). His grade reports showed him to be on the first grade level in reading, and not doing well in other subjects. Late in the first semester his teacher referred him for a child study. She commented on her referral form that he had 'difficulty working independently, especially in tasks in reading, writing and spelling . . . reversed letters . . . had trouble remembering visual cues or focusing on written work'. On the other hand, his ESL progress was fine, and he was 'very verbal and cute'. The school nurse visited Gilberto's mother as part of the child study. The mother reported that aside from his being very active and some-what accident-prone, his early life had been normal and uneventful. After testing by the school psychologist, Gilberto was diagnosed as learning disabled due to severe auditory and visual deficits. He had subsequently attended LD classes four times each week.

Gilberto's LD teacher recommended a further speech and language assessment, to 'improve his coarticulation skills for maximally intelligible speech'. The language therapist, Ms. Martin, concluded that he suffered from 'verbal developmental dyspraxia'. He was assigned to receive language therapy twice a week. He also continued to attend ESL classes. Therefore, by the second semester of second grade, Gilberto had been placed in three special categories – ESL, LD and language impaired – and began the complex 'pull-out' schedule which we observed in our study. At the beginning of third grade, language screening placed Gilberto at the highest level of proficiency in English, and his language therapist remarked that he was nearly ready to transition out of bilingual instruction. But he was still reading in Spanish at a first grade level. Both Ms. Santana and Ms. Osgood named him as at-risk both because of his low achievement, which they attributed to his language difficulties and because they had concerns about the stability of his home life. Ms. Osgood gave a layperson's definition of 'dyspraxia' for us as: 'he has the thought but cannot physically move the muscles of his mouth to communicate and get his messages right'. The teachers believed that he was the youngest of ten children who had more than one father, and that more than one family lived in the home. One thought that he was a 'foster child'.

Parents and Home Experience

Gilberto was the middle child in the largest family in the sample. He had two older sisters, an older brother and three younger brothers, the youngest of whom was not yet 1-year-old. The older siblings were the children of an early marriage that ended before Gilberto was born. According to his mother, her former husband had returned briefly; but when her pregnancy (for Gilberto) was discovered, the father and his family denied his responsibility and accused her of 'running around'. She said she was advised not to tell social services he was the father; otherwise, she might not receive support for the baby. Gilberto's father had wavered in his acceptance of the boy through the years. Sometimes he included presents for Gilberto in his Christmas package, but most of the time the boy was excluded.

Thus, Gilberto's young life had been a center of family conflict. His mother traveled back and forth between a Mexican border town, another small town in Southern Arizona, and Suroeste, in her efforts to make a new life for herself and the children. She said they were hungry sometimes, and life was very difficult.

Gilberto was a healthy baby who walked and talked early and was quite agile. His mother said he climbed everywhere, including up to the roof at her mother's house – his uncle cured him of that with a good spanking. Once she left him on an upper bunk and he fell and got a nosebleed; otherwise, he seemed to have survived his adventures well. His mother called him 'tremendo', that is, difficult to handle. She explained that in spite of his advanced physical skills, he refused to toilet train as early as her other children. Though he could say anything he wanted, including many vulgarities, he would not tell her when he needed to use the bathroom. What's more, his grandmother would clean Gilberto up and 'cover up' for his toileting 'accidents' whenever she was around. The mother still seemed frustrated remembering those days.

Gilberto's mother described him now as very friendly, daring, enterprising, and clever – as well as lazy. She said he took off after whatever interested him, often without telling her, and this caused her a great deal of worry. He was always very sure of himself, she said, friendly and willing to start a conversation with anyone, 'rich or poor'. She worried that one of these days it might be with someone who wanted to hurt him, since 'there are many people here who like to hurt children'.

At home Gilberto liked to watch cartoons on TV and to play with his friends. His mother said he learned quickly from TV and was very good at telling stories. Gilberto also liked to play ball with his older brother or to spend time with the next younger one, his favorite. He would often bring his younger brother little things from school and would also protect him from punishment.

Gilberto's relationships with his older sisters, however, appeared to be more distant and less positive. The two girls seemed to identify more closely with their father. Family difficulties apparently stemmed from conflict between the girls and their mother's current male companion (referred to here as 'stepfather'). Many times, she said, it had to do with the stepfather's efforts to discipline the children – in these situations she ended up in the middle.

Gilberto's mother seemed puzzled about Gilberto's problems in school. She speculated that he might simply become distracted there. He was so quick and clever at home, she could not imagine why he would have trouble learning in school. Gilberto himself did not complain to her of any problems in school; on the contrary, he appeared eager to attend. His teachers had also told her that he was a good boy in school, respectful with teachers and classmates. On the other hand, his first grade teacher had mentioned that Gilberto would think of something and then forget what he wanted to say. The mother admitted that at home he also would not respond sometimes when she called. She was preparing him for his First Communion, and noticed that he had been slower to learn the catechism than her older children, though now he could read it quite well.

Perhaps his teacher this year was too easy on him, she said. The year before, she had gone to school every Friday at his teacher's request, to pick up material she could use to help him at home. When she was unable to go to the school, the teacher came to the house. These contacts were opportunities to find out how he was doing. She had not heard from Gilberto's teacher this year.

Gilberto's mother commented that she had always wanted her children to do well in school. She worried about her son's future, but felt it was up to God to control what would happen. She thought that Gilberto was the one to decide what kind of career he wanted; she simply wanted to make sure that her children grew up to be 'good people who don't cause problems'.

School Personnel Perceptions of Gilberto

In an interview in December, Ms. Santana said that Gilberto had a lot of difficulty early in the year 'adapting' to the classroom. He had an especially hard time with writing, and would 'just sit there' not knowing how to start. Lately, however, he had been getting 'right to it'. She could not 'see much about this dyspraxia thing', and seemed to think it was part of the specialist's realm. She simply viewed him as a 'different' kind of student, average in his skills. He was interested in, and enthusiastic about, his school work, active in class, and a 'fighter', not one to give up on himself. Ms. Santana had visited Gilberto's home on one occasion, when he was afraid another boy would beat him up on the way home. The mother told her that there were problems in the neighborhood with that kind of thing.

Ms. Santana described Gilberto as a 'noble personality', very warm and kind, with a 'smile that could break your heart'. As she put it, 'his personality helped him a lot with me and with other kids'. Because of his complex schedule, on most days Ms. Santana did not work with Gilberto until the afternoon. She thought that Gilberto looked forward to seeing many different teachers and working with them, because it 'brought out his sparkling personality'. After all, he was getting a lot of attention from a lot of different people in a lot of different environments.

The LD teacher commented that Gilberto came from a large, low income family. His love of school 'treats' to her seemed an indicator of the lack of such things at home. She described his reading as 'labored', at the 'sound level', and thought that he was becoming impatient with learning. On the other hand, she said, 'I don't look at him as being real, real high risk.' His assets were his charming personality, his positive attitude or 'spirit', the fact that he was making progress. He accepted being LD and needing help, and it was not a 'trauma' for him. She saw this as a healthy outlook. She was working on his fluency and his sight vocabulary.

The ESL teachers, asked to name at-risk children in their classes, did not name Gilberto; neither did the nurse have any comments about him. The school psychologist could remember only that he was a 'Spanish LD' student.

By April, Ms Santana described Gilberto as no longer 'at-risk'. He had made a lot of progress, and would do well in the fourth grade. According to the language therapist, he would soon be phasing out of her program. He was now more independent, understood English very well, and was reading at the second grade level.

Gilberto's Perceptions of School

The interviewer quickly realized why all of Gilberto's teachers referred to him as a 'charmer'. He smiled often, and when he did, his whole face lit up. Among the six children interviewed at Escalante School, he was the most articulate and relaxed. He also seemed to be aware, early in the study, of the researchers' interest in him. His ease in addressing the researchers was an example of Gilberto's mother's description of him as ready to talk to anyone, anytime, regardless of class or position.

School for Gilberto seemed to be a continuous commuting trip, as seen in his description of his daily routine in Chapter 1. In spite of his hectic schedule, Gilberto said he liked school, his classes, and all of his teachers. Gilberto was less clear about what he was learning in school. His descriptions of what he learned in his classes were vague, for example, 'in music a whole bunch of stuff'. He wondered about the need for attending some of his classes. For example, he did not know why he needed to go to his LD group to learn how to read, since he believed he already knew how to read.

When asked about the reason for attending school, Gilberto's responses appeared to reflect adult opinions of the importance of school. He said he must learn to work hard, and that what you learn in school will be necessary in your job later. His most genuine response toward school was reserved for science activities. He was excited about magnets, about how they stuck together when placed one way and rejected each other when placed another way. He became animated, his eyes bright, his words tumbling on each other, as he explained how it all happened.

Gilberto explained about the magnets in Engish, but he seemed equally comfortable speaking either Spanish or English. He said he used both when speaking with his friends; but when asked he chose Spanish as the language for the interviews, though he would sometimes lapse into English. As with most coordinate bilinguals, Gilberto would shift unconsciously from one to the other language. Sometimes he would stop in mid-sentence and point out that he was speaking English while the interviewer was speaking Spanish, or vice versa.

Gilberto appeared to be popular among his classmates. He said he had lots of friends and that they helped him when others threatened him. This perception of friends as those who will stand up against threats was consistent with Gilberto's explanation of why he used to fight in years past, because he had a friend who was always getting into fights. He claimed his behavior was only 'so-so' but better than last year when he used to fight all the time.

Gilberto's opinion of himself as a student was not as positive. He classified himself as the worst in the class, since he never received 100s in his work, only Cs. However, he believed his low performance was due to the fact that he did not work hard enough. He also said that he often got very tired in school, perhaps because he got up too early.

Gilberto had a very good opinion of his present homeroom teacher, but remembered another teacher as one he could not understand at all. He was not sure whether this was due to his lack of English language skills or to the teacher's speaking style. He said he liked teachers who were 'good' and disliked those who got mad easily. If he were a teacher, he said, he would never say anything bad to children.

Classroom Observations of Gilberto

Gilberto was very friendly toward the classroom observer. He was curious about whether if somebody hit somebody else, she would write it down, and if she would tell the teachers. He also asked about the tape recorder, and about a co-researcher who spoke to him in Spanish: 'Can't she speak English?' When the class went out for a free playtime one Friday, he asked the observers, 'Aren't you guys coming?' In other words, Gilberto was at ease with school adults, even relative strangers. Moreover, because he was so talkative, Gilberto provided the observer with a running commentary about himself and his view of school.

An additional factor in his task completion was that quite often he seemed dependent on teacher assistance, especially on independent writing assignments or math problems which required reading. If the teacher left him too long without reminders or monitoring, he seemed to become bewildered. Rather than spending much time in confusion, however, Gilberto usually sought out teacher advice quickly. Just a brief explanation, a small nudge and a smile, seemed sufficient to keep him going. If a teacher were not available, Gilberto might ask another child for advice. He did not seem to become anxious about such incidents; in fact, Gilberto did not seem to 'sweat' anything about school too much.

Not that Gilberto's difficulties with school tasks were slight. When he read aloud, it was haltingly, and he needed teacher assistance with many words in his second grade reader. He read aloud in an odd sing-song style, with rising intonation at the ends of words, in a regular rhythm unrelated to the meaning of the passage. Ms. Santana complained that there was something about the stories he wrote which was not 'logical'. He also confused certain letters and sounds. Ms. Santana pointed out to him that he made frequent 'careless' errors on his math problems, because he did not 'use his head', 'follow directions', or check his work.

On the other hand, Gilberto seemed to have good comprehension for most lessons, and lots of practical knowledge. He seemed to be the most able reader in his LD group. His comments about his own work were positive; in fact the word 'know' cropped up in his speech quite often. When a teacher presented information he had already encountered, he would pipe up, 'I already know that'. He used this one day as an excuse for not having attended to a teacher's directions. Other remarks were, 'I know how to do that because we already did it', or 'That's easy'. He also commented on overlap or repetition among the lessons presented by his many teachers.

Gilberto also commented on his understanding of school routines and rules. He knew how many children in his class went to ESL and when, what time all of his special groups began and ended, how the reward system worked in every classroom, how Ms. Santana wanted the class to lift their slates – with no 'special effects' (banging noises). His routine had familiarized him with the layout of the entire school and with many of its staff, so that he could adapt to a variety of social expectations with poise.

Like Juan, Gilberto's school life took him away from Ms. Santana's homeroom for long periods of time. The observer followed Gilberto, to understand his schedule and its consequences. It was an exhausting experience. Pull-out groups left Gilberto with a very fragmented schedule, more like secondary than elementary school, on every day except Friday. The only other child Gilberto saw consistently was Juan, and Juan was not exactly the 'buddy' type.

Gilberto's interactions with other children were positive and cooperative, but he did not seem to have any special friends in his homeroom. However – and this seemed important to the boys at the school – he was included in the recess soccer game. Most important, he maintained jovial relationships with every teacher on his schedule. One might say that Gilberto's best friends at school were his teachers.

Discussion

For Gilberto school appeared to be a pleasant experience that allowed him the social contacts he seemed to enjoy. His understanding of the value of schooling, however, appeared to parrot adult advice (perhaps in his effort to please the interviewer). It was clear that his understanding of the purpose of instructional activities was hazy at best, though he was a willing participant. Some 'of his comments during the observations indicated that he was already beginning to question the reasons for his special classes and the repetitiveness of his program. This should be a warning flag for his fourth grade teacher to make sure that Gilberto is stimulated by more than just the social aspects of his schooling.

Gilberto's complaints of tiredness should perhaps be seriously explored. His tiredness may have been related to early rising, as he pointed out, or it may have been the result of staying up late, although the mother said the stepfather was firm about bedtimes. It was also possible that Gilberto was working below his capacity and becoming bored at school. His perception of his reading ability, his comments about 'knowing' things, and his excitement about hands-on activities such as the work with magnets, suggested that he might benefit from more experiential instructional approaches. Finally, it could be that Gilberto, a member of the largest, least affluent family in the sample, was not as healthy as he might be.

A question brought up by Gilberto's case is the importance of social adaptability of students in teacher assessments of their at-riskness. As Gilberto had become more and more comfortable with his school, his schedule, his teachers and with the English language, he was considered less and less at-risk. However, his basic academic problems still needed much attention, as the LD teacher pointed out. He presented a challenge to those who would remediate these problems without insulting his obvious intelligence and causing him to doubt the purposes of schooling. Charm could only take him so far in an increasingly achievement-oriented system.

Juan

At age 10, Juan was the oldest child in the study. Despite his age, he did not stand out in his physical appearance as older than the other third graders in his class. He was a small and rather frail-looking boy with a generally serious expression. The times when he smiled, and when he seemed excited about school, became notable to the observer. He seemed to be inwardly focused, unless something special happened to draw him out.

Juan had the longest history of identification as a child with special problems in school because of an early childhood head injury which had impaired his speech. He began his school career in the 'special needs' category of the Head Start program in a border town south of Suroeste. Head Start had referred him to Ms. Martin, a speech and language therapist at a hospital in Suroeste. She concluded that Juan's auditory comprehension was 'significantly reduced' and his expressive language was 'severely disordered'. He had received speech and language services through Head Start, under her direction. He attended his first year of school across the border in Mexico, where all instruction was in Spanish. There were no records available for this year. The next year, he entered a school in Raintree District as a first grader. During his very first week, his teacher recommended him for special attention. On an Adaptive Education Screening form she indicated 'yes' for *all* indicators of need in social/emotional, language, intellectual and physical areas. Juan soon transferred to another school, where again the teacher immediately referred him for special services.

Language assessments indicated that Juan was completely Spanish dominant, with no listening comprehension skills in English; that his speech was difficult to understand; and that even in Spanish his language skills were limited. His teacher placed him below grade level in all subjects, and noted that he needed improvement in all 'habits and attitudes' except 'getting along with others'. In December, his teacher filed another form indicating that he had 'highly critical needs' in intellectual skills and speech and 'critical needs' in school progress and social/emotional areas. A conference in March attended by the nurse, special education representative, the principal and the teacher, concluded that Juan should be retained in first grade and should receive special education services. However, he was inexplicably placed in second grade after all. In second grade, his school performance appeared from the records to be dismal. His teacher recommended him for a child study.

The school nurse conducted a home interview for the child study team, in which Juan's mother reported that she had had a difficult pregnancy with Juan, and that her ex-husband had been abusive. She said that Juan had a 'violent temper' at home. The school psychologist's testing found Juan to score only sixty-eight on the WISC-R, in the 'mentally deficient' range. The psychologist also noted Juan's 'distractibility, fatigue and resistance' and his severe speech impediment. Juan was labelled Educationally Mentally Handicapped (EMH), and the team recommended that he be removed from the regular classroom for special placement. But by chance, Ms. Martin, Juan's language therapist from Head Start, was now working for Raintree District. She again evaluated Juan, whom she referred to as a 'challenging, friendly little boy,' and recommended that he be mainstreamed, with pull-out services. Apparently her recommendations were taken.

Juan transferred to Escalante School, because it offered bilingual special education services. Though he still had considerable problems in some areas, his school progress appeared to have taken an upturn after his transfer and he was promoted to third grade. Early in third grade, he performed at level five in Spanish, the highest level on a language assessment scale; but his performance in English was still at level one. A written comment said that 'severe speech and language disorders' made it impossible to administer parts of the test. When our study began, Juan was still reading at the first grade level. His teacher, Ms. Santana, named him as at-risk because of his learning disabilities and speech problems. She saw him as having such discouraging difficulties that she wondered what could continue to motivate him in school.

Parents and Home Experience

Juan was born in a border town, the youngest child and only boy in a family of four siblings. Juan's parents were divorced, and he lived with his mother and sisters. His oldest sister was married; thus the household also included her husband and 3-year-old daughter. According to the mother, Juan's father was very close to him and came to visit often. The family also maintained ties to relatives in Mexico, where they travelled several times a year.

The mother recalled being very depressed while carrying Juan; the pregnancy was accidental and unwelcome. She said that unlike previous pregnancies, she experienced strong fears about giving birth when carrying Juan. Nevertheless, Juan had a normal birth and learned to talk and walk as expected. His mother remembered him as being very mischievous and 'always falling'. According to his mother, when Juan was just a few months old, one of his sisters fell while carrying him, breaking his leg. The break was apparently set incorrectly, so that he developed a limp which required two operations to correct.

After the last of these operations, only a year or so before, Juan had to wear a body cast.

An even more serious accident occurred when Juan was about 1-year-old. His mother said that he fell from an upstairs porch at his grandmother's house to the street below and fractured his skull. His brain swelled and became very soft. She remembered she had to exercise great care in handling him in order to avoid complications. After a while she noticed that he no longer used all the words he had learned before the accident. He would only say 'ta-ta' when he wanted something, and would become very angry when he was not understood. At first she did not pay much attention, because his skull had healed and he had improved; but she finally decided to have him checked at a clinic. After many tests, doctors told her that the fracture had injured Juan's 'voice box' where speech was produced. They explained that the correct words emerged from his brain, but become scrambled in this 'box'.

In addition to these physical traumas, Juan had felt the loss of some important adults in his early life. When he was a baby, an older woman who lived next door took a fancy to Juan and practically took charge of him. Juan became very attached to her; but she moved away suddenly and they had seen her only once since then. Juan's grandparents, particularly his grandmother, were also very close to him; they used to take him to their house for days at a time. The mother thought that the grandparents' deaths within days of each other had been an important event in Juan's life.

Playing with other children and children's activities did not appeal to Juan, according to his mother. He liked to be with adults, and his father and an older male cousin were his favorite companions. He had copied his cousin's 'punk' hairstyle, and said he wanted to be 20-years-old. The two men had taught him to drive, and he was allowed to steer when his mother drove on the highway. She told a story of how Juan had recently asked her for the car keys and, without her knowledge, moved the car from the front to the back of the house all by himself. He then announced that now he *really* knew how to drive.

Juan was described as very 'feisty' by his mother (and 11-year-old sister, also present at the interview). He did not get along with his 3-year-old niece because he was 'jealous' of her, his sister said. The mother said she could not get him to do anything around the house – he insisted that he was 'a man' and therefore should be waited on by his mother and sisters. Until very recently, he would not even bathe himself. His favorite home activity was watching TV, especially videos of horror movies.

187

Juan had attended several schools, beginning as a pre-schooler in Head Start. With each school change, he seemed to have had a difficult adjustment. After Head Start, he attended school in Mexico; but he did not receive speech therapy there, and in his mother's opinion the year was 'wasted'. On the advice of a language therapist who had worked with Juan at Head Start, the mother had decided to move to Suroeste. However, Juan was unhappy about leaving his friends in Mexico. At his first school in Suroeste he was teased by other children, fought with them, and cried all the time. He also cried when he was moved to Escalante School to receive special services in Spanish, but he gradually adjusted. The presence of Ms. Martin, his ex-language therapist at Escalante seemed to have made both Juan and his mother more comfortable.

The mother remarked that Juan had a lot of trouble with his home-work, and sometimes she was unable to help him. He also rushed through his work so that he could watch TV. She said the school generally kept in touch with her, and from what she had heard he seemed to be doing well. In any case, she did not worry too much about him, since he seemed fortunate to be leading a 'normal life' in spite of his handicap.

School Perceptions of Juan

When Ms. Santana, Juan's third grade teacher, recommended him for our study, she described him as an LD student who was 'mainly monolingual' in Spanish and had speech problems. She said that the other children were 'very understanding' of Juan's difficulties; they did not 'mock him or anything'. But she wondered if he might get to the point where he 'just got tired of going to speech'. 'Will he keep striving?' she asked. Ms. Santana seemed to wonder what would continue to motivate a child with so many handicaps. She was instructing Juan entirely in Spanish, though the school policy stated that third grade was the 'English transition' year. The teachers also felt he was profiting from the services of the 'wonderful speech pathol-ogist' at the school, Ms. Martin.

All of Juan's work was 'below average'. His learning disabilities, especially his lack of reading skills, limited his achievement in every area. In addition, Juan was not a 'risk-taker' – his reading teacher had pointed out that sometimes he could do things even when he said he couldn't. For instance, in writing he used only a few words that he felt 'comfortable' with. He also had a hard time with 'motor skills'.

Sometimes he became impatient with himself, the classroom and the other children.

On the other hand, Juan usually communicated with his teacher, and felt fairly comfortable with the other children. He generally had a 'positive outlook', was 'putting in considerable effort', and liked doing things creatively with his hands, for example, working in the school garden. He participated in group discussions in class and brought his homework back every day, an indication to Ms. Santana that he was receiving 'encouragement from home'. She had contacted Juan's mother earlier in the year, when he was not bringing his homework regularly, and was pleased that the mother had cooperated

Ms. Santana felt that Juan needed more practice in writing. Until he could write more on his own, she had accommodated his needs. For instance, she had him dictate stories for her to write, and his ideas really 'flowed'. In addition, she quizzed him orally, or read him questions and had him write the answers. She felt that to evaluate Juan fairly she had to consider both the conditions in his past which had created his handicaps and the fact that, no matter what his level of achievement, he *was* trying.

The speech therapist, Ms. Martin, confided that the head injury which had set off Juan's educational difficulties was probably not from a fall. She had learned during her work at Head Start that other children in the family had also suffered 'green stick' fractures, commonly recognized indicators of child abuse. Ms. Martin also explained the medical basis of Juan's problems. Speech-related areas of his brain had been bruised, and his brain still 'moved around' inside his skull. She said that as a result he could understand much more than he could express. He had a wonderful imagination; for instance, the summer before he had told her he was going to Russia for his vacation. It was obvious that she enjoyed working with Juan.

The LD teacher said, on the other hand, that Juan had 'poor work habits', did not like school work, and tried to avoid it by lying and other strategies – becoming 'uptight' when he was found out. He 'put down' other students and 'ratted' on them to boost his own self-image. His handicap was severe, she granted, and he was dependent on help in reading. But she thought that he knew he was 'not expected to perform' and therefore put out little effort. Her solution would be to treat Juan 'like everyone else'. She was also concerned that Juan seemed preoccupied with violence and death, and talked about watching 'horrendous' movies at home.

The ESL teachers named Juan their 'top contender' for the 'at-risk' title, and projected that he would always be dependent on others. They noted that he had a poor memory and as a consequence needed constant repetition. One remarked that 'of course with Juan you have to under-stand the circumstances [referring to his physical injury]. He will never have true language.' In the meantime, the other children were helping him, and this was 'beautiful to see'. On further reflection, they decided that Juan was not the most problematic student in their classes. Compared with a multiply handicapped boy in another classroom who 'looked vacant', at least Juan had a 'questioning look'. In one lesson he had whistled at a picture of a pretty girl, and one commented laughingly, 'we thought it was a great reaction, especially for Juan'.

The nurse and school psychologist had few remarks about Juan. The nurse said that the family was too poor to take care of his many medical problems; she described him as 'chronically ill'. The school psychologist said Juan had a 'severe need' for special services.

In a final interview in April, Ms. Santana seemed to have changed her opinion about how hard Juan was trying and how limited his abilities were. She said, 'He doesn't try hard enough, but he does have ability'. If he tried hard, he could do a 'beautiful job'. Juan had also missed a lot of school (twenty-seven days for the year, according to the records), and she felt that this had limited his progress. Juan had made a lot of progress, nevertheless. He was 'pushing forward' in reading and usually succeeding in math, unless he 'got desperate'. Ms. Santana also recognized that he had a special talent for telling imagin-ative stories, and she had encouraged him to write them on the computer. Next year, in Ms. Santana's opinion, Juan's teacher would need to continue instruction in Spanish while working to improve his English. His fourth grade teacher would also need to continue to 'push him' and not 'let him slack off'.

Juan's Perceptions of School

Our interview with Juan was not very productive, first, because he had a noticeable speech impediment, and second, because he was evasive. During the period of the study Juan appeared to be spontaneous and trusting with only one adult – the speech and language therapist with whom he had been working for five years.

Juan was interviewed twice. Each time he found other things to take his attention away from the interviewer. He colored a worksheet during one session and carefully observed playground activities during another. In each case he began to display signs of boredom or tiredness after only a few minutes. Juan described his school day by naming the teachers he saw in sequence: first Ms. Santana, then Ms. Kiley, then the LD teacher. In response to questions about what he did in these classes he mentioned the name of one of his books which he described as 'bueno' (good). When he was asked about the book he said it had many pages and also many songs.

Singing and dancing had been mentioned by Juan's mother as areas of interest for him, and Juan confirmed this. In fact, his only excited moment during the interview was when the interviewer asked him what he liked to do. In an effort to get him to respond, she offered to tell him first about something she did well. When she mentioned dancing, Juan's eyes lit up as he looked at her and exclaimed: 'Me too!'

Juan was vague about what he was learning in his classes: 'muchas cosas' (many things), he said. He said he liked to do mathematics; and as for reading, he mentioned a series of children's storybooks in Spanish as his favorite. Juan was asked if he could recall any of the stories, and he summarized one in a few sentences.

Asked about his previous school, Juan said that he had liked it better because he had many more friends there – twenty-eight to be exact! He said he had come to Escalante because 'he had been sent' by 'the school people'. To questions about why this had happened, he responded that there had been no teacher for him at the other school and that he needed a special teacher 'porque hablo mal' (because I speak badly).

Classroom Observations of Juan

Juan usually began the day in a quite business-like manner, keeping up appearances at least of completing his school tasks. However, by the end of the day he seemed tired, rubbing his eyes, yawning, putting his head down on the table, and watching the clock up until the moment when he could leave. Since he was a bus student, he left school fifteen minutes before the others and seemed reluctant to begin any new activities during the last minutes of the day. Juan's eye rubbing, his tendency to put his face very close to the page and incidents when he moved closer to the chalkboard, also raised a question about his vision.

Juan spoke Spanish almost exclusively, even in his ESL group. He was also instructed almost entirely in Spanish, with ESL as the exception. However, Juan demonstrated some comprehension of English in ESL lessons. For example, one day the group was playing a 'secret object' game, in which students had to guess the identity of a hidden object through descriptive clues. In response to the clues 'square, hard and smooth', Juan answered 'dados' (dice), a very good guess indeed. When it was his turn, he gave the clue 'una cosa que tiene dientes' (a thing which has teeth) for a comb, with a grin showing his quiet delight in stumping the other children. Whereas the ESL teachers encouraged other children to use only English in their classroom, they did not request this of Juan.

Juan's speech was somewhat difficult, but far from impossible, to understand. His sentences were complete and correct in their general structure, but he tended to leave out certain sounds, such as the 's' on plural endings and the 'l' in Spanish articles. His teachers seemed to be able to communicate with him without much difficulty, and with his language therapist he was positively gabby. He rarely conversed with other children, however.

Juan attended to, and participated in, the lessons we observed for the most part, until late in the school day when his interest seemed to fade. He was particularly excited about writing stories, when he felt invited to contribute from his vivid imagination. The language therapist, Ms. Martin, nurtured any and all oral expression from Juan, and he lit up with ideas in her sessions. He seemed to like 'scary' touches such as adding a tombstone for the wolf in drawings of 'Little Red Riding Hood'. In an LD lesson involving a story about bears, bees and honey, Juan dramatically 'acted out' the bees stinging the bears, and drew lines around the word 'murieron' (they died) at the end for emphasis. In Ms. Santana's room, Juan was most animated the day she asked for ideas for a group story. He suggested the idea of 'fantasmas' (ghosts), but the example story turned out to be about a desk. Undiscouraged by this mundane topic, Juan suggested that the story include jumping and putting one's feet on the desk. Ms. Santana smiled and shook her head, and brushed these suggestions aside.

It was clear that Juan did have severe difficulties with completing tasks involving reading and writing. Routine tasks, such as putting his name and date on his papers and copying spelling words, seemed tediously slow. Reading aloud, he needed teacher assistance with many short, common words. He had difficulty helping the teacher by returning papers to other children, because he could not read their names.

In one lesson, Juan's reading teacher read the assigned story aloud to him, and on this basis he was able to participate in the group discussion. For writing assignments, he depended on Ms. Santana to sit near him and proceed slowly, word by word, through the task. When other children came up to talk with the teacher, he seemed completely stalled without her help. As a consequence of this dependence, he completed many fewer tasks than other children. On the other hand, Juan seemed to understand basic math concepts like 'borrowing', and participated enthusiastically in the 'Mad Minute' exercises which so frustrated Carmín. Of course, 'word problems' were a barrier to his math achievement. He could also tell time, seemed interested in science lessons, and expressed an active curiosity about just about everything in his one-on-one sessions with Ms. Martin.

If Juan could complete a task independently, he worked with great concentration and an appearance of diligence. If not, he would matter-of-factly approach a teacher for help – his main strategy for making it through his lessons. It was generally at the end of the day, or when he knew a transition to another class was coming up shortly, that Juan avoided tasks and had to be reminded. One avoidance strategy he used was to stack and restack, or fold and refold, the papers on his desk to keep up an appearance of useful activity.

In comparison with all of the other target children at Escalante, relationships with other children were a missing element in the observations of Juan's school behavior. Even though he spent most of his days in the company of Gilberto, the two did not seem to interact as close friends. Juan, for instance, was not included in the recess soccer group, as Gilberto was. One factor may have been that Juan was limited to Spanish in his interactions, while code-switching Gilberto had a wider range of contacts. In addition, Juan's speech may have been a barrier or stigma separating him from others. Gilberto was also very outgoing, while Juan was withdrawn.

At times Juan seemed to be shunned by the other children. In the ESL 'secret object' game, he was among the last children chosen by the others, even though he raised his hand high and even tapped a girl on the shoulder to catch her attention. When he was finally chosen it was by 'default' (the teacher said a boy had to be chosen, and he was the last unchosen boy). Still another factor in Juan's limited interactions with other children may have been that he spent so much time in contact with teachers. This may have been a long-term pattern; in pre-school he had been singled out for extra teacher attention and special lessons.

The 'helping' strategies which Ms. Santana employed generally reinforced Juan's dependence upon her. But giving Juan extra help may have seemed like the only way for him to have successful experiences, especially in writing. There were no observations of the use of peer tutoring or cooperative learning experiences in his classes, and he did not seem to ask for help from other students. In language therapy (where he had individual attention) and LD (where he was one of three students), it was easy for Juan to get the one-to-one attention he demanded. However, giving this amount of assistance in the regular classroom was considerably more difficult, and Ms. Santana's ability to balance Juan's needs with those of the other children seemed stretched to the limit at times.

Discussion

In summary, Juan was the only child in the target group whose learning problems could be clearly traced to a physical injury. In contrast with the others, his handicap had been recognized, diagnosed and treated at an early age, before he came to public school. Teacher expectations for him to perform independently seemed lower than those for other children, and Juan also seemed aware of his limitations. In response, he appeared to have made an adjustment to school which had worked for him so far. He depended largely on teacher assistance and certain strategies for 'keeping up appearances'. Compared with Carmín, he did not seem to become too discouraged with his learning difficulties; in fact, he seemed rather detached and blasé about school.

Juan had not only his physical handicap to cope with, however. His early history suggested that he might have been abused. This, in combination with his abruptly broken early attachments to caring adults, might have contributed to his cautious behavior. His painful experiences of stigmatization by other children may have extended this caution to his interactions with them, as well. (Interestingly, however, other boys in the sample mentioned Juan as one of their friends.) His acceptance at Escalante School, and his placement in a mainstream rather than EMH classroom, had undoubtedly been positive for his social development.

Those who had known him for several years spoke of Juan's progress in speech, attributed to Ms. Martin's efforts. His current problems seemed to be in speech production, not processing. Juan's future in school was likely to be closely allied to his continued progress in speech and language therapy. As his pronunciation improved, his teachers might rate his academic abilities more highly. It was interesting that some of his teachers were already attributing his low achievement not only to his handicap but also to his lack of effort. That is, once Juan's speech had improved, he would be left with 'motivation' problems, perhaps tied to his long years of dependence on adult assistance.

Juan's speech improvement was also bound to enhance his social relationships with other students. However, his learning of English had been delayed compared with most of the others, and we wondered how that would affect his future schooling and social acceptance in a system which emphasized the transition away from Spanish, especially after fourth grade. How would Juan both transition to English and close his academic gap in one short year?

There is a temptation to end, as Juan's mother did, with the conclusion that for him simply to lead a 'fairly normal life' was quite enough. In contrast with the other students, Juan had surpassed low expectations, rather than disappointing high ones. The challenge for his teachers was to keep this hopeful trajectory going by developing his social skills, his sense of responsibility for his own learning, his creativity and love of language, and his strong desire to be perceived as 'adult' and competent in spite of his 'handicap'.

Lina

7-year-old Lina was one of the youngest children in the Escalante group; like her classmate Mateo, she was born in August, less than a month before the cut-off date for school entry. She was always conservatively dressed and neatly groomed, with barrettes or braids in her long hair. For the most part she seemed quiet, serious, inexpressive and often tired. She would slump at her desk with her head down, often with one leg dangling off the chair onto the floor, as if she could barely hold up her weight. Two of her teachers made remarks about her 'tiredness'. Given this general pattern, the occasions when Lina was animated or active became notable by contrast.

Lina's records showed that her first school experience was in a pre-kindergarten program in Suroeste District. She attended kindergarten at three different schools. The first two were in Suroeste District. On her withdrawal from the first school after two months, her teacher noted that she 'had a difficult time staying in circle at listening time; liked to explore the room by herself'. Her second school was in the old downtown barrio, and offered bilingual instruction in some classrooms. But on the entry form, someone (usually parents fill out this form) had written, 'quiero que estudie in ingles' ('I want her to study in English'). This statement seemed to have been symptomatic of a misunderstanding between Lina's parents and school personnel about Lina's language of instruction. She was apparently placed in an English-only classroom at this school.

Lina transferred to Escalante School during the second semester of kindergarten. The transfer form said that she had made satisfactory progress on physical and emotional growth, but 'had difficulty relating to and interacting with other children'. The teacher added, 'I feel Lina would have functioned better in a bilingual classroom. Her mother, however, did not agree'. On the entry form to Escalante School, Lina's mother indicated that her daughter spoke Spanish at home and English with her friends. A language assessment indicated that Lina scored higher in English than in Spanish dominance. Lina, therefore, had subsequently not attended ESL classes. Her final kindergarten report placed her 'on grade level', though the teacher remarked that she needed improvement on completing work and working independently.

In first grade, Lina's school progress took a downturn. Because of the school's policy of grading students in reading at their level of placement her reading grades appear to be satisfactory. But by second semester her grades in math, social studies and penmanship had plummeted to Ds and Fs. Her Iowa test scores for vocabulary were particularly low, 27 per cent compared with a class average of 50 per cent. In May the school's promotion-retention team considered Lina's case, which meant that her teacher had recommended her for retention. Everyone on the team – her classroom teacher, the principal, and Ms. Osgood (later her second grade teacher) – agreed to this course of action. However, in large letters across the report someone had written: 'This decision inaccurate since dominance in Spanish'. A later report showed that Lina was promoted after all. The principal, Ms. Bolivar, wrote on this report: 'Student is dominant in Spanish and had been in English reading in first grade. Teacher is on maternity leave. LAS was given'. The Language Assessment Scale (LAS) indicated that, contrary to previous assessments, Lina's language proficiency was higher in Spanish than in English.

When our study began, during Lina's second grade year, her grades appeared to be satisfactory. She was named as at-risk by her teacher for other reasons. Ms. Osgood said that she was the 'goat' of the classroom, a child who was ostracized by others. The teacher thought that Lina brought this treatment on herself by being mean to other children. She also displayed some LD kinds of problems, reversals of letters and numbers.

Parents and Home Experience

Lina was the second child in a family of four siblings, and the first from her mother and father's marriage. The mother explained in confidence that the oldest child, a boy, was born from a 'mistake' with a different father — this did not seem to be common knowledge in the household. The youngest child, a second boy, was born just a few weeks after our interview.

Lina and her sister were born through natural childbirth in the presence of their father. In fact, the mother shared pictures of Lina's birth during the interview. According to her mother, Lina was a very desired child, and a healthy baby except that she cried often during her first few months. After that she had few problems, and learned to walk and talk early.

The mother characterized Lina as more mischievous than her older brother, but less so than her younger sister. For fun, Lina liked to watch TV and play 'dolls' with her younger sister. She also played with her brother, but the mother had to separate them sometimes because they became so noisy. The mother also described Lina as 'irresponsible' and messy at home and considered her to be easily distracted.

Lina's mother presented a portrait of a very close-knit family. She had always been Lina's caretaker, with the exception of one year when she worked outside the home. Lina was 3-years-old at the time and stayed with a Spanish-speaking baby-sitter. There were many pictures of Lina's early years in company of extended family members. The mother said her husband 'spoiled' the girl, and he appeared to be close to all of his children. He was also supportive of his wife. For example, he was waiting for the new baby's birth in order to use his vacation time to stay home with the older children.

According to her mother, Lina had always enjoyed school. Lina's school-related problems, in her perception, were recent, and she thought that Lina's lack of responsibility was at least partly to blame. If she would only concentrate on her schoolwork instead of playing, she noted, Lina would finish her work. However, the mother also recognized that changing schools during kindergarten had been hard on Lina, and that Lina just seemed to learn more slowly than her older brother.

Lina's mother had found communication with her daughter's teachers difficult at times. She said that when Lina began first grade she had requested a Spanish classroom. Later, when the teacher complained that Lina was not finishing her work, she found out that

Lina was receiving instruction in English. The teacher suggested leaving Lina in the English classroom for the rest of the year because otherwise she might get 'confused'. The mother was told that placement in English was based on a test which indicated that Lina was dominant in English. When the teacher threatened to retain Lina in the first grade, her mother made a strong protest to the school. Her objections apparently led to a reevaluation of Lina's program and a decision to promote her to a bilingual second grade.

This year, Lina's mother and her second grade teacher had been communicating more effectively through the use of a journal, an idea of the teacher's. The journal contained information about homework assignments and Lina's school progress, and Lina carried it back and forth between school and home. By checking the journal, her mother could make sure that she got her homework completed. The mother could also use the journal to communicate with the teacher.

Lina's mother said that she only wanted what was best for her daughter in the future, and would like her to go as far as possible in school. She hoped that Lina would finish at least high school with no problems. She was trying to do her part to encourage Lina's school achievement through the use of rewards and punishments at home. Lina also liked dancing and singing, and her mother thought she might choose a career in those areas. She and her husband had discussed dancing lessons for Lina, but that would have to wait until they could afford them.

School Personnel Perceptions of Lina

Ms. Osgood attributed Lina's social problems at school to her home environment. She argued that since Lina's older brother was also picked on, and he was in a different class with a different teacher, the problem must lie with their family. She traced Lina's academic problems, on the other hand, to having spent first grade in an English-only classroom and experiencing a 'full year of failure'. Ms. Osgood reported that though Lina was improving academically, especially in reading, she still did not complete her tasks. She was also sloppy; as Ms. Osgood put it, she let 'mold grow in her desk'. The 'chic' Spanish-dominant girls at her table shunned her. One girl told her 'she was not of God's children' — the 'supreme insult'. Ms. Osgood thought that Lina's mother might be the source of her problems. The mother was demanding that she have homework every night, but Ms. Osgood argued that 'That's not going to work. Lina herself is the key.'

Ms. Wilson, who began teaching part-time in Ms. Osgood's classroom in November, described Lina in January as a child who was making herself unlikable by not being 'nice' to other children, by poking them and bothering them. Lina did not finish her work and 'wasted a lot of time'. Ms. Wilson did not know at that point how Lina was doing academically, but she thought that Lina had less 'potential' than another girl who had similar work habits. She thought Lina would probably need two years to improve.

These teachers said that they had tried several strategies with Lina. Ms. Wilson had talked about her relationships with other children: 'Would she like to be a child who sat close to her?' Ms. Osgood talked with her about 'being a friend'. Ms. Wilson took Lina home after school and talked with her parents. They reportedly told her that Lina had the same problems with children outside of school. Nevertheless, Ms. Wilson thought that Lina had seemed better since she had developed a one-to-one relationship with the parents.

Ms. Osgood was the one who had initiated the 'journal program' with Lina; however, she had doubts about whether the mother would follow through. Recently, Lina's mother had complained at a PTA meeting that no homework was being sent home. But when Ms. Osgood called her and arranged to send work home, it seemed that the mother found it difficult to keep Lina on task, and 'slacked off' on her responsibilities. Nevertheless, Ms. Osgood wanted to keep trying with Lina's mother, and said she was anxious to talk with her again.

In a final interview in April, Ms. Osgood no longer classified Lina as being at-risk. She joked that Lina was still an 'intrinsic slob', like herself. However, she was improving academically; for instance, she now had fewer reversals in her writing. Ms. Osgood predicted that Lina would be 'real successful' in Spanish and then transfer to English. But more than academic improvement, Ms. Osgood focused excitedly on Lina's social development: 'She's bloomed!' Ms. Osgood attributed Lina's new-found security to having a new baby brother in the family, her feeling of being very 'big sisterly'. She was starting to get along better with other children, because she was feeling successful and had a higher self-concept. In spite of all these positive changes, Ms. Osgood would still advise Lina's third grade teacher to keep reporting to Lina's mother and to follow up on the issue of Lina's sense of responsibility.

Ms. Wilson, in contrast, said in her final interview that Lina was still at-risk. She was 'just not very motivated', to the point where 'I can see her not finishing school'. Lina's family had been supportive when the teachers asked for their help, but they were not comfortable in the school-environment — she guessed because they were primarily

Spanish speaking. She had been surprised, however, to hear them speak up assertively at a recent parent meeting.

Lina's Perceptions of School

The two interviews with Lina were not very productive. She was somewhat shy and her responses may have been guided by her perception of what the interviewer wanted to hear. She chose Spanish as the interview language, but seemed equally comfortable in English.

Lina said that she enjoyed school and all her classes, but she was not able to say much about her classes and what she was learning there. Interestingly, when asked in Spanish if she was learning how to read she responded affirmatively and said (in English) 'in reading (class)'. But to a follow-up question she responded that she was learning how to read in Spanish, not English.

According to Lina, she did not have any friends, and yet she seemed to be actively engaged with other girls at the lunch table. She was also approached, while in the company of the interviewer, by another girl who wanted to 'borrow' money from her. Lina refused the girl's request and pointed out to her adult companion that 'they' were always doing that. Her response, and her comments to the interviewer, were adult-like, almost 'gossipy' in style.

Lina said she liked to dance and sing as well as play with dolls. She appeared to be very fond of her newborn brother and explained that she helped take care of him. She also mentioned playing with her sister and older brother.

After reading a short passage from a children's story (third to fourth grade reading level) to Lina, the interviewer asked her to retell the story. Lina's response was brief and incomplete. However, comprehension questions from the interviewer elicited very accurate responses from Lina and plausible predictions of the story's outcome. The girl was also able to demonstrate good decoding skills when she attempted to read another paragraph from the same story. She was also able, when asked by the interviewer if she knew the meaning of the Spanish word 'escoger' to provide a rather complete definition of the word. She was not able to say what the word would be in English, but when given the equivalent 'to choose' she added that 'to pick' could also be used.

Lina said that she saw herself as an average student, not too bad, not too good. She thought reading was the most important thing in school. Asked if she was going to pass to the next grade, Lina was at first not sure, but then guessed she probably would. In any case, she expected the teacher would tell her. She thought she would be very sad if she did not pass.

Classroom Observations of Lina

Lina was a study in contrasts. She could seem very lethargic in the classroom, but excited a few minutes later, running and playing with other girls at recess. Daydreamy or distracted during a whole group lesson, when Lina was assigned to complete her seatwork with a partner she could be chatty, entertaining and absorbed. Shy and uncomfortable as the center of attention in the Christmas program and on 'share and speak' day, Lina could be critical, assertive, even down-right bossy with other children, especially boys. Sometimes she would suddenly 'light up', as in a reading lesson when the teacher mentioned locusts. Her head popped up from its resting place on the tabletop as she called out, 'They eat clothes!'

Lina used both Spanish and English informally with other students. Her conversations with the girls at her table were in Spanish, but when she called out requests to others and when she reprimanded boys for 'picking on her' she often used English. Given a choice, she chose Spanish as her language for 'share and speak' time. She initiated a playground conversation with the observer (who she could probably tell was a predominantly English speaker) in English. Lina demonstrated some code-mixing in both her speech and writing, but not a great deal. She was assigned to Spanish reading and science groups in Ms. Bernard's classroom, and Ms. Osgood and Ms. Wilson also instructed her in Spanish, math and language arts. However, many of the task instructions and routine directions in their classroom were in English only.

Another notable characteristic of Lina was that she seemed very attached to little 'things' of her own. Her desk was usually overflowing with papers and other possessions: barrettes, headbands, coloring books, bits of pretty cards and pictures. Very often she carried some little thing in her hand from activity to activity, room to room. During lessons, she would stare at and handle these material companions.

Lina's group participation, attention to lessons, and task completion were spotty. She seemed to tune in and out of whole group activities, sometimes volunteering and attending very closely, sometimes putting her head down, playing with things or watching other children. Teaching style may have made a difference; for instance, when Ms.

Osgood turned on her animated, entertaining style it generally drew Lina's wide-eyed gaze. Working on her own, she was distracted by almost anything. Consequently, Lina worked very slowly on individual tasks, and dragged out their completion while other children moved on to new things.

As mentioned above, Lina seemed more productive when she was assigned to work with a partner. However, she may not have been a popular choice among the other children. In two observations she had to ask for the teacher's help to find a partner. Once assigned, she seemed to cooperate well, taking a genuine interest in the other child's work. The disadvantage of cooperative learning for Lina was that she and her partner (always another girl in our obsrvations) could both become distracted. In one lesson the two girls played 'hairdresser' with the scissors rather than cutting out a science puzzle. Having a partner could bring out Lina's more playful and boisterous side.

Lina could also complete her work successfully when she was isolated from others and from the distractions at her desk. For instance, Ms. Wilson had her sit at a desk in a corner of the room, turned toward the wall. In this lesson, Lina finally completed several pages in her math workbook on time. Lina herself chose to work alone in one reading lesson, despite her reading teacher's encouragement to work 'with the other girls'. In this lesson, she worked steadily and deliberately (though not with any obvious enjoyment) and her pace matched that of the others.

The characteristics of Lina's work which could be observed were that her writing was of variable size, sometimes with a messy appearance. This improved over the time of the study, however. Her writing did demonstrate the reversals Ms. Osgood had mentioned in her interview. Sometimes Lina paid attention to, and spent task time on, small 'aesthetic' details like adding extra wavy lines or curlicues. She also could be rigidly methodical in her efforts while others buzzed along, talking quietly with each other and enjoying themselves. She sometimes appeared to watch what others were doing in relation to her own pace and progress.

Lina's quiet style meant that she rarely drew teacher attention to herself. Nonetheless, she seemed comfortable enough asking for teacher assistance. In our observations she sought out attention and affection from Ms. Wilson and from Ms. Bernard, her reading and science teacher, and even from the observer. She also signalled that she wanted to be noticed for being helpful. For instance, in one observation she went out of her way to straighten up a box of markers for Ms. Osgood before going to recess. But when she received praise or a hug from a teacher in return, her reponse was characteristically stoical. Whatever satisfaction she took from these encounters, she kept to herself.

As for her interactions with other students, Lina's encounters with girls and boys were very different. (However, boy-girl divisions were also typical of student social pattern at Escalante School.) Girls were Lina's chosen companions on the playground and in the classroom. Once in a while she seemed to have a small 'spat' or be irritable with another girl. She also initiated much more contact with the 'chic' girls at her table than they did with her. At recess she seemed most often to play with girls from other classrooms. But in general her most shining moments in the classroom were when she was able to work and/or socialize with other girls.

Despite both Ms. Osgood and Ms. Wilson's warnings, the observer did not see Lina picking on other children. However, there were incidents in which Lina herself was picked on, and these all involved boys. In one incident she was putting together a chain of plastic cubes when Victor attempted to grab them away. She squealed 'No!' and held the blocks close to her protectively. He smiled, went over to her desk and 'karate chopped' her pencil, saying 'Here's yours!' with a menacing look. Another boy needlessly kicked a pile of her things as she was cleaning out her cubby, and she assertively said, 'Don't kick my things!' There were two other incidents of boys teasing her.

In no case did Lina directly provoke this behaviour, but this is not to say that Ms. Osgood and Ms. Wilson were incorrect in their observations. The behaviours of the boys may have had a history that involved Lina's behavior toward them; for whatever reason, Lina's relationships with the boys in her class were strained. Lina could be irritable, bossy and loud (for her) with boys, especially calling attention to their mistakes.

Ms. Osgood's classroom strategy with Lina was to try to keep her involved. This teacher had a preference for cooperative activities, and she seemed to choose partners who worked well worked with Lina. Ms. Osgood also knew how to 'grab' children by being dramatic or funny, and this seemed to draw Lina's attention. On the other hand, Ms. Wilson's style was quiet and serious. She sternly emphasized staying on task, and isolated Lina from others when she could see her becoming distracted. She told Lina, 'Look, math is hard for you. You play and walk around. You don't have time.'

Discussion

In summary, Lina was a child who may have been placed at-risk for school failure by her mistaken placement in English-only kindergarten and first-grade classes. She had been identified as socially isolated since kindergarten, and perhaps this, too, could be attributed to her linguistic isolation. After one year in a bilingual classroom, with Spanish-speaking classmates, at least some measure of parent involvment, and two different sets of teacher strategies, she may or may not have left 'at-riskness' behind — depending on which teacher one asked.

Lina on the surface seemed to have recovered well from her misplacement experiences. She did not talk about those days in her interview, and did not mention any present unhappiness regarding school. However, as was noted above, she was very reserved in her interview. Also evident in the interview, Lina's Spanish reading skills appeared to be at least average for her grade, a great improvement from the previous year.

Lina's academic improvement suggested that the Principal's decision to promote her to third grade was appropriate. And her English competence suggested that, given sufficient psychological and academic support, Lina might be able to make a smooth transition to an English classroom. It had probably been to her advantage that Lina's parents had been willing to complain about school practices.

Lina's social relationships were more difficult to understand. She seemed to be highly adult-oriented, but her complaint about having no friends at all did not seem to be borne out by the observations. It was possible that Lina's new responsibilities as an older sister may have helped her become more self-confident and mature by the end of the year; if so, hers is a case in which outside-of-school factors, rather than school efforts, had made the difference.

Because at least some of her longstanding school patterns seemed to be persistent, there was a sense that her third grade teacher would need to attend closely to Lina's progress, both academic and social. This might not be immediately obvious to that teacher, since quiet, undemanding, daydreaming Lina could so easily be ignored or written off. Her slow task completion, her distractedness, could be confused with low ability. The difference in teacher perceptions of Lina at the end of our study suggested that her new teacher's response to her could be a factor in her continued success at school.

Mateo

Mateo had a round, very pleasant face, sandy brown hair and eyes, and a usually placid expression. He was always clean and neatly dressed in plain, practical clothes. Though like Lina he was one of the younger students in the class, he appeared somewhat older than the others. He was taller than most children in his class, and also slightly plump. His physical movements were slow and smooth, never sudden. A word for Mateo would be 'low-key'. Until the observer focused more closely on him, the changes in his behavior and expression seemed almost unnoticeable. Moreover, he rarely called adult attention to himself.

School records showed that Mateo had attended kindergarten at a school in Suroeste District not far from Escalante School. He had an extensive kindergarten file with records of many screening and testing procedures. After a first round of screening, he was referred to a Chapter 1 kindergarten class, where he would receive extra attention. His original teacher's referral form said that his English proficiency was low, his Spanish high. She also indicated that he was 'somewhat below average' in self-development and independence, social skills, motor skills, and communication skills; and 'well below average' in creative development and thinking skills. Later screening results said that he needed help with listening skills, had 'immature speech and limited vocabulary,' and in general exhibited 'poor communication skills'.

On a Home Language Inventory, his parents responded that he mostly spoke Spanish at home, and they had given permission for him to be placed in bilingual education. By the end of kindergarten, Mateo showed progress in his acquisition of English. His teacher's final report indicated that he had made satisfactory progress in other areas as well. She commented: 'Gets along well with others, positive attitude toward school . . . Needs more confidence in speaking, using speech to express ideas'.

Mateo's parents enrolled him in Escalante School at the beginning of first grade. At this time they approved his continued placement in bilingual education. From his grade reports, it would seem that Mateo had a very successful year. For the second semester he received As in all areas except penmanship, PE, art and music. He 'mastered' all first grade skills on the Raintree criterion-referenced tests given at the year's end. A language assessment indicated that he demonstrated moderate proficiency in both Spanish and English. His reading instruction was in Spanish, and he attended ESL classes. But in second grade, when our study began, Mateo's grades had taken a downturn to Bs and Cs.

Not only had his reading grades dropped, but he was still reading in the same basal reader as in first grade. His teacher Ms. Osgood, named him as marginally at-risk. She said that he really had no academic difficulties; in fact, he was 'bright' and 'capable'. His problem was work completion. As she explained it, 'What he does finish is good, but there's a three week lap'. The teacher had a hunch that his mother did too much for him at home, and as a result he had become rather unambitious.

Parents and Home Experience

Second grader Mateo was the older of two brothers; the younger of which was eight-months-old. His mother and father had met in Mexico, and they married and moved to Suroeste when she was already pregnant with Mateo. This was still a source of embarrassment; she blushed when she described how difficult it had been for her as the favorite child in a very reserved, proper family. Nevertheless, in spite of her fears and embarrassment, the baby was well received by both sides of the family. In fact, her mother seemed to suspect the problem and came to visit just in time to take care of her daughter after childbirth.

Mateo's birth was difficult and required a Caesarian section. Both mother and son suffered with fevers after the delivery, and they had to remain in the hospital for five days. In addition, her husband lost his job soon after the birth, and mother and baby went to Mexico with her parents for a couple of months. Since then, they had always lived in Suroeste.

The mother displayed many pictures of Mateo, showing a strong baby, large for his age and physically accomplished. She recalled that he developed normally, except that he seemed delayed in putting words together in sentences. She became worried about this and asked the doctor when she took him for his immunizations. The doctor reassured her that he was quite within the normal range.

Many of the pictures showed Mateo with his father, being hugged and carried. Mateo's mother explained that the father and son were very close. There were also pictures of Mateo with his cousins in the small southern Arizona town where they lived. The family traveled to this town often, and Mateo had visited his cousins there for short periods of time. Several pictures also captured Mateo's mischief; the mother said the camera was always ready to catch him in these situations.

Mateo seemed to have a pleasant, unexceptional home life. He and his mother liked to do jigsaw puzzles together, and he played 'men's games' such as wrestling with his father. The family watched movies together on their VCR, and the mother said she was careful to select movies appropriate for Mateo. *Pinocchio* was one of his favorites. They also participated in church activities, and Mateo was preparing for his First Communion.

Mateo's mother appeared to be very sensitive to her son's needs. She said she had enrolled him in Head Start as a pre-schooler because he often cried with strangers and did not get along well with other children. In her opinion, Head Start resulted in positive changes not only in Mateo, but also in his parents. She learned how to deal with Mateo better, she said, by learning how to correct him without losing her temper and screaming at him.

According to his mother, Mateo had always enjoyed school, but his attitude towards school worried her. She believed he was intelligent enough to do well; however, he 'played' instead of doing his work. This behavior was causing him problems in school. She pointed out more than once that he had no problems with English, and had even learned to read a little in English, although he had received reading instruction only in Spanish. She reported that his teachers had also agreed that he had no language problem, and that his only school problems were paying attention and getting his work done. She said she had tried to emphasize the importance of schoolwork, and how he must use his time for work as well as for play.

As for her participation in Mateo's education, the mother said that she used to go to school more often, when Mateo was in kindergarten, but now only attended special activities. She went to meet the teacher at the beginning of the year; after that she expected the teacher to call if there were problems. Mateo's teacher, Ms. Osgood, had worked out a communication system with her using a 'journal' which he carried between school and home. The journal allowed her to keep track of the work he needed to complete, and he was expected to finish his schoolwork before playing outside. The mother said she helped him when there were things about his schoolwork he did not understand.

Looking to the future, Mateo's mother wanted him to study and develop a career, but she said the choice of career was up to him. She also wanted him to be a 'good person' and a 'good husband'. She believed it was important to teach her son about God and to instill in him sound moral principles.

School Personnel Perceptions of Mateo

In an in-depth interview a month after our study began, Ms. Osgood said that Mateo was already doing much better. He was interacting more with other children 'in a rumbling sort of fashion'. Before, 'his world was just very tightly related just to him'. She described the 'journal program' she was trying with Mateo, which from her perspective was paying off. He was even writing his own stories in the journal at home. His mother seemed to be cooperating in this venture, and she had also come to school to participate in class activities.

However, Mateo still had a problem with slow work completion. In addition, while he was reading with a third grade group successfully, he was not demonstrating his potential in written expression. He was also getting into a little 'social' trouble. The boys at his all-male table fought among themselves, but also acted as 'armed guards' for each other. Nevertheless, Ms. Osgood felt that it was good for Mateo to have friends. Even if he did get into more trouble, it was preferable to his former isolation.

Ms. Wilson, Ms. Osgood's teaching partner, took a dimmer view of Mateo's troublemaking. She remarked that he disobeyed rules often, 'not just with me' but with other teachers, too. She was concerned that when apprehended, Mateo would not explain his side of the problem. He just shrugged his shoulders and 'took his punishment' without argument or emotion — 'he just didn't take responsibilities for his actions'. On the other hand, he was 'awfully smart'. She theorized that maybe he had just been allowed to 'get away with it'. In her opinion, the danger was that boys like him might go on causing trouble in school and eventually drop out. She said that his behavior had improved when she gave him a 'ticket', part of Escalante School's system of consequences for rulebreakers.

Interestingly, when his ESL teachers were asked to name any children in Ms. Osgood's class whom they considered to be 'at-risk', they did not name Mateo at all. At the end of the study, in April, Ms. Osgood still had some concerns about Mateo. Certainly he had improved a lot. He was talking to her more, which was encouraging since she had heard that in first grade he barely spoke at all. She jokingly said, 'He's still not "Chatty Cathy" '. For example, at the end of April, in a follow-up observation, Mateo voluntarily participated in a sharing time at the beginning of the day, telling the class in Spanish that his uncle was in the hospital with heart trouble. The ESL teacher had told Ms. Osgood that she considered Mateo and Victor the 'most improved' ESL students in the entire school. Nevertheless, Ms.

Osgood still classified him as bright but 'lackadaisical'. As she put it, 'He's over-mellowed.'

A disturbing piece of news which Ms. Osgood added in this interview was that Mateo had reported a case of sexual abuse by a peer. The follow-up on this case mostly involved the other child. She was also concerned because Mateo had told her that when she saw his report card, his mother hit him with a stick. She didn't want to condone such treatment on the mother's part, but had talked to Mateo about what he might do to prevent making his mother so angry.

In her final interview, Ms. Wilson said excitedly that Mateo had 'just taken a turn for the better!' He still had trouble communicating; she thought that 'if he could just write everything down, in every academic area, it would be a lot better for him'. But he was developing better skills, his grades were improved, and most important to her, he wanted to 'be caught up in his work'.

Mateo's Perceptions of School

Mateo was the least communicative of the six children interviewed. His responses were mostly monosyllabic, and he initiated no topic of conversation. He was often silent in response, and the interviewer tried to give him ample time to respond, waiting him out. His most common response was 'No Se'. (I don't know.) He chose Spanish as the language of the interview, though he was assured that he could choose either language.

Mateo said he liked school but was silent when asked about his daily schedule. To get any idea of his schedule the interviewer had to prompt him with questions such as: 'What do you do first in school?' To this he replied, 'Trabajo'. (I work.) When asked what he worked at, he answered, 'Español'. To the next question about what he was studying in Spanish he responded 'Letras pegadas', (the term the teachers used for cursive writing, literally 'letters glued together'). When asked if he read stories, he said no, he was learning letters.

The only description of his school schedule which could be elicited from Mateo was an ordered list of the teachers whose classes he attended. First, he said he was doing 'mas español' (more Spanish) in Ms. Kiley's class, and learning to write. After more prodding, he said that next they would go out to play, at mid-morning, and then 'nos ponemos en linea' (we get in line). For what? He answered, to go to class. To study what? His first response was 'No se', but then he said 'centers'. When asked what 'centers' were, Mateo answered that they were like games, but not really games. He did not like centers, he said, because he had trouble rhyming words. When asked about the purpose of the centers, Mateo answered, 'Para ganar premios'. (To win prizes.) He did not know whether he learned anything in these centers.

Mateo was slightly more animated when asked what he liked to read. He mentioned a series of Spanish storybooks called 'Barbapapa'. He also said he did not have much schoolwork to do at home and that he did most of it alone, although his mother helped him when he needed her. He would not answer questions about the kind of student he, or his teacher, might consider him to be. His only comment about teachers was that they should be 'buena' (good). However, he could not, or would not, elaborate on that. He was equally hesitant to speak of his quality as a student or about his friends. When asked to comment about his performance in school, whether good, bad or normal ('regular' in Spanish) He asked 'Que es regular?' When the word was explained to him he chose that term to describe himself. He finally named Paulo as his best friend.

At the end of the second interview Mateo was asked to read a page from the story *El Pizarron Encantado*. He read very well, stumbling only a few times with some of the longer or uncommon words, for example, 'oscureciendo' or the protagonist's name 'Adrian', an unusual combination of sounds in Spanish. He was asked to discuss what he had read and, as usual, said he did not know. But when he was prodded with specific questions about the facts of the story he responded correctly. He also suggested what might happen next in the story.

Toward the end of the interview Mateo admitted that he did not like to talk much, but that he did talk at home and with his friends. He said he liked Escalante School, and did not seem to remember going to a different school for kindergarten. His responses to questions about school suggested little understanding of the instructional activities in which he participated. It was difficult to determine whether this was due to the sparsity of his responses, to a real confusion about the purposes of instruction, or to an unwillingness to spend any effort in discussing those issues. The interviewer's impression was that all three of these reasons contributed.

In contrast, when Mateo discussed other issues, for example, that he would soon get a puppy, he became somewhat more talkative. He also asked occasional questions when he did not know something (as when he asked what 'regular' meant), and sometimes became impatient when the interviewer happened to repeat a question.

Classroom Observations of Mateo

Mateo rarely participated in his classes unless called upon. His attention was good for question-and-answer sequences when he tended to watch others participate. He watched when the teacher actively demonstrated a task, but he yawned and his gaze wandered when the teacher read or talked for extended periods. Independent seatwork was Mateo's greatest downfall; it simply did not seem to hold his interest. For instance, students in his classroom were expected to complete a certain number of math workbook pages per week. They worked independently on this assignment during math time each afternoon under Ms. Wilson's supervision. Mateo fell behind in his math work under this arrangement. He would work for a while and then begin to watch others or try to distract the boys at his table.

Mateo liked to watch other boys who seemed to be 'getting away with something'. A sly grin would appear on his face as he watched. During seatwork Mateo would also initiate games at his table using easily available materials: flying scissors like airplanes, cutting off the points of pencils with scissors and then sharpening them again, 'karate-chopping' pencils. Some of the other boys resisted his attempts to distract them and plowed on with their work; others were only too willing to join in. Once when Mateo kept talking and leaning toward him during math workbook time, Paulo resorted to setting up a cardboard screen on the table between them. Another boy, Richard, worked with such concentration that he seemed able to 'tune out' Mateo. Victor, on the other hand, was usually off-task himself, and affected a sort of bravado about the consequences. Perhaps this was one of the qualities which seemed to make Victor attractive to Mateo.

Mateo communicated primarily in Spanish, which Ms. Osgood thought was a factor in his close relationships with other Spanish-speaking boys. His reading and vocabulary in Spanish seemed quite good. When called upon to read aloud, he read smoothly, clearly, with ease. His written production was slow but passable, with a few spelling errors. It was apparent that Mateo could succeed at the tasks given to the whole class. When he did perform, he did well, and his work generally drew the teachers' praise. The teachers seemed to wonder why their approval was not enough to motivate him to perform consistently.

When Ms. Osgood or Ms. Wilson made a special effort to get Mateo on-task, he could complete his work on time. Ms. Wilson demanded that Mateo finish his work, even if it meant working while others were going on to other things or getting ready to leave at the end of the day. Mateo could put in a last-ditch effort to redeem himself with her. In one observation, she gave Mateo one of her 'motivational talks', pulling him close to her and asking him in Spanish, 'You know how to do it. Why haven't you done it?' and 'It's only three pages. Can't you do one page?' Mateo did not respond to any of her questions. He simply stared at her blankly or hung his head.

It was notable that in his ESL class, Mateo was more expressive than in any other classroom setting. The ESL Program was primarily designed to stimulate oral language development. There was little 'academic' pressure; and activities, usually language games or art projects, were conducted in small, personal groups. Mateo joked in a very relaxed way with the ESL teachers. Something which he expressed in ESL and occasionally in his home classroom was a joking self-deprecation: 'I'm not doing it right.' 'Mine looks ugly.' He teased one ESL teacher by telling her that he threw away his projects when he got them home. Yet he seemed to enjoy completing the projects and invited the ESL teachers' responses to them. Another feature which undoubtedly made the ESL class a comfortable environment was that it included three of his closest friends: Luis, Victor and Paulo.

Something else which might have slowed the pace of Mateo's work was that when he wanted teacher attention or assistance he could be ineffective at getting it in a large group setting. It seemed that Mateo was shy with most adults. However, he had a quietly rich social life in his relationship with other students, especially the boys at his table. Smiles and laughter lit up his usually sombre face when he 'played around' with other boys. As was typical for boys at Escalante school, Mateo's interactions with other students were almost entirely with other boys. He sat at an all-male table and carried these relationships over to his ESL and recess time. In reading in Ms. Kiley's room, however, he did not sit near other boys from his room and seemed very isolated. In this classroom, he spent more time 'watching'.

Mateo seemed to be especially attracted to Victor's exploits. However, Mateo sought Victor out more than vice versa. It appeared to be a case of 'following' or 'hero worship' behavior on Mateo's part. Mateo saved seats for Victor in ESL, sat by him at lunch, watched when Victor was fighting or fooling around, followed him about at centers time. But at recess Mateo did not seem included in the very active group of soccer-playing boys to which Victor belonged. Mateo more often walked about with small groups of other boys from his classroom.

Discussion

In summary, Mateo was a capable student with a 'motivation' problem which his teachers felt placed him 'marginally at-risk' for school failure, or at least underachievement. They expended most of their efforts with Mateo in attempts to find a way to motivate him to complete his schoolwork. In this, they seemed to have been partially successful. Somewhat inspired by the rewards offered for work completion, Mateo on the other hand seemed uninspired by the work itself. On the positive side, Mateo's home situation appeared to be stable and supportive, a definite resource for him. The journal program seemed an effective link between home and school.

Mateo was quiet and fairly unresponsive toward his teachers, seemed bored with the usual school tasks, and did not often demonstrate his potential. However, he responded socially (if not always in acceptable ways) to the other Spanish-speaking boys at his table, and these friendships seemed to be a very important aspect of school for him. Less daring at acting-out than Victor, Mateo was attracted to and entertained by Victor's exploits. The question his teachers faced was: What could make 'academic' work equally appealing for him?

The observations suggested that humor, conversation, 'exciting' or personally relevant content, and small-group cooperative activities might motivate Mateo and bring him out of his shell. That is, Mateo's need for social involvement might also serve to nurture his learning potential. A more challenging instructional program might also be helpful for him. It seemed that he failed to relate the activities presently being offered to any significant learning on his part. His teachers also felt that getting his mother involved had been a positive step, and the mother agreed; hopefully this home-school link will continue.

Mateo's story ended on a rather hopeful note in comparison with those of some of the other children. Though far from tragic, there is a lesson in his story nonetheless. Mateo reminded us that extrinsic rewards for achievement such as offered at Escalante School may take a child only so far; beyond that, the child must perceive some personal interest and meaning in schoolwork which will deepen his/her involvement. There is a sense that much, much more could be happening for Mateo at school — if his schoolwork were as stimulating to him as the social milieu in which it occurs.

Victor

Second-grader Victor was a slender boy with thick, unruly hair. His most noticeable features were his large and heavy-lidded eyes, which on first glance gave him the appearance of being tired or even sullen. There was also something indescribably 'old' about his face; he did not have the naive, open childlikeness of his other classmates. He spent a great deal of his time involved in the nonacademic aspects of schooling, socializing, playing and scrapping with other boys. While he seemed socially successful, Victor's difficulties with academic tasks were quite obvious to the observer.

Escalante School was the only one Victor had attended. Though his kindergarten records were not extensive, it was clear from comments on his grade reports that his teacher had identified him as a student with learning problems. He was often absent. It was not clear if he attended a bilingual or English-only kindergarten class. Language screenings indicated that he was Spanish dominant but had begun acquiring oral language skills in English. Victor's first grade year began poorly, according to his low grade reports, and in January the teacher referred him for a child study. She said on the referral form that Victor was 'below grade level in all academic areas' and in her opinion was disruptive because of frustration with his inability to do schoolwork. He was 'usually tardy and frequently absent' and missed his ESL class 'a lot'. She cited 'minimal parent involvement [and] a poor home environment'.

In her role in the child study team, the school nurse made a home visit, where the mother reported that there had been complications at Victor's birth and that she had noticed him stuttering at home. But his early development had progressed normally, and he was quite competent at doing home chores for her. The mother told the nurse that she thought that recently meeting his biological father for the first time had been very difficult for Victor. He fought a lot, did not listen, and angered easily. In addition, she talked with the nurse about having been reported by the school to the Child Protective Services for slapping Victor. According to the nurse, the mother said she had been referred for counseling but had not kept the appointment.

The school psychologist's report showed that Victor performed within the 'average' range on the WISC. The final diagnosis was 'learning disability based on manipulative processing deficits'. Victor was placed in the LD resource program at the end of first grade in order to receive special services in Spanish. The promotion-retention team also met about his case and recommended that he be retained in first grade. But he was promoted, despite the fact that his grades had declined even further.

Early in second grade, Victor was screened for language proficiency. The results placed him at level three in English, and level five in Spanish, indicating a moderate degree of proficiency in English and the highest proficiency in Spanish. He continued to be pulled out for ESL classes, as well as LD services. His grades continued to be poor; however, his attendance this year had greatly improved. His teacher, Ms. Osgood, named him as one of her at-risk children both because of his low school performance and what she considered a neglected home environment. From what she had observed, he was the 'caretaker' for his younger brother and sister. According to her, the stories he brought from home were so upsetting that the other children did not want to hear them during 'sharing time'.

Parent's and Home Experience

Eight-year-old Victor was born in a Mexican border town when his mother was only 15. She was eager to have a child, and said she wanted a boy because he 'would have more strength to face life'. But she admitted that she had no idea what it meant to be a mother, and that had she realized the responsibility she might not have had him. Her parents and older sister took charge of the baby's care. Nevertheless, she remembered Victor as a happy, healthy baby who walked and talked early and was very attached to his grandparents.

When Victor was only 2, both grandparents died within five months of each other. His mother found herself suddenly alone and in charge of the toddler. Her older sister had moved to another border town by then, and Victor's mother followed her there. There she met a young man, married and had two more children, a girl and a boy. However, she and her husband had been separated for four years and he seldom visited. Victor's natural father had seen him only once.

When Victor was 3-years-old the family moved to Suroeste, to the Escalante School neighbourhood. At the time of the study they lived right across the street from the school. The household consisted of the mother, her three children, and the mother's sister — the aunt who had helped care for Victor since his birth. They had no other relatives in Suroeste.

According to his mother, Victor was very helpful at home; he liked to clean house and take care of the younger children. However, she had to be careful about placing him in charge of his brother and sister, since he treated them 'as though he were their father', ordering them around and threatening punishment for misbehavior. Family activities consisted of trips to the country, going for rides, and eating out together. The mother said she took the children with her everywhere, except to parties at night — she did not think that children belonged at dances.

Victor began his school career in kindergarten at Escalante School and had attended there ever since. The family had moved just once since coming to Suroeste, within the Escalante attendance area. Victor's mother said he was not too eager to start school, but soon thereafter his worst punishment was missing school. She never had any problems getting him ready to go in the morning. Becoming very animated when she recalled Victor's first year of school, she said that he had excellent grades, that she was often congratulated on his achievement, and that Victor himself was enthusiastic about learning. She found it 'incredible' to see her own son learning to read and write, and said it brought back memories of her own early school experiences.

Victor's mother said she became aware that Victor had school problems in first grade. From talking with his teacher, she found out that he was not bringing homework or notes from school. He would swear to her that the teacher had sent nothing home. She said she had missed parent meetings because Victor did not bring her the notices. Since then she always asked him about notes from school and about his homework, and did not let him watch cartoons or play until he did his work. Victor had also 'taken off' from school once in first grade. The teacher called her on the telephone, and she went to the school. She was impressed that the teacher talked to Victor about this incident as though 'she were his mother'.

As far as his mother was concerned, Victor's main problem in school was his feistiness. She counseled him against fighting, although she also told him not to let others hurt him. She mentioned that he frequently brought home good grades and 'presents' from his teacher, a sign that he must be doing well. While claiming that he was not behind in reading, she also said that he did not know the names of the letters, and forgot them as soon as she told him. He 'read' to her in Spanish, but she had noticed that he seemed to stop and think about what 'should' happen next in the story and then continue with that. She suspected that he did this 'reading' from memory, since he could read isolated words only after studying them.

Though she recognized his learning problems, Victor's mother was confident that as he matured and developed more understanding, he would improve. In her view the first year of school was 'almost nothing', and the second one was to learn to read and write. With time, she said, 'he will gradually learn all those things'. Her optimism was reflected in her aspirations for Victor — to be a 'professional', perhaps a lawyer, or a technician. She would prefer a career that would not cause him problems or involve danger, since as she put it, 'After all, I am his mother, no?'

School Personnel Perceptions of Victor

Ms. Osgood said she wondered sometimes if 'school made more problems for Victor 'cause he's too busy trying to live'. She reported that Victor's mother did not feel it was 'her job' to send him to school. He got himself ready, since his mother rarely rose before noon. The mother did not respond to teachers' requests concerning his school progress or needs; she may have given Ms. Osgood an incorrect telephone number. Victor had also, she had heard, taken 'quite a few blows to the head'. She remarked that he seemed happy with his home life recently, since his mother had bought a VCR and they were watching 'raunchy movies late at night'.

Academically, Victor had reached a 'learning plateau' and needed another evaluation, Ms. Osgood believed. His major difficulty was with retention. He was also disruptive in class at times. The solutions she had tried so far were to give him love and to allow him physical contact. She was also going to try a new 'pull-in' plan with his LD teacher, bringing the specialist into the regular classroom to work with Victor and the other LD students.

The other teacher, Ms. Wilson, said that one of Victor's problems (which he shared with some other boys) was 'bad citizenship' — he 'infringed on others'. He then became upset when he had to face the consequences of his behavior. She felt that this attitude stemmed from Victor's home. He also was not keeping up academically, and even if he did pay attention and cooperate he was 'lost'. Therefore, he simply said 'forget it' to academic work. As for solutions, Ms. Wilson thought that Victor could be turned around by a special teacher or through a method designed especially for him. He also seemed to be responding to the system of rewards for work completion in the classroom. She thought it probably would not help to consult his mother; it might even hurt, according to what Ms. Osgood had told her. She also thought that retention would not be the solution for Victor this year.

The LD teacher said of Victor, 'I worry about him more than the others because I think he's so susceptible'. She reported the same concerns as Ms. Osgood about Victor's home life and the same as Ms. Wilson about his social behavior, remarking that he 'fits in negatively'. She felt that he would always have a need for special services because of his severe memory problems. Her concern was that in the meantime the 'system could lose him' if he did not get what he needed. She favored more 'hands on' work for Victor, and a positive environment where 'he could have room to make mistakes and not be a failure . . . just be a leader and just feel good'. Though Victor wanted to appear 'cool' and uncaring, she felt that he did care very much about school.

The ESL teachers were also concerned about Victor. They saw him as inconsistent and sometimes disruptive. Though being 'tough' had helped him survive, they thought perhaps he was taking it too far, to the point of lying and hurting others. They attributed this behavior to his low self-esteem. One teacher, who had been at the school for several years, also knew about the reports of child abuse levelled at Victor's mother, and traced his problems to her. The other, new to the school that year, said that she did not know about his home background, but she could not help 'liking the kid'.

The nurse confined her comments to Victor's mother, who she believed had recently come to school 'stoned' and was neglecting Victor's health due to her lack of medical knowledge. The school psychologist could not recall anything specific about Victor, one among the dozens of students he had seen over the past year.

In a final interview, Ms. Osgood could see that Victor had 'grown academically' over the year. In fact, the ESL teacher had named him one of the most improved students in the school. He could 'see his progress' now, and as a consequence he had a better self-concept. In addition, the grouping in the classroom had changed, and he was sitting at the 'higher echelon society' table, with higher achievers. Ms. Osgood believed that this heterogeneous grouping related to his gains in self-concept. She had also decided to test Victor at the first grade level, so that he could 'show gains'. She reported that she was encouraging Victor to define himself as separate from his home. She felt that his home life was so abusive that he must 'outgrow' it, become independent of it or 'compensate' for it, as he was beginning to do. She did receive a telephone call at home about once a month from Victor's mother, but was very doubtful of the sincerity of his mother's concern.

Ms. Wilson considered Victor still 'at risk' at the end of the year, because of both his learning problems — which seemed severe and permanent — and his 'attitude'. In her opinion, he knew he had a learning problem, but 'he needed to feel like another regular student'.

Ms. Wilson recommended that Victor receive one-to-one daily tutoring in third grade, not on 'special assignments' but on the same ones as the mainstream students. Because he did not have adequate family support, Ms. Wilson thought, Victor 'felt bad about himself' — to the point where he turned against others.

Victor's Perceptions of School

Victor was interviewed twice. He was articulate about what he wanted but generally evasive about school. According to Victor one of the most important things he had learned in school was to 'no pushar' (a not uncommon 'Spanish' version of 'not to push'). Asked how he had learned this lesson, he said his mother had spoken with him about it.

The interviewer had observed Victor's classroom antics and asked him about his behavior. He smiled a knowing, very adult smile, and said 'es verdad' (it's true) very quietly. He added that if he were the teacher and a student behaved that way he would put the student's name up on the board. (This was the rule at Escalante school.)

Victor said he preferred math in school, and his best work was in writing (probably meaning penmanship). He noted that sometimes he misbehaved when he was angry, and that he got angry when he could not do something right. He seemed aware that he needed to use the learning strategies, since he explained that when he had trouble with something he was able to figure it out by 'thinking'.

Asked about his progress in learning to read, Victor claimed that he was learning to read in English (although in fact he was learning to read only in Spanish). He may have been trying to avoid being embarrassed if asked to read in Spanish, because when the interviewer pulled out a book he asked if it were in English. When told it was in Spanish, he said then he did not know how to read it. The interviewer read a passage from a children's Spanish storybook (estimated to be at about third grade reading level). Victor was able to give a detailed summary of the passage. Asked to predict what might happen next, he provided a very plausible narration as a continuation of the story.

After this successful interaction, the interviewer asked Victor to read from the book. He behaved as his mother had reported, making up the story, but hewing very closely to what he remembered from listening to it earlier. He was then asked if it was not true he had trouble reading, and he admitted his problem, adding that he wanted to learn to read in English. Asked why he preferred to read in English, Victor said that he stuttered badly in Spanish but not in English. He also commented that his mother wanted him to learn English so that he could teach her.

As for his frightening stories from home, Victor told the interviewer about how robbers had broken into his house and how he had gone after them with a gun. Victor also continually referred to his mother. She had said in her interview that she told her children stories before bedtime, and Victor confirmed this. His 'reading' strategies also matched her descriptions. He connected his eagerness to learn to read in English with her need to learn English; and changes in his behavior, he said, were due to her influence.

Classroom Observations of Victor

While Victor did seem tired on a couple of occasions (once he fell asleep listening to a taped story in centers time), for the most part he was physically active and very quick. He often found an excuse to wander about, at times engaging in semi-serious punching or 'karate' matches with other boys. At recess he joined a group of boys from more than one classroom who played soccer every day. The game took up a large part of the playground, as the teams swept across the open dirt spaces like herds of antelope. Since the game was managed by the boys themselves, sometimes heated disputes arose, and Victor was always in the thick of things.

Victor was also very talkative. Most of his informal conversations in the classroom were in English, but he was fluent in Spanish. For this reason, he could communicate with all the other children in his classroom. He was instructed in Spanish in language arts, LD reading, math and science. However, aside from these lessons, he generally communicated with his teachers in English. Once Ms. Osgood had to remind him to switch to Spanish in a language lesson, and he switched with ease. The observer heard very few instances of code-mixing in his speech.

Another notable aspect of Victor was his appearance of confidence. Despite his many experiences of failure in school, Victor did not seem defeated. One sensed, however, that sometimes his 'confidence' was made up of more than a little face-saving bravado. Victor was generally assertive with his teachers, speaking out during lessons, taking charge of 'helping' tasks without being asked, questioning why he was not receiving the same rewards as another, or trying to bluff his way out of negative consequences. While anyone might doubt his academic prowess, no one could question his knowledge of school routines or of the social skills necessary to survive in that setting.

Victor participated in group discussions in small groups where he could get through to the teacher and became part of the arena. In larger groups, when the teacher was mostly presenting information, he would tune out, wander, socialize, and need to be called back to attention. In one science lesson he even disrupted the teacher's talk with loud 'burps', hiccups', and comments about 'GI Joe', to the entertainment of the other boys. In his Spanish LD lessons in the classroom, he was distracted by the more interesting discussions going on in the English reading group nearby. Victor was also often off-task during independent seatwork assignments.

In our analysis we looked for evidence of learning strategies used by at-risk children. For Victor, a much larger category emerged of 'avoiding strategies', ways he devised for not completing his work or complying with teacher expectations. 'Avoiding' may be too negative and teacher-centered a term for these behaviors, which probably served to save Victor from repeated experiences of failure. The problem was that these strategies, more than learning strategies, were monopolizing his abilities.

Victor's avoiding strategies included: going to the rest room: taking advantage of confusing transition times to socialize, hiding out in the reading corner until discovered, getting his friends to do his work, getting 'lost' on the way to classes, making excuses and negotiating-with the teacher to avoid consequences of unfinished tasks, leafing through his book in an appearance of being on-task, disrupting a lesson with 'news' from school or home, wheeling and dealing with other boys over toys, money, etc., refusing to work because his clothes were wet, and hurriedly going to recess before anyone checked out his work. On three occasions he interrupted a lesson to tell one of his 'stories from home'; one story about a break-in at his house was so exaggerated that the observer wondered if he were consciously trying to engage the teacher's compassion and distract her from the work at hand.

The characteristics of the work Victor did not avoid (based on a small number of observations) were that he confused certain consonant sounds, that he used auditory strategies to read painfully slowly, and that his writing was also slow and tedious. Even with words he had practiced repeatedly, he had a tendency to omit letters when spelling from memory. His handwriting was large and erratic. Ms. Osgood on at least one occasion allowed him to compensate for this by responding orally. In another incident, he was not able to read his classmates' names, and Mateo helped him. His written work was difficult to observe because once he was aware of the observer's presence he guarded it closely. (He accused her of 'copying'!)

Victor seemed very comfortable with his teachers. Though he could be angry and argumentative if things did not go his way, for the most part he was careful not to overstretch the teachers' limits. He seemed to value the rewards presented by the teachers at Escalante School, and to know that being too resistant would jeopardize his chances for prizes. In return, the teachers seemed very tolerant of his behavior, more than with the other children. For instance, on three occasions boys involved in off-task behaviors with Victor received 'consequences' while he did not. Ms. Osgood seemed to try to ignore Victor's off-task behaviours until they became too obvious. She also tried having personal 'heart to heart' talks with him about his problems. Ms. Wilson was somewhat less tolerant. When she caught Victor hiding in the corner rather than completing his centers, she said, 'How dare you be playing when your work is not finished!' Despite his attempts to dissuade her, Victor was required to stay in after lunch and work. In one observation, Ms. Wilson had him bring his math workbook to her desk where she could monitor him more closely.

The LD teacher, Ms. Ramirez, was very firm with Victor but also gave him every possible chance to succeed. The difficulty was that given his good oral language skills, Victor seemed limited by the syllable — or at most word-level lessons in his LD program, which was geared to his admittedly poor reading and writing levels. In LD lessons he consistently tried to turn syllables into words and words into conversations. However, the teacher persisted at the syllable level, since he could not remember his syllables from lesson to lesson, even though he had been practicing them for a year. She kept him motivated through a reward system: a prize after every twenty stickers on a chart.

His social life may have been the centerpiece of school for Victor. He was a good friend and a tough enemy for other boys. Quiet Mateo was one of his most frequent followers, helpers and admirers; but unlike Mateo, Victor did not limit his friendships to boys from his table or classroom. For someone who put on a show of 'toughness', he could be quite open with his affection and concern for others. When Luis left for a trip to Mexico, Victor gave him an emotional embrace. When Carmín became defeated and weepy during an LD lesson, Victor — himself not one to give up easily — tried to help her by spelling a word in the air with his finger.

Granted, sometimes Victor could be feisty. One day he got into an angry punching match with another boy in science. When the boy ran to the teacher he called out mockingly, 'There! Tattle tale! Crybaby!' and the boy came back for more. Victor also seemed to be involved in various mysterious 'scams' involving money and trading for little toys. He liked to tease girls unmercifully. However, in a follow-up observation in April, Victor was chosen by chance as the 'special person of the day'. A huge cheer went up from the class, a testimony to his general popularity among the other students.

Discusion

Victor's case was a study in contradictions. The first contradiction was between his mother's perceptions and those of the teachers. It was impossible after one meeting with the mother to make a judgment about the existence of abuse and neglect in this home. We did learn that Victor's mother had been very young and unprepared at his birth, had not completed her own education, had lost both her parents and lived fairly isolated from extended family support in Suroeste.

The mother was not concerned about his learning problems, yet the interview with her revealed that she was quite aware of them problems. Indeed, her description of his memory problems matched closely with that of the LD teacher, and her description of his 'reading' strategies was confirmed by the interviewer's work with Victor.

The perception in the school was that Victor's mother was abusive and neglectful. This may have aroused the teachers' compassion toward him to the point where they seemed extremely protective and tolerant of his behavior. If he acted out, it was ultimately blamed not on him, but on his mother. The mother was not enlisted to help with Victor's academic difficulties because there was an assumption that she was uninterested and incapable. She was not informed of his misbehaviors because of the fear that she would further abuse him. The teacher with major responsibility for him, Ms. Osgood, had an intense resentment of the mother that must have affected their communications. The communication breakdown led to another contradiction, between the mother's perception that Victor was doing well in school because he often brought home 'prizes' and the teachers' perceptions that he was among those students who were most 'at risk'.

We wondered what the school could do to guide the mother toward the most appropriate ways of influencing and helping Victor. The school's well-intentioned efforts to shield Victor from his mother may have contributed to his development of a manipulative style that allowed him to 'play both ends against the middle'. (In fact, Victor himself contributed to the communication breakdown by not taking notes from the teacher home to his mother.)

The final contradiction was between Victor's apparent potential and his academic performance. Victor displayed many of the characteristics attributed to 'learning disabled' students. His oral language, his appearance of confidence, his social adaptation, were matched by severe problems with regular classroom tasks. As a consequence, he avoided these tasks when at all possible. Victor's leadership in the classroom and his 'charismatic' personality might well spell trouble later on unless he developed the basic academic skills necessary to succeed at school in socially acceptable ways.

The 'remediation' for his disability, however, may have placed him at greater risk for avoiding school tasks. Except through the guarantee of material rewards, it was dificult to keep his attention on the repetitious tasks in his LD lessons. It was obvious that Victor was a student who wanted to be working at his level of comprehension and interest, and needed at the same time to improve his simple 'decoding' skills. Rather than the fragmented, decontextualized system currently prescribed for the treatment of learning disabilities, a method which incorporated his love of exciting stories could both develop his basic skills and meet his social/emotional needs.

Ann

Ann was a sandy haired, chubby, 9-year-old Anglo girl in the third grade. She often came to school with her hair uncombed and in clothes that never seemed quite to go together. She appeared to be the 'perfect student' and she worked hard at this portrayal. She maintained perfect attendance. Initially, she was considered marginally at-risk for social reasons by one of her teachers, Ms. Jones. She described Ann as a marvelous student but was concerned with her low self-image, her past experiences and problems she seemed to be having in the foster home.

Ann's school records began in the second grade. There was nothing in her file about her kindergarten and first grade year. Information gathered from other sources indicated that she had attended at least two different schools during that period of time. In the second grade, she had perfect attendance and did very well academically. She received As in all areas except spelling and handwriting where she received Bs.

Her ITBS scores were above average and ranged in the 70s and 80s percentile in every area except math where she was in the high 60s.

Ann enrolled in Plaza School in the fall of her third grade year when she was placed in a foster home which was located in an area from which students were bussed to Plaza. She liked this new school, the teachers and other children. She said, 'I think it's a really good school. It's the best school that I've been to in all my life.' Ms. Jones, one of her teachers at Plaza, was concerned about her being a loner, her lack of friends and a 'few strange things' that she did for a third grader. She said she worked too hard on being 'Miss Perfect' and thought this was an indication of other things that were causing her problems. At that time, her other teacher, Ms. Green, saw her only as a good student and did not consider her as at-risk.

Parents and Home Experience

Ann was the oldest of four children. She had two brothers ages 5 and 7 and a sister who was 4. All the children were living in foster homes, with the two boys living in a different home than Ann and her sister. No contact could be made with the mother during the study.

According to Ann and her teachers she had been molested by her father when she was in kindergarten. It appeared that all the children were taken out of the home and then sent to Oregon to live with their grandmother. Later, the mother came and got them and Ann was enrolled in the second grade in a bordering district. At some time during that next year the children were again taken out of the home and placed in foster homes. Their mother seldom came to visit them.

Ann's foster mother was an oriental, middle-aged woman who spoke broken English. She reported that the children had been in several foster homes and that no one would keep them. She said that the girls did not know 'how to brush their teeth or flush the toilet' when they came to her. She described them as being 'tight, closed' and not willing to get close to her. She said that Ann did well in school but had problems keeping friends because she lied. The foster mother said that Ann lied at home too and was not 'into doing jobs around the house'. She said that Ann 'just went through the motions' and had so sense of 'doing a job well'. She didn't know how long she would be able to manage with the girls and 'just took it a day at a time'. She did not hesitate to say that she had 'no expectations' for Ann or her sister. She also reported that Ann's mother didn't visit them and did not send presents at Christmas time.

The foster mother was concerned about Ann's weight and talked about her problem. Ms. Jones had previously reported that the foster mother would not allow Ann to bring money to school for popcorn on Fridays because 'she is too fat already'. In conclusion, the foster mother did not share one positive contribution about Ann or her sister.

School Personnel Perceptions of Ann

Initially, Ann was considered marginally at-risk for social reasons by only one of her teachers. By the end of the school year, both teachers were very concerned about her socially and emotionally and considered her to be at-risk for these reasons. Ms. Green had gotten 'a lot of feedback in her writing and she has a lot of very negative feelings about herself, bad self concept about her sex, her weight and her looks. Real bad self concept about goodness and badness.' She discussed an incident that had occurred a month earlier. The class was scheduled to go on an overnight field trip to an environmental camp. Two days before the trip, Ann reported that she was being punished and couldn't go. When asked if the school should contact the foster mother, Ann replied, 'I don't know.' Ms. Green understood this to mean that Ann would get in trouble if they did contact her. Eventually, she did contact the foster mother as it was a required school activity and her foster mother allowed Ann to attend. Ms. Green found it difficult to understand why Ann never talked about her foster mother unkindly or felt 'that she has been treated unfairly'. She concluded by saying, 'Beautiful student, academically. Always does what she's supposed to do. I think there's a lot of repressed hostility there. To me she's a perfect candidate for teen suicide.'

Ms. Jones, who had been concerned with Ann since the beginning of the year and had described her as marginally at-risk, considered her at-risk by the end of the year. This change was influenced by the things that what had happened to Ann and through the things that she had observed and learned about her during the school year. One of these was the treatment that Ann received in the foster home. Ms. Jones said, 'The school called the Child Protective Agency (CPS) once about the terrible treatment Ann receives from her foster mother . . .' CPS talked to the foster mother and Ann, but it seemed that they believed the foster mother's story. Ms. Jones added, 'They don't believe Ann. Ann is not a mean child. She'll do anything to please. She gets good grades and does every chore you ask her to do, yet she's tormented.' She was very concerned about Ann's self concept and her feelings that she 'didn't measure up'. She talked about the story Ann wrote about being molested by her father and reported, 'She (Ann) said when she was a little girl, her father molested her and then her parents got a divorce and now she was safe. But now she's also in a foster home.' Both teachers appeared to care very much about Ann but felt that there was little they could do to change the home environment. They tried to compensate for this by giving her special attention at school that might help build her self-concept.

The school nurse had never worked with Ann but knew that CPS was involved with her. She said, 'They (CPS) get involved when a child is made a ward of the state'. She added that this doesn't happen unless there was severe abuse in the home and in Ann's case 'this must have been a real abusive situation'. The classroom aide thought Ann was 'doing great'. She said, 'I see no problems with her. She does her work, she understands, and when she writes stories, she writes pretty good stories'.

The school counselor had worked with Ann. She said, 'At the beginning of the year, she had some adjustment problems socially. Does not have any real self-concept. Very loving. Every time she speaks to me, I get a big hug'. It was the counselor who had contacted CPS because the 'foster mother was very physical in her discipline . . .' CPS was working with the foster mother and the counselor said that she 'made it a point to keep in contact' with Ann. She was concerned with her social and emotional well-being. She thought that Ann didn't 'see herself as having friends or doing real well'. The counselor felt that she had seen growth in Ann during the year. She said, '. . . when she first came, she was like a downcast child, a child in her approach to kids, she was isolated, and now I see more of a sparkle in her eyes'. She found it interesting that Ann and Jerry were good friends and played together often. Ann was one of the few friends that Jerry had in the school.

Ann's Perceptions of School

Ann seemed to respond to any adult that gave her attention. She liked being asked questions about school and appeared to be anxious to answer each one thoroughly. Her ease in handling the formal interview seemed to indicate that this was not the first time she has been involved in such a process. She was not uncomfortable with the situation, appeared to be relaxed and talked in a mature manner.

Ann talked about the reason she was in a foster home. (Her actual words can be found at the beginning of Chapter 1.) She said she was molested by her father when she was in kindergarten and that didn't make her feel good but she 'still loved him'. After that happened, she and her sisters and brothers were taken to a center for abused children. Later they were sent to Oregon to live with their grandparents. At Christmas time, her mother came and got them and they lived with her. She did not say why they were taken from her the second time, but this is the first foster home they had been in. She discussed having two moms and said, 'It feels kind of complicated because you have to be able to get used to having them both and having to cooperate with one mom and the other and it's really hard.' She doesn't see her mom very often and this bothered her and her sister. She said, 'When I'm really bored and stuff like that, I'll think about her and I'll start to cry because I miss her so much.' It also bothers her sometimes that she lives in a foster home. She said, 'Sometimes they'll (other students) make me feel really bad 'cause some kids will say, "Are you in a foster home?" and I'll say "yes" and they'll say, "Is it fun to be in it?" and that's a hard question for me.'

Ann considered the worst thing that had happened to her during the school year was being told she couldn't go on the field trip. She had been half-an-hour late getting home and she hadn't done her job. When asked what the job was she answered, 'I usually clean the bathroom floor 'cause my foster mom babysits kids and it gets pretty messy and so I have to clean the bathroom floor.' She did not seem to think that her foster mom had been unfair but she was very appreciative that her teachers and the counselor had intervened. In fact, she thought that being able to go was the best thing that had happened to her and said, 'I felt really proud and I felt that teachers are the most important people in the whole wide world'. Later she added, 'It makes me feel good because I know that two or three people care about me'.

Ann liked attending Plaza and thought it was a good school. She appeared to have confidence about herself as a student and felt that she was smart. She added, 'I know I am because I'm really good in reading and spelling and math and I think I'm good in it 'cause I get my work done mostly everyday except on Monday, 'cause I have to be taken out of work time 'cause I work here at the library'. She felt that it was important to be good in school because 'if you're good in school, you always get to do something special'.

Ann liked school and most of what happened there. In discussing this, she said, '. . . math is one of my favorite subjects' and later added, '. . . reading is my most favorite thing'. She also thought that other activities such as being read to, doing art and working in the computer room were fun. There was only one thing that she didn't like and that was 'the daily oral language'.

Socially, Ann seemed to grow more confident in herself but there was a tone in her voice when talking about friends that led one to wonder how much she really believed in what she said. She thought the students in the room treated her nice 'because on the field trip, I got to be in a cabin with girls that I usually don't hang around and I got to know that they really did like me. They said, "Ann, I think you're a really good friend because you were cooperative with us." ' She also thought they treated her well because they didn't tease her. She said, 'I think they treat me very good and what I like about this school is they don't tease you'. She had been teased at her other school. She said they teased her 'about the way I am, how chubby I am, but I don't care about that because it helps me'. When asked how it helped her, she replied, 'When I'm hungry, I'm not that much hungry, 'cause the fat on me helps me survive'. It appeared that she was going to need more than that to survive.

Classroom Observations of Ann

Observations of Ann did reveal that she was a 'good student'. The kind of student that teachers like to have in their classroom. She was successful academically, behaved well in the classroom and was usually on task. During Silent Sustained Reading (SSR), she always read for the entire fifteen minute period. She made certain that she had several books by her in case she finished one before the period was over. She was never seen talking to anyone during that period. During other group activities, she was able to do all the tasks, complete her work and was willing to help others. She may even have needed more challenge in some areas.

Yet with this background, there were times when she sought out additional support and reinforcement. On one occasion, in a letter writing activity where the observer was working with another student, Ann repeatedly kept coming to her and asking if she thought the letter she was writing was good. She then drew a picture on the back of her paper and came up again and asked, 'Do you like my picture?' It appeared that even though she always did the 'right thing' and said the 'right thing', deep inside her she didn't feel sure that she had approval.

Ann did deviate from this pattern of being the perfect student in one way which indicated that she was a 'normal kid' in some ways.

She usually came in the classroom in the morning five or ten minutes late. Upon checking, it was found that she was in the breakfast program at the school and the teachers thought she was a slow eater. Later, it was learned that during this time of the morning daily oral language was conducted, and this was the only activity in school that Ann did not like. When talking to Ann about her being late she said, 'Usually it's because we'll walk as slow as we can 'cause we really don't want to get into daily oral language and we try to be as late as we can but we're never later than 8:15 because we like silent reading'.

Ann never missed school and was always on time other than in the above instances. School probably was a haven to her. When asked to tell how she felt about school, she summed it up in three words — 'wonderful, great, fantastic'.

Discussion

Ann is one of those students that cause teachers much concern; however they have few avenues available to them through which to help. At the end of the study, Ann was doing well in the classroom academically. Her ITBS scores at the end of the year ranged from the 80s to 90s. She was unstable, however, in her social and emotional well-being, both of which were influenced by factors outside the classroom. She had experienced trauma in her early years and kept it inside her. Her living conditions seemed to be compounding the problem rather than alleviating it. She seemed to have placed a great deal of the blame for all these things on herself and had suppressed any hostility she experienced towards others.

She desperately sought acceptance from adults, and in school had tried to gain this through being the 'perfect student'. This did not seem to be a problem then but could cause her further emotional stress later on. Ann was fortunate because the classroom that she was in focused on social and emotional skills as well as academics, something that other classrooms might use as a model for working with students with similar problems. They offered her a supportive environment that seemed to be helping Ann make progress socially and feel better about herself. Still, both teachers felt that she had 'deep problems' that they were unable to touch. Schools currently are not equipped to deal with these kinds of serious problems. Yet there seems to be a growing demand for this kind of help. Two of the six students studied at Plaza School were referrred to CPS for child abuse during the study along with two others in the classroom who were not in the study. Several others were in foster homes or lived in environments that were not supportive. Still others lived with violence in the home and/or had family members in prison. One child had lived in a car for three months before they found a home and another was withdrawn from the school when authorities located the family because he was the object of a national search in a divorce case. As one of the teachers said in discussing the problems of at-risk students, '. . . I think that the few children who do have dyslexia or have some visual or auditory problems . . . is so minor compared to the problems that have emotional family-based reasons and I don't think for a long time that they were given as much credence'.

Travis

Travis was a 10-year-old, black boy in the third grade. He was tall, well-coordinated with handsome features. He was accepted socially, had many friends and appeared to be confident and well-adjusted in school. One of his teachers, Ms. Green, described him as a 'very lovely child' who was 'thoughtful and kind' and appeared 'well cared for in the home'. She also considered him marginally at-risk for academic and attitudinal reasons. She thought he was 'below grade level but not tremendously below' and was concerned with his past school experiences which seemed to be influencing his participation in her classroom.

Travis was new to Plaza School in the fall. He had been in another school in Suroeste School District for the previous four years. There he had been retained in second grade, and comments in his school records from that school included 'will not do any of his work' and 'will not participate in classroom activities'.

Ms. Green had seen him 'shy away from an activity' in her classroom but had found that with encouragement he would do the activity. This was not always true when he was working with other personnel. The LD teacher had told Ms. Green that she had difficulty getting him to participate in her classroom. Ms. Green concluded that he would be at-risk 'depending on the personality that he's working with or the situation that he's put in'. Her goal was to help him overcome some of the bad experiences that he had in the past.

Parents and Home Experience

As a baby he was quiet. His mother said she called him the 'lonely child' because he did not want to play with toys by himself. He wanted to be around other people. As a young child he often stayed with his grandparents (his mother's parents) while she worked. His mother did not mention his father but in an interview Travis said, 'I don't never see my dad and I don't know where my real dad is'. He walked at nine months. His mother said that he 'enjoyed being independent' and that 'by the time he was 2-years-old, he could do just about anything'. This changed when he started school.

His mother related that from the very beginning he didn't like school. Kindergarten wasn't too bad but first grade was a 'struggle'. She 'had to push him and push him and push him'. In the second grade, she decided that she couldn't do this any more and that she would 'let him learn for himself'. This did not work either and he had to repeat second grade. She felt that he just didn't seem to like the idea that he had to go to school and that he would rather stay home and play. His second time in second grade seemed to be a more positive experience. He was placed in special reading and math classes and received an hour of individual instruction each day. His mother felt that that was his best year in school.

At the end of that year, Travis' mother moved to another part of town near her parents. Travis moved in with his grandparents, an aunt and two cousins. They lived in a well-kept house in a middle-class black neighborhood. The home environment was warm and friendly. His mother lived around the block with another aunt and came daily to visit. Travis said he chose to live with his grandparents 'because it is funnier'. It also helped with the babysitting as his mother often worked from 7.00 am to 6.00 pm.

Travis' grandparents live in an area from which Plaza School bussed students. His mother had attended Plaza as a child. (At that time she was one of the few black children going there.) Travis' mother thought that he was doing better at Plaza and that repeating the second grade had contributed to this. She said, 'We had a lot of trouble trying to get him to go to school and do his work. I'm proud of him cause he's come a long ways.' She felt that he was an above average student now and validated this opinion with the grades on his report card.

Travis' mother had gone to the first conference at Plaza to check on how he was doing. She also wanted his teachers to know that 'if there's anything that he needs help in, be sure they call and let us know'. At the conference, she was told that he was doing well and they (the teachers) were impressed '. . . cause he had adjusted just right'. She had been in contact with the school since that time. She realized that he still didn't talk about school very much and still didn't seem to like it. She had few concerns with the school because Travis 'can take care of himself'. She seemed to hold him more responsible for his learning than the school. She said, 'he's got to learn to make it'.

School Personnel Perceptions of Travis

The school's perception of Travis brought into focus the concept that at-riskness may be socially constructed. It also illustrated the fact that what may be considered at-risk to one teacher might not be considered at-risk to another. In Travis' case, one of his teachers, Ms. Jones, did not view him to be at-risk while the other teacher, Ms, Green, thought he was marginally at-risk. She was also concerned with his lack of participation at the other school and was hopeful that this would change at Plaza. Although she felt that 'he also has to understand that you can't always do just the things that you want to do'.

Other school staff knew little about him indicating that he was not seen as a problem in the school at large. The nurse said she knew nothing about him. She had seen him once in a while, particularly in the fall when he had a fractured finger, but other than that she had little contact with him. The counselor also said that she really didn't know him. When he first came to the school it was noticed immediately (she did not say by whom) that he was a child 'who had some special needs'. At that time, his records had not arrived from his previous school so she intervened and had him placed in the LD program on an informal basis until she got his records. (The records were later received but were misplaced at Plaza School and still had not been found at the end of the study.) She said that he was now officially in the LD program. The aide did not discuss him when asked to talk about students she thought were at-risk in the classroom. She did mention him and another student when asked if she thought there were any students that were marginally at-risk. She said, 'Travis, he's really bright, he can read, he understands but there are times that I don't know if he's a perfectionist or not but he's slow getting his work done. He doesn't finish it.' She reported that she did work with him at times, especially when he had to write stories. It took him a long time to do this activity. She thought other students had similar problems. She concluded by saying, 'They're slow but when they do their work, it's good'.

The above findings appear to match the view that Travis' mother had expressed about his progress in school. They were also similar to Ms. Jones' perception at the end of the study. In her final interview, she said, 'Travis is doing very well. I wouldn't consider him at-risk now.' These sentiments were not in agreement with Ms. Green's. She said that his work was 'probably low average, at best' and thought that 'he has a poor self-concept because he has been a retained child'. Later she added, 'He'll probably be at-risk forever because no matter what I say, his self-concept still comes through as very low . . .' This was the first time in the study that his self-concept had been mentioned and it appeared that this was truly a concern of hers because she said, 'I have really tried to make a point of at least, every other day, making sure that he knows what a wonderful person I think he is'.

Ms. Green discussed some of her observations of Travis that she had made during the school year. She thought that 'color seems to be important to him' and maybe that was caused by 'some bad confrontations with white teachers'. This, too, was something that no other school personnel had observed. She felt that he was a 'tough little guy to figure' and difficult to get to know because he was so quiet. She had assessed his reading skills to be average but that 'the math skills seem to be his real weakness'. To help him in this area, she said, 'Academically, I spend as much time with him as I possibly can and he does receive extra help, resource-wise'. She did not discuss what she meant by 'academically' or what she had done to help him.

Ms. Green had not contacted the home concerning Travis' problems in math even though initially, she had said that 'there seems to be a real interest in school' at the home and she had been told, during the fall conference, that help would be given at home if needed. She did not discuss why she had not contacted the mother concerning Travis' problems in math.

Travis' Perceptions of School

Travis' perceptions were ascertained through his involvement in the initial and final parent interview, at which he was present, observations in the classroom, communication during individual instruction, informal interviews and a lengthy formal interview. He had a story to tell about school and it seemed to be the first time anyone had asked him about it. He gave considerable thought to each question before responding and the wait time required for his responses was much longer than what is normally provided in the regular classroom. He later shared that he went to a special teacher for help in his talking because 'when nobody asks me questions, then I got to tell somebody something, I just don't say it right'. The depth of the responses during the interview reflected that this might not be a problem when adequate wait time was provided and/or when the subject matter was relevant to him.

Travis didn't like school, couldn't think of anything that would make him like it and found it boring. The things he thought were 'fun' were those things that don't occur often in the classroom like visits from famous authors, field trips and releasing helium balloons during a science/language arts activity. He felt that the teachers didn't notice that 'most of the time I do my work without talking'. He also felt that he doesn't 'get picked' as often as those who are 'smart' and that he never gets 'free time' because he doesn't get his work finished. Yet he wouldn't change school 'because it would be different for the teachers and they would probably forget things and the kids might not get as much learning'. He also thought that 'it wouldn't be fair for the other kids' if he changed school to suit him.

He seemed to have an understanding of what his 'problems' were in school and where he needed help. He said, 'I did second grade over because I was too slow in my reading and then I got slow in my math'. He doesn't like math but knew he should get help at home with his 'times in math'. He related that his mother had told him 'to practice more on it'. He said, 'Yeah, I knew I should of practiced but when I go home, I don't practice cause I don't have anyone to write it'.

He wished he could have someone help him at this school like Jenny (the LD teacher) over at his other school. He said, 'She helped me. She brought me gum. She sometimes would bring me presents when I earned it . . . I did earn it . . . I treated her like she was my teacher.' He recognized that he got some help at Plaza but said, 'Well . . . I do but then I don't. Sometimes they tell me to go sit down and sometimes they don't. Sometimes I'll sit there with my hand up and sometimes they'll tell me to get to work.' This bothered him because it made him feel 'like they don't pay attention to me. Like they're not wanting to teach me. It seems like the worst ones get the most attention . . .' Travis appeared to want more attention in the classroom. He said, 'When I'm around them, they don't have hardly nothing to say to me'.

One of the things that Travis thought was 'hard to do' besides math was 'writing stories'. Neither teacher had mentioned that this was a problem for him but the aide had said that it was the area that she most often helped him with. His main difficulty appeared to be his inability to 'finish a story'. When asked why he thought writing stories was hard he said, after a long pause, '. . . somtimes I just don't know what to think of and sometimes I just think that there's . . . it's not too fun in the classroom'.

He was concerned with his inability to 'finish work in the classroom'. When asked what was his favorite thing to do in the classroom, he said, 'getting my work done'. His main reason for wanting to finish centered on being able to then participate in the 'other activities'. Presently, he rarely got to have 'free time or play a game' but he didn't know how he felt about this '. . . cause I don't hardly think about it'. Later, he said that 'he got mad' about it.

Travis couldn't think of anything that he did well in the schoolroom but said, 'I got an S in writing and reading'. Outside the classroom, he thought he was good in sports like soccer and football and playing games (PE). Even though Travis doesn't think he is smart or good in school, he still has hopes for when he finishes school. When asked what kind of a job he might want when he was older, he replied, 'Something that gets a lot of money cause I plan to have a big house'. He added that he'd 'probably be a lawyer but I'm not smart enough. Or work for the government. Or maybe be a sports player cause they get lots of money. And I'm good at sports.'

Classroom Observations of Travis

Travis was a student who did not appear to be 'into school'. Many of the activities conducted in the classroom did not seem to motivate him and he had difficulty completing or responded to them with minimal participation. This lack of participation was often unnoticed by the teachers because he seldom 'acted out' or caused a discipline problem. An example of his behavior can be illustrated through the following description of an observation made of him during a large group presentation. The lesson focused on the 'Words of the Day'. As Ms. Jones wrote the words on the chalkboard, Travis gave no indication that he was interested in the activity. He talked to his neighbor, stared at the table and at other children, and did not look at the board. When Ms. Jones asked for volunteers to pronounce the words, Travis was not among those who raised their hands. He scooted his chair back and forth from the table. When the lesson was concluded, Travis had not participated verbally nor had he been asked to participate.

As mentioned, on other occasions when Travis did participate he had difficulty completing the activity in the designated time frame. He seemed to work at a slower pace and would have to struggle with the activity much longer than most of the other students. When this happened he would become unhappy with the task, resent that he was not able to go on to the extended activities and sometimes withdraw from the task with it unfinished. Once, after it took him fifty minutes to write a seven line poem during an activity to develop handwriting skills that most of the other students completed in twenty minutes, he demonstrated his resentment by saying that he didn't like to do it and that he thought the task was boring. At another time, he simply 'gave up' and did not complete the task. It was during a timed, ten-minute math test in which he was having difficulty doing the task. He erased, stared, tried another problem and finally after forty minutes he quit and just sat with the test unfinished. When asked why he was not working, he said, 'I don't know how to do these and I don't know the answers'. Again, it was observed that the teacher did not seem to notice his behavior nor did she attempt to help him or urge him to finish.

This same behavior was observed almost every day during Silent Sustained Reading (SSR). Travis rarely read during this fifteen-minute period although it had been determined that he had no problems in reading and appeared to be a fluent reader. He often sat with his book closed or simply looked at the pictures. Several times he did not even have a book. Again, his behavior went unnoticed and only once was he given something to read during that period of time.

Many of the activities were 'timed' in the room. This may have been to motivate the students to work faster and/or to get them ready for the test. In either case, this had little influence on Travis. He often did not finish the task in the given time although he worked on the task during the period. He was never seen to ignore a task, it just seemed that he worked at a slower pace and was not motivated by the usual competition in a classroom. This caused him problems because he then had to 'finish the task' at another time and miss some of the activities that he did like. But even knowing this, he couldn't seem to work faster.

He did have academic problems in math. On several of the timed tests he was able to complete only a few of the problems. Much of the work centered on the multiplication tables and he had not learned the 5 through 12 tables. It was not observed that he received individual help in this area and, in fact, was told with the others, that he should work on them at home. It did not appear that he had done this as he continued to have difficulty.

There were some activities that did motivate him. He liked working on maps and art projects. On these occasions, he gave the teacher full attention, acted like he enjoyed doing the activity and did not appear bored. The problem was that these kinds of activities did not occur often in the classroom or when they did he was finishing his work.

Socially Travis got along well with others and seemed to have their respect. He often moved from table to table to be by friends. For a period of time he sat at a table with Ann. In her interview she said, 'He (Travis) does really good and instead of bothering you, he'll only say something when he really needs it.' Brad considered him his friend and liked to wrestle with him in the grass. He thought that Travis was smart and was good in reading. Travis was a responsible person in the classroom and would sometimes remind others at his table to 'be quiet'.

Discussion

Travis appeared to be one of those students to whom the typical process of schooling was not meaningful or motivating. He had a rich, full life with many social and real-life learning experiences outside of school. He had participated in many extended family activities, been treated in an adult manner, gone hunting and fishing with his grandfather, traveled with his grandparents, understood and handled some of life's complexities such as not having a father, and seemed to have an awareness and maturity about him than many other third grade children do not have.

He seemed to find little relationship between school and real life. He found school boring and was not motivated by much of what was done in school. He knew how to get along in the classroom and rarely 'got into trouble'. Travis' lack of motivation to participate in many of the activities in school appeared to have been something that he had been struggling with for some time. He seemed to have a sense about what was a meaningful activity and withdrew from an activity when it was not. At times, the tasks he found boring also seemed so to the observer; but most schools are not organized to allow students to make decisions as to when to participate. He suffered the consequences of his decision by missing out on the activities he enjoyed and being viewed as a student with problems.

As one solution, it seemed that his teachers needed to make an extra effort beyond what they were doing to help him. They needed to find ways to make the learning activities more meaningful and motivating for him. Each day he became more disillusioned with school and his dislike of it grew which, in turn, affected his level of achievement. Tests (ITBS) at the end of the year showed him below the norm in all areas including reading where he appeared to have no problems. Part of the test scores were influenced by the fact that he did not complete several sections of the test. Regardless of this fact, these scores will follow him and he will eventually become labelled and viewed as a low-achieving student when he has the potential to achieve at a much higher level.

The above problem was complicated by the fact that he did have difficulty in the academic area of math. His lack of knowledge of the multiplication tables was influencing his level of achievement as well as his participation. In this area, he knew he needed help and wanted it. The home had not been asked to give additional help and the aide nor his teachers provided it. There appeared to be a need for better communication between the home and school in order to alleviate this problem.

A second solution to his problem might be to explore the reasons why Travis could be considered at-risk by one of his teachers and not the other. What was it about his behavior and/or expectations of him that would make this possible? This difference in expectation is important as it could work to his and other students' benefit in the learning environment. Studies have long shown the importance and effect of positive expectations and view of the learner by the teacher. In Travis' case, higher expectations might have encouraged him to participate more in classroom activities.

A third solution might be to attempt to understand Travis' lack of motivation and participation though the resistance theory (Erickson, 1985). Erickson states that resistance theory 'explains the puzzlingly low school performance of students who in the literacies of practical reasoning in everyday life display impressive competence' (p. 537). Resistance theory proposes that students knowingly disadvantage themselves by refusing to learn as a form of political resistance to the mainstream values and expectations. If his learning problem was viewed in this manner, neither he nor his teachers could be blamed for his lack of success. Instead, this theory suggests: 'intervention to break the cycle of school failure must start by locating the problem jointly in the processes of society at large and the interactions of specific individuals' (p. 538). The first step would be to recognize that such a situation could occur and strive towards trying to understand what was happening to Travis.

The system needs to be changed but, at this point, it appears that it is Travis who has little choice but to change his attitude towards school if he is to succeed. His mother, who feels that school is important and wants him to finish, holds him, not the school, responsible for his learning. In the parent interview in which both Travis and his mother participated, she told him this in response to his statement that school was boring. She said, 'You're not there to be bored. It's what you make it. You still have eight more years to go.' It appeared that the next eight years may be long ones if nothing is done to change the pattern that has already developed.

Andy

Andy is a tall, quiet black boy in the third grade at Plaza School. He attended pre-school and kindergarten in a small town where his mother had been raised. His family moved to the Sureoeste District at the beginning of his first grade year. He was enrolled in another school for a short period of time and then transferred to Plaza. He had attended Plaza since that time.

Andy liked going to school. In fact, he had liked school since he started kindergarten and all his teachers had said that they liked him. He went to school every day unless he was sick and his mother said that he had always been happy in school. Andy's school records, however, did not indicate that school had been a successful experience for him. His kindergarten report card showed that he needed improvement in phonics and math and that he was performing unsatisfactorily in the language arts. In the first grade his report card grades indicated that he had made improvement but that he was not doing satisfactorily work in any of the academic areas. In the second grade, his grades were still lower and he received N's, which meant that his skills needed improvement, in all academic areas. By third grade, both his teachers, Ms. Jones and Ms. Green, considered him at-risk for academic reasons. They described him as having low reading and math skills. But even though his skills were low, they both appeared more concerned about his home life than his school life. They felt that the home situation was responsible for his lack of success in school.

Parents and Home Experience

Andy is the oldest of two children. His sister is three years younger than him. She was in the first grade at Plaza at the time of the study and was having difficulty in school. Andy's mother was a single parent and had been since he was 3. She worked long hours as a clerk in a convenience market. His mother's sister and her two children, as well as her brother, lived with them. They helped each other out with babysitting. They lived in an apartment that is located in a neighbourhood from which students are bussed to Plaza.

Andy's mother was a student in a business college when she became pregnant. She was sick all the time she carried him and had to quit school. She hoped to go back to school when the children were older. She said that he was a large baby and described him as being 'hyper' when he was little. She said, 'he was constantly running around getting into stuff', but that he 'mellowed out at the end of his first grade year'. She felt that 'it's kind of hard for Andy . . . 'cause he doesn't have a father or a father figure'. She wished she could do more for him but she was always working and had no transportation. She portrayed Andy as being a sensitive person who did not like to be teased. He was also a responsible person. He watched out for his sister and the two cousins, picked up his room and took out the trash. She said, 'I feel sorry for him cause I think that most of the responsibility is off on him cause he's the oldest'.

In discussing school, she indicated that he had always liked school and was glad to go. She thought that he was really happy with school and said, 'I think they've done real good with him.' She indicated that she tried to help him when he needed something but added, 'I don't really spend that much time with them (Andy and his sister) cause I'm always at work or something like that'. She had little contact with his teachers and reported, 'I've talked to his teacher probably once on the phone. There's conferences and stuff but I didn't make it to the conferences'. She said she didn't have a car or means of transportation to get there. She felt that she was doing her part though and said, '. . . I think I've done pretty well. Course my kids have probably had some little problems in school, but as far as keeping a roof over their heads and feeding them, I think I've done pretty well.'

When asked how Andy felt about school, she said, 'I think he thinks he's doing really well. I think he's a real good kid and real responsible. He tries real hard.' Andy's mother was not aware that he was having serious problems in school. She reported that 'a man had been there last year and said that they were going to have him (Andy) in special

classes . . . They were supposed to let me know but they haven't . . .'
She said, 'I don't worry too much about school cause I think that
they're there and they'll learn okay on their own'. His mother stated
that she listened to him read, encouraged Andy to do his school work
before he went out to play, and had her sister help him with his reading
and writing. She felt that she could do more and wanted to 'give him
a little more of my time and help him and try to explain to him and
stuff'. She would also like him to participate in Big Brothers because
'if he can be out and probably be away from home and probably see
different things and participate in different activities.' it would help
him in school. Lack of transportation made this impossible as Big
Brothers was located on the other side of town.

The goals Andy's mother had for him reflected her experience with
life. She said, 'I hope that he doesn't get a girl pregnant at a young
age and that he makes some kind of a way for himself first. I hope
that he does something good in life.' She planned to be there if he
needed her.

School Personnel Perceptions of Andy

As mentioned previously, Andy's school records indicate that he was
not a successful student. His report card grades were low as were his
achievement test scores. In kindergarten, his California Achievement
Test (CAT) percentile scores were 53 — listening,83 — letter forms,
72 — letter names, 34 — letter sounds,39 — visual discrimination,
pre-reading — 49 and 19 — math. There were no comments on his
report card about his lack of success and he was promoted to first
grade.

On his first grade report card, Ms. Green did comment that he
needed drill at home on reading and math but nothing specifically was
mentioned. His test scores that year on the Iowa Test of Basic Skills
(ITBS) were not as low as the grades on the report card (all Is which
meant 'improvement shown but not doing satisfactorily'). His test
scores in percentile were as follows: listening — 62, word analysis —
69, vocabulary – 30, reading — 48, math concepts — 67, math problem
solving — 59 and math computation — 65. He was passed to second
grade.

In second grade, his report card grades moved down to Ns, the
lowest category on the grading scale. His ITBS scores, in percentiles,
were as follows: listening — 57, word analysis — 52, vocabulary —
44, reading — 43, spelling — 27, math concepts — 56, math problem

solving — 47 and math computation — 66. During the second grade, he was recommended for testing and put into the LD classroom. The LD teacher wrote in his folder that Andy's main academic difficulties were in reading, math and written language. There was no indication what those difficulties were but she did add 'these difficulties may be due to visual processing defects'.

By the third grade, he was considered at-risk for academic reasons by both of his teachers. Ms. Jones said, 'Very much below level, goes to LD, but a real interesting kid. He's the one who never gets out of bed at night because his mother tells him that there are snakes on the floor.' His other teacher, Ms. Green, who had been his teacher since he entered Plaza, described him by saying, 'He is again an LD student. He's a third grader probably functioning at a second grade level. Enthusiastic child, very artistic, but low reading skills, very low math skills . . . he's been with us since first grade. I've had him for three years and I've never had a conference with the mother. We've tried and tried.' She had talked to her on the phone but since she wouldn't come to school Ms. Green said, 'I get the feeling that she's not real supportive of the school situation'. She also said that Andy had told her that he always stayed in bed at night because of the snakes. When asked what she thought caused his lack of achievement, Ms. Green said, 'probably pre-genetic. That might be a lot of it, although I think if he had more support from the home he would be doing better.'

The aide in the classroom had worked with Andy since the first grade and felt that he had made improvement and she was proud of him. She reported how, after hearing a story read, Andy could 'just stand up and literally tell you the whole story . . . every little detail'. She did think that he had a reading and a math problem. She said, 'There are times when he just writes any old answer down. I guess he wants to finish too. If you're sitting down with him, one to one, and working with him, he can do it. He can really do it.'

The counselor had attempted to help the teachers in contacting Andy's mother. She had gone to the apartment once and reported, 'The mom will meet you at the door in a bathrobe, regardless of the time of day and just sort of pass the time of day without really giving answers. Specific questions are glossed over so that you never really get any truthful answers.' The counselor thought that Andy was a 'very, very slow student' and that 'he is not one of the best to grasp concepts'. She also told the story that Andy had told her about having to be in bed by a certain time, if not snakes would get him. She said, 'kids always have an imagination' but that 'some things that stem from the home (Andy's) that are almost cult, in thinking'. She appeared to have little knowledge of his home situation as she said, 'I think maybe this year, they are in a separate house but last year we had an extended family situation and it varied from night to night, cousins, aunts, kids and uncles . . . so the kids were exposed to not a lot of supervision but the supervision that they did have came from a variety of sources and probably a varied assortment of men.'

The underlying philosophy of Andy's classroom was to build students up and let them be leaders in something in which they excelled. In Andy's case, his teachers asked him to give drawing lessons. This may have helped him socially but at the end of the year he was still considered at-risk for academic reasons. Ms. Jones said, 'I love Andy. I don't think he's ever gonna be great in school work. Andy just goes along at his own pace. I don't believe we've ever seen his mother but he and his little sister do come to school. He's quite an artist. He's beginning to really write stories and he does minimal math. He's just never gonna be a good student.' His other teacher, Ms. Green, who also thought that he was at-risk, said that he 'probably will be for a long time'. After having Andy for three years, she felt a fondness for him and didn't want 'to see him go on to another teacher'. She finished by saying, 'he's made some progress in self control, reading . . . he's never been a discipline problem but controlling himself as far as what's going on in the class. His life is difficult. I spend a lot of time telling him how much I think of him.'

Andy's Perceptions of School

Andy is indeed an 'interesting kid' as Ms. Jones said in her interview. It would seem that his daily experiences in school, his lack of success, his inability to finish his work and his difficulty in reading and math would make him dislike school. This did not seem to have happened. In his interview, Andy made very few negative remarks about school life, thought school was fun and said, 'the only time I've been absent is when I had the chicken pox'.

He said his favourite activities in the classroom were field trips, pizza parties for reading a certain amount of books, 'soccer, library and classes they have . . . and the cafeteria and volleyball'. If he could make school be exactly the way he would like it, he said, 'everybody gets how much lunch they want and they could check out three books at a time and they can have a cookbook for free . . . have free time after they do math and watch a movie'.

He liked his teachers and also the substitutes that came once a week while his teachers are involved in a district project. He liked Ms. Jones because 'she likes to make me do hard stuff . . . she lets us pick out stuff, and every time we have music she lets us have free time. She takes us to her house for a swimming party'. He liked Ms. Green because of 'her truck . . . and her sunglasses . . . and she lets us make kachinas'.

Since interviews and observations had indicated that Andy had difficulty in the areas of math and reading, he was asked about these subjects. In talking about math, he said, 'sometimes it's hard but sometimes it's fun'. He thought he was pretty good in math. He knew he didn't know his multiplication tables and needed help and indicated this by saying if there were more teachers in the room he would ask them to 'help me on my multiplication and on the times that are hard'. When asked how Ms. Green, who was mainly responsible for teaching math in the classroom helped him, he said, 'I don't know, she never helps me in math'. He thought reading was a little fun but that he didn't like reading a whole long book. He indicated that he did not like SSR by saying, 'cause you have to read with your eyes . . . I would rather read out loud'. His favorite books were *Bears on Wheels, A Fly Went By*, and *Hop on Pop* (all books which are listed as 'beginning readers' and 'easy-to read'). He said that he would like someone to 'tell me what the words are that I need and don't know' because there were lots of words in his reading book that he didn't know.

Andy indicated several times in the interview that he didn't get as much help as he wanted. This did not happen in the classroom he said, 'cause there's a bunch of people and everybody tells me to do it myself'. He couldn't always do that so sometimes he just skipped that question. He said that he stayed in his seat and raised his hand for help but he doesn't get called on 'cause there's a whole bunch of people that raise their hands and they're too busy telling a whole bunch of people to get back into their seats'. He liked the help he got last year when there were five teachers. (There were student teachers in the room.)

Since the issue of the snakes had been mentioned several times, Andy was asked about snakes. In the interview, he did not mention the 'bed story' but talked about the time when a boy brought three snakes to school. He said he was scared of snakes because 'the way they bite. They're poison. The way they feel.' During the interview with mother she had also said that he was scared of snakes, that she was too and so was her mother.

Andy was not considered a discipline problem. When asked what he thought one had to do not to get into trouble, he said, 'To not talk out loud and not to be rude . . . Don't fool around and try to get it all done . . . Don't be walking around when the teacher tells you to stay in your seat.' He felt that sitting at the little desk in the corner of the classroom helped him to get his work done, kept him from getting into trouble for talking to other kids and he didn't have to put up with kids fighting over pencils. He said he also liked it ' . . . cause I have my own privacy and I can turn it into neat things when I'm sitting there. I try to make an office . . .'

Classroom Observations of Andy

During initial observations in the classroom, the researcher attempted to identify the students named as at-risk by the teachers in their interviews. Andy was the last student to be recognized. His ability to function in the classroom without being 'spotlighted' was excellent. He always sat in the far corner of the room at a small table with another younger, black student. On most occasions, he tried not to let school 'bother' him. He was not a behavior problem and seldom was reprimanded for misconduct. He displayed a 'good attitude' and never complained about anything. This was true whether there were books left lying all over his desk, the assignment was too difficult or when he missed out on activities because he hadn't finished his work.

Through observations of Andy, it became apparent that he had his own way of coping. As the year progressed, he started coming in late from breakfast so he missed out on Oral Language which he didn't like. He would also appear to be taking part in a lesson but in actuality he would not be attending, and would 'mouth the words'. He seldom read during SSR but was rarely spoken to about this. He would leaf through a book, look at the pictures or talk to his friend. He and his friend had worked out a system for talking that seldom 'got caught'.

Andy was often observed having difficulty with the math lesson and he always seemed to be behind. He would attempt to do the tasks but, lacking skills, often resorted to putting down any answer to get finished. Only on one occasion was it observed that this bothered him. The math group in which he was working was given a timed test and he was first one done. He took the paper to Ms. Green and, without looking at it, she asked: 'Did you think about these? You'll have to correct the ones you miss'. She corrected the paper and handed it back with many errors circled. He went back to his desk, attempted to correct the problems and then began to quietly cry. The researcher went over to him and began to help him. It was observed that his problem stemmed from the fact that he had not learned the mutiplication facts that the test covered. He had been instructed to learn them at home and had not done this. A system of marking was shown to him and he quickly grasped the concept. The individual help appeared to have helped him but it was observed that no one else gave him any additional instruction or rechecked his paper. He did not raise his hand or ask for help.

Andy had difficulty completing his work and keeping up with the pace of the class in other academic areas as well. His slow pace caused him to miss out on much of the follow-up instruction. On one occasion, during a ten-minute timed letter writing-copying activity, when many of the students were finished, Andy had eight words on his paper. While the teacher was explaining the mistakes in the letter, Andy was still struggling to finish copying the letter. In a similar activity, the students were asked to copy a letter from the board and correct the ten mistakes that were in the letter. Andy struggled to complete the task and 'found' ten mistakes in the first few lines. His paper looked like this:

1.811, Loper Avenu
Rockford Illinois 6.1104
March. 10, 1987

It appeared to the observer that this quality of work resulted from his waiting to finish the task and from not having fully learned the concept for which the activity was designed to provide practice.

Discussion

The descriptions above portray Andy's life in the classroom. He appeared to lack the knowledge necessary for successfully completing many of the academic tasks in the classroom. Due to his slow work pace, by the time he was ready to refine and practice one skill, the class had moved on to a new one. This left him confused and unable to do the new tasks as well as not having fully learned the previous task. To cope and not draw attention to this fact, he did not act out or complain, and he tried to make himself as inconspicuous as possible. This appeared to have worked as he was seldom observed getting into trouble and his teachers liked him. This was to his disadvantage, though, because his needs were not dealt with and he did not receive the help that he wanted and needed. Andy's teachers gave him support to build his self-confidence but they also needed to give him individual help in building his academic skills.

This mismatch of instruction may have occurred because the school identified his home rather than the school as being responsible for his problems in school. The home may not have been as supportive as the school might have wished but there were reasons for which the school did appear aware. The home lives of many children has changed, recently, because of the many single-parent families. The schools need to realize that these parents may not be able to support the schools in their academic endeavours as in the past. They may need to accept the fact that if the parents feed, clothe and send them to school regularly, this may be the limit of what their time allows them to contribute. The schools may have to assume the role of assisting the child and his/her family with homework by providing more time at school, or providing more explicit directions to parents.

Andy's case also illustrates how 'myths' can start about a family. With little contact with the home and a lack of understanding of extended families and the difficulty of being a single-parent, they drew some conclusion that did not appear to be valid when all the information was put together. This 'myth' may have influenced how the school dealt with Andy. They felt the home was not supportive because the mother had not attended conferences. They were concerned about weird activities in the home because of the 'snake story'. They felt the children were not getting proper care because several people were responsible for them. They had very little information from which to draw these conclusions. Further, it seemed to influence how they worked with Andy. For example, they did not think Andy's mother helped him at home, and never sent any instructions home to her concerning what he specifically needed help with. However, both Andy and his mother mentioned that help was given in the home when Andy brought work home. More direct instructions to the home concerning ways in which the mother and other members of the family could assist Andy would have helped.

The school staff almost seemed resigned to the fact that Andy was never going to be a good student. The teacher expectation literature illustrates why such an approach can lead to problems with the self-fulfilling prophecy (Cooper and Good, 1983). In addition, they did not seem to focus on Andy's potential. Several separate incident gave clues to this potential. The aide reported skills that he had that indicated he had a good auditory memory. She also reported that he was able to learn concepts when working with her, one-on-one. The researcher observed that Andy was able to generalize his math knowledge to a new task quickly and effectively when given individual help. That individual help was needed was indicated not only from observations but by the grades on his report card and his achievement test scores. His scores, in percentiles on the ITBS at the end of the study year were as follows: vocabulary — 13, reading — 16, spelling — 30, capitalization — 39, punctuation — 54, usage and expression — 45, math concepts – 32, math problem solving – 29 and math computation — 44. It should be noted that the one area in which the students were often given direct instruction, punctuation, Andy scored with the national norm although his class's average was at the 63 percentile.

At the same time, it appeared that the particular individual instruction that Andy received in the LD room had not provided Andy with the skills he needed in his classroom activities. At the end of Andy's third grade year, as at the end of his second grade year, the LD teacher was still reporting that he had academic problems in math and reading and that they may be due to visual processing. Her goal remained that of trying to improve his visual processing as well as his academic skills. Helping him learn his multiplication tables and providing additional experience in the reading of books would have related more directly to the difficulties he was experiencing in the classroom. Her instructional time might have been more to his benefit had she worked more closely with the classroom teachers to determine what his 'everyday' needs were in the classroom.

Gary

Gary was included in the study as a marginal at-risk student. Ms. Green, who considered him a bright student, was concerned that his lack of motor skills would affect his ability to communicate in written language. When his parents were contacted for permission to include him in the study, they indicated that they were very concerned with this problem which they described as perceptual. They were afraid that it would interfere with his achieving to his level of potential. His other teacher, Ms. Jones, who had been his teacher since first grade did not appear to share these concerns and did not consider him at-risk.

Parents and Home Experience

Gary's home experience appeared to match what the literature suggests is the kind of background that prepared students to be successful in school. He was the only child of upper-middle class parents, of whom both had college educations and were employed professionally. He had a very stable environment and had been born and raised in the same town. When he was small, his mother worked part-time and had a sitter come to the home when she worked. As he grew older, his mother resumed full-time work and Gary was put in private pre-schools. His mother said, '. . . he couldn't wait to go to kindergarten . . . he loved his teacher'.

He had spent two summers in Vermont with his parents, when his father was involved in a program there. He had enjoyed being out in the country and visiting his grandparents who also lived there. His mother said that he also enjoyed going out to dinner, playing board games (with them) and computer games, and having conversations with them. They were concerned that he watched too much TV as he liked to watch the educational channel, news, cartoons and game shows. His father was also concerned about his moodiness while his mother was worried about the way she saw him interact with other children. She felt he was too bossy.

This latter pattern seemed to typify Gary's home environment. He was the child of two people who wanted him to achieve at a high level and they were concerned about anything that might stand in the way of his success. This concern was the reason they were interested in having Gary included in the study. They hoped it would reveal something more about 'his problem'. The problem that they were referring to was Gary's perceptual difficulty. Gary had been in pre-school when it had been diagnosed. A psychologist friend of his mother's had recognized it. They had been attempting to deal with this problem ever since. Upon a doctor's recommendation, they had asked the school to have him placed in the LD program. They had also purchased glasses for Gary. They knew he didn't like them but the doctor had said he needed them and they felt he should wear them.

Gary's parents saw their roles as supporting and guiding Gary in his process of growing and learning. His father said, 'I want him to be open to whatever it is in life that will enrich him . . . but I want him to do that with enough discipline in his life to be able to find something that he can be useful and productive doing, whatever it is. I want to push him toward doing well, whatever he wants.'

School Personnel Perceptions of Gary

Gary had attended several pre-schools before entering kindergarten at Plaza School. It was the only elementary school he has ever attended.

Records showed that he did satisfactory work in kindergarten but that at the end of the first reporting period his teacher had commented 'needs more writing — tends to be messy'. At the end of the year, she noted that he was getting better.

In first grade, Ms. Jones was his teacher and she gave him 'E's (excellent) in the areas of listening, speaking, math and reading and noted that he was reading at fourth grade, second level. He did receive an 'S' (satisfactory) in spelling and writing and an 'I' (improvement shown but not doing satisfactory work) in penmanship. His test scores on the CTBS were above the average but not as high as his report card grades.

His experience in second grade was also successful. He remained with Ms. Jones but Ms. Green also became his teacher when she joined Ms. Jones in a team teaching arrangement. He received 'E's in all subjects on his report card except in penmanship where he got an 'S'. His test scores were still above the average but down somewhat from the previous year and were as follows in percentiles: listening — 65, word analysis — 69, vocabulary — 75, reading — 68, spelling — 59, math concepts — 69, math problem solving — 67 and math computation — 67. Nowhere in his files was there an indication that Ms. Jones was concerned about his handwriting. His parents were and they had taken him to a doctor who recommended that he be placed in the LD program.

It was in the third grade that Ms. Green expressed her concern with his extremely poor motor control and thought that it might interfere with his schooling. She said, 'he had extreme visual problems and had difficulty doing any kind of art projects, anything that requires hand/eye coordination'. She thought he had an excellent family life, that they gave him lots of support, and that Gary was aware of his problems. She concluded her discussion of him by saying, '. . . I would say he's marginal. He is also on the LD roster. He was tested and found to have problems in visual discriminations.' Ms. Jones did not mention him in her initial interview.

Other school personnel knew him but not because he was seen as having problems. The classroom aide had worked with him since kindergarten. She was surprised to be asked to talk about him. She said, '. . . he's smart, intelligent, and he gets his work done . . . He understands what he's doing . . . I don't see him as at-risk.' The nurse knew who he was because he came in to see her when he had headaches. She reported that she called him 'my little old man' because he's so very serious and said, '. . . he comes in more to just talk so I think when he has the headache, he does have the headache but to him it's a major catastrophic illness.' She did not see him as having any problems. The counselor did not mention him in her discussion of at-risk students.

At the end of the study the teachers were again interviewed. When Ms. Jones was asked about Gary she commented that even though he was in the LD program, she did not think he was at-risk. She said, 'There's nothing except his handwriting. He's a marvelous student.' She had never seen the LD teacher's report on Gary as it was mailed directly to his parents. Ms. Green, who had considered him marginally at-risk at the beginning of the study, said that knowing what she now knew, she would not have considered him even marginally at risk. She saw his life was pretty much ideal and that he was an excellent student. She said, 'His handwriting perception . . . whatever Miss . . . (the LD teacher) has done has really helped him. (She appeared not to know that he was also receiving perceptual training with a physician.) So he's LD too but it was not something that I recommended. It was his mother's request because of a physician.' She added, '. . . he's gone through several ophthalmologists and he seems to do almost as well without his glasses as he does with them'. After working with him during the year, she did not feel that his perceptual problems had interefered with his activities in the classroom.

Gary's records also indicated that he had a successful year. On his final report card, at the end of third grade, he received 'E's in listening, speaking, reading, writing, spelling, math and in penmanship. His percentile scores on the ITBS were as follows:vacabulary — 90, reading — 86, spelling — 83, capitalization — 86, punctuation — 96, usage and expression — 88, math concepts — 96, math problem solving — 92 and math computation — 88.

Gary's Perceptions of School

Gary's interview was facilitated by the ease with which he was able to converse with adults. He did have a tendency to answer questions on a 'surface level' and seemed to know what to say that would please or impress an adult. He thought Plaza School was a nice school, that the teacher and Principal were nice and that the kids were nice. (He was the only student to mention the Principal but this might have been because his parents were friends of the Principal.) He said, 'I've heard a lot about other schools, but it doesn't sound good to me. I've just always loved this school.'

Gary said that he liked both of his teachers because of the way they taught, that they didn't really get mad, and that they gave him chances. He had already thought about who he wanted his teacher to be next year. He said he wanted Mr . . . because 'he's a good teacher and he does things that kids want to do, like Ms. Jones, and he gives good rewards'. He didn't necessarily think it was important to get rewards but he liked getting them.

Gary liked SSR but wished it were longer and he said, '. . . usually when I first start reading a book, I just get into it and I don't want to close the book'. He also liked working in the math group and writing stories. He said, 'I love writing'. When asked about his problems in writing he said, 'I had trouble with handwriting. Writing is something that you feel and handwriting is something that you do with your hand.' The thing he liked the least was Oral Language. Interesting enough, Happy Hour, an after-school, activity program was his favourite time of day. He said he liked it because 'they have games and they have free time and they have choices for what you can do'.

Gary said he felt that his teacher thought he was a good student, a smart student. He also felt that Ms. Jones liked him and that Ms. Green liked him a lot. When asked why he thought that he said, 'I don't know, surely not the way I look. . . . I think she likes me cause of the way I work and the way I act.' He then said, 'I think I'm a good kid. I don't like the way I look, but . . .' Since this was the second time he had mentioned his looks, the topic was pursued. He replied, 'I just don't like the way I look in glasses'. This was the only part of himself that he didn't like and if he could be different he wouldn't wear his glasses. He said he wore them because, 'I have a weak muscle in my eye'. He said he had been wearing them for about four or five years and that they had helped a little but that they didn't really seem to affect his school work.

Classroom Observations of Gary

Gary was an average height, average size, Anglo boy. He had blonde hair, wore glasses and dressed in casual (but not jeans) clothes. If he were an adult, one might describe him as being conservative looking. He was the kind of student teachers like to have in their classrooms. He was observed usually on task, completing his work in minimal time, doing quality work and relating well to others in the classroom. During SSR, he always had a book and either read it or quietly shared it with his friend that sat next to him. (He and his friend, who was also a good student, were never reprimanded.) He read non-fiction as well as fiction. He participated actively in Oral Language even though it was later learned that he did not really like the activity.

He missed school occasionally and during one quarter was taken out for several days to visit Disneyland. Gary did not exhibit any behavior that indicated that he had problems in school. Only on one occasion was it observed that he might feel pressure to succeed. It was during an activity in which they were to describe 'love' by completing sentences about love. In the sentence, 'to be loved_____', Gary wrote, 'be smart'. He then highlighted and drew a box around the words. In another sentence, 'how people show love_____', Gary wrote 'my mom shows her love by giving me a home with a swimming pool'. This second response seemed to illustrate the home environment that existed for Gary. A background that appeared to contribute to his success in school, allowed him to feel little if any discontinuity between the home and school environment and dealt with his perceptual problem in such a manner that it did not interfere with his learning.

Discussion

Gary's school experience was so different from the other students in the study that it was difficult to view his perceptual problem as a problem. His mother was often in contact with the school and knew the Principal and Ms. Green. This may have been the reason Ms. Green was concerned about his motor coordination and viewed it as more of a problem than it appeared to be. As she worked with him during the year, she too came to the conclusion that it did not make him an at-risk student.

Gary's parents were still concerned with his perceptual problem but it may be that as he continues to succeed in school their concern will also diminish. At that time, they were still searching for ways to help him. Even though they liked Plaza School and the social and emotional support it offers, they would have liked a stronger academic program for Gary. They were making plans to send him to a private school that had smaller class loads and a strong academic program when Gary enters sixth grade.

It was amazing that all this concern had not influenced Gary more than it had. The only indications that it had some effect on him was noted in his discussion about his glasses. They may represent some of the frustration that Gary felt towards the concern for his perceptual problem. It was also thought that he had 'worked this out' though by his comment to the researcher that he did not have problems in writing but in handwriting. It would be fortunate if other students, who had problems in school, could be allowed to view them as rationally.

Brad

Brad was another student who had been enrolled at Plaza School since kindergarten. He was well known by his teachers as he had been with Ms. Green since first grade and with Ms. Jones since second grade. Both teachers had worked closely with him and his mother during this time as there were problems in the home. Now in third grade, Ms. Jones felt that Brad had come a long way and was doing better both academically and emotionally. She was still concerned about his difficult home situation, felt there was violence in the home and, for these reasons, considered him at-risk for social and emotional reasons. Ms. Green, who had worked with him the longest, said that he read fairly well, was excellent in math but was on the LD rolls. She was concerned with his poor self-concept and considered him marginally at-risk because he had the tendency to allow his self image to take over. She worried that he might go back to his old habits. She thought that his troubled home life, which had lots of ups and downs, contributed to his problems.

Parents and Home Experience

Brad lived with his mother, an older brother who was 15 and a freshman in high school, and two younger sisters who were 9 and 7-years-old. They lived in a small house in the neighborhood from which students were bussed to Plaza School. He was born in this town, left for two years and returned when he was three. His mother had worked since he was born. She was presently employed as a waitress in a truck stop and was the sole support of the family.

His mother remembered that when Brad was small, he was very quiet and shy. She said, 'When I introduced him to anyone, I always said he's my shy one cause he's the one behind me'. She added that he was active as a little boy, didn't go to strangers very easily and loved being outside. She thought that one of the most important happenings in his life was when he was four and learned how to ride his bike. She described him as basically a loner but that he loved to help his dad work on his truck.

Brad's mother indicated that he didn't want to go to kindergarten and said, 'He raised "holy devil". . . . He was scared. The school scared him cause it was so big.' She explained that he didn't handle change well. She thought that kindergarten was his worst year in school and said, 'He got into fights cause he wasn't used to being around kids his own age and having to handle things'. She then talked about the problems Brad had in school. In discussing them, she was very supportive of the school and the teachers and said, '. . . if it wasn't for the school, I wouldn't know he had any problems. There is nothing wrong with him. He just has a visual/memory problem that needed working on'. She visited school often, went to most of the conferences and felt that she knew Brad's teachers well, especially Ms. Green. She also knew the Principal and the counselor and she talked about the help the counselor had given the family. She reported, 'When . . . (Brad's father) would come over here drunk and it would be the violent drunk. Not the hitting but the anger . . . the counselor would talk to the kids and find out if anything had happened at home the night before.' She appreciated the support the school had given her children.

Brad's parents were divorced when he was in the second grade and his father moved out of the home. School seemed to start getting better for Brad at that point. His mother reported, 'His confidence grew a lot more . . . He's a whiz at math and they put him helping the younger kids.' Brad had been very close to his father but it was the father who had put so much pressure on him in the first grade. His mother said that his father would call Brad 'an illiterate' and 'stupid'. 'He still has a lot of anger towards his father', she added. She did not indicate that she put pressure on the children although Brad perceived that she did. He is afraid to get into trouble at school. He didn't want to get suspended or grounded. He said, 'I wouldn't be able to sit down for a week. She (his mother) would spank me bad.'

Brad's mother did not talk about any other problems in the home. She did say that her oldest son had just been suspended for the rest of the school year. Brad said in his interview, 'He's just gonna have to be in the ninth grade next year. That's his third time being in the ninth grade.' Brad's two sisters were apparently doing satisfactorily in school and liked it. The only mention of violence in the home and its effect on Brad was in the mother's conversation concerning the counselor. Other school people who had worked with Brad reported that his father had an alcohol problem and there were many family fights. The mother did not discuss these issues.

In general, Brad's mother doesn't worry about him. She said, 'My kids have a good, strong sense of responsibility. They have a good sense of who they are and what they can do and cannot do.' She would like Brad to be a lawyer, doctor or computer technologist but she thought he was going to be a football player or an auto mechanic. She will help him any way she can but added, 'It's gonna be his life and he's gonna have to make his decisions. I can't make them for him.' At the present time, she was concerned about his moving to fourth grade and said, 'I dread next year cause it's gonna be a change for both of us. I've gotten used to trusting Ms. Jones and Ms. Green . . . I don't know how he's (Brad) gonna do, especially if he has a man teacher but he's never had a male teacher to cope with everyday.'

School Personnel Perceptions of Brad

Brad's records showed an irregular pattern and some discontinuities. In kindergarten, his teacher gave no indications that he had problems. He received Ss in all areas including attitude and social development. The teacher had written 'good' beside them.

An immediate reversal seemed to appear in first grade. During the first month, he was referred to the Speech and Language Pathologist and it was determined that he had a lisp and needed special help. Five months later, Ms. Green referred him to special education for testing. On the referral she wrote, 'poor memory for basic concepts . . . can't spell name, recognize numbers or letters out of sequence'. The grades he received on his report card at the end of the first grade were lower than in kindergarten. He got an 'S' in listening, 'I' (improvement shown but not doing satisfactory work) in reading, 'E' in penmanship and 'S' in math. Ms. Green had made no comments on the report card until the fourth quarter when she wrote, 'Brad starting to work in reading'. His tests scores on the ITBS did not reflect this and were higher than his report card grades. They were above the average in all areas and were as follows: listening — 72, word analysis — 63, vocabulary — 57, reading — 71, math concepts — 67, math problem solving — 82, and math computation — 73. He missed eighteen-and-a-half days of school that year.

In the second grade, Brad was released by the speech pathologist but was placed in the LD program. He began to make progress in the academic areas. His report card reflected this growth. During the first report period, he received Is in speaking and reading and 'N' in spelling. At the end of the year, he received Ss in all areas except math where he received an 'E'. His test score on the ITBS did not reflect this improvement. They were as follows: listening — 57, word analysis — 52, vocabulary — 44, reading — 43, spelling — 27, capitalization — 62, punctuation — 56, usage and expression — 67 (above the average of 62), math concepts — 56, math problem solving — 47 and math computation — 66 (above the average of 65). His attendence did improve and he missed only three days.

In the third grade he continued to improve and made good gains. Still, both his teachers were concerned about him. Ms. Jones considered him to be at-risk for social and emotional reasons and Ms. Green described him as marginally at-risk because of his poor self-concept. They were still concerned with his home environment and considered it to be influencing his success in schooling.

Other school personnel knew Brad and had worked with him. The classroom aide who had known him since kindergarten said, '. . . I've seen a lot of improvement in him, a great deal . . . last year he was having quite a bit of trouble and this year is a complete turn over in him . . . he's been doing great in reading and math, academically and socially'. The nurse knew who he was but had not worked with him very often. All she said was, '. . . Brad is not a frequent visitor here'. The story was quite the opposite with the school counselor. She had been working with him and his family since he had been in the first grade. She said that in the first grade, when his parents had gotten separated, he was devastated. She reported that Brad got very depressed and had told his teachers that he wanted to die. She involved him in a divorced parents' group and that seemed to help him personally but he continued to struggle in school. She worked with his teacher and they tried several approaches but he still struggled. She attributed this to his low self-concept. She reported, '. . . he improved in the second grade, was still having some difficulty with academics but at least his attitude was changing and he'd make a try'. This year, in the third grade, she saw still more improvement and he was getting along better with other kids. She thought that he was still at-risk emotionally because of his self-concept. She said, 'I think he's a child who adults need to continually be aware of because of this emotional lack of strength situation . . . that does affect academic progress.'

At the end of the study, Ms. Green thought that Brad had made much improvement during the year. She said, 'I've just been thrilled with his progress. He's really coming into himself.' She did relate that he was very apprehensive about going to fourth grade and changing teachers as he had been with her for three years. She reported, '. . . he has begged me to please change grades and teach something else'. It was interesting that even with the progress Brad had made and the fact that Brad reluctantly went to the LD class at times, Ms. Green was not going to recommend that he be taken out of the LD program. She said, 'I think that Brad has really done well with her (the LD teacher) and he enjoys that individualized attention. His scores have really increased. Next October, he'll come up for review. Let's see how he's doing in the fourth grade . . . it's very difficult to have them removed and then have them put back in. So I'm hesitant to have him removed.' Ms. Jones did not comment on whether she felt Brad was still at-risk but she too thought the LD had helped Brad through the one-on-one instruction.

Brad's final grades on his report card were similar to last year although they were lower in the area of math. He received Ss in listening, speaking, reading, writing, and penmanship, an 'E' in spelling and an 'S-' in math. Ms. Jones wrote as a comment for that quarter, 'Brad, practice your multiplication facts this summer. I'll miss you.' Brad's test scores on the ITBS were above the average in all areas except vocabulary. They were as follows: vocabulary — 40 (the average was 48), reading — 73, spelling — 57, capitalization — 61, punctuation — 79, usage and expression — 91, math concepts — 82, math problem solving — 83 and math computation — 76.

Brad's Perceptions of School

Brad had mixed feelings about school, his ability, his teachers' perception of him and about life in general. He said that he wished that he could have more than one teacher because 'it's good to know how they all act' but later he said he didn't want a new teacher in the fourth grade. He wanted Ms. Green. These kinds of contradictions ran throughout his interview. At one point he would say that he didn't like school much and then at another point, he said that 'it was alright'. He would say that his teachers didn't think he was smart and later comment that they liked his work. When asked how he felt Ms. Jones thought about him, he answered, 'Nothing, she just probably likes me the way I am. She hates me.' (The word 'hate' came up often in the interview.)

Brad was not a discipline problem and was usually observed on task in the classroom. When asked about this, he said that he did try to do a good job most of the time and that he did this 'just so I don't get in trouble'. He said he didn't like being quiet but he seldom talked in the classroom. He explained this by saying 'cause I'm not getting in trouble and losing fifteen minutes of my lunchtime . . . playtime'. He usually got his work done and he gave his reason for this as '. . . so I can get a Panther Pass and I don't have to do it at lunch'. He said that he never raised his hand in class because 'it's just boring . . . school is boring and raising my hand'.

He was aware that he had made improvement in school. In the area of reading he said, 'I didn't know how to read when I was in the second grade . . . That's how I felt . . . Now I do.' The reason that he was able to learn was because his teachers just told him to keep trying and he did. He thought that he had made the most improvement in math but said, 'I do hate it.' He was concerned with the multiplication tables and this may have been what influenced his final report card grade in math.

Brad did talk about his home life. He felt his mother couldn't help him with his math because she was too busy. He said, '. . . from 6 in the morning till 2 . . . she works 7 days a week. . . . on the days she shouldn't be working but she wants to . . . she works 6 to 1'. He and his sisters get themselves ready for school in the morning. He said that even though his dad lived in town, he didn't see him very often. He did not want to see him more often either and added, 'No, because I hate him'. When asked if he really meant that he replied, 'I mean it because when I saved up a whole bunch of cans, I should have had twenty dollars and he gave me eleven and spent the rest on beer'. He added that his dad had been gone about a year and it had made a difference in the home because 'there's never no fights'.

He wanted to graduate from high school but he was not going to go to college and said, 'I'm sick of school where I am'. He shared his concern about going to fourth grade. He said, '. . . fourth grade is gonna be harder . . . math was gonna to be hard . . . following the rules would be harder'. He hoped that he'd be in Ms. Green's room. He wanted her to be his fourth grade teacher. He was definitely worried about making the change.

Classroom Observations of Brad

Brad was a wiry, light-brown haired, Anglo boy. His body was always moving and when one got close to him, you could sense that his body was 'tight'. He always seemed ready for whatever could happen to him. His guard was up and he was defensive. During the student interviews, he was the only student to ask what was going to be done with the tape. He didn't appear to trust people and therefore kept himself aloof. He was very quiet in the classroom and seemed to try to be 'unnoticed'. He avoided trouble and moved away from students that talked or got 'into trouble'. When attention or praise was given him, he became very embarrassed and had difficulty accepting it or dealing with it.

During the interview, he bounced around and appeared uneasy. He just couldn't seem to relax. This behavior was similar to his behavior in the classroom. It was difficult to understand how he kept all this energy under control. In the classroom, he was usually observed working on the assigned task, often the fourth or fifth one finished, doing good quality work and hardly ever talking or bothering anyone.

On more than one occasion, he came to school looking very tired. He would put his head down and rest during SSR. The teachers never said anything to him about this. They felt that he may have had a difficult night at home and needed the rest. On one occasion when this was observed, it was informally discussed with Ms. Green. She said, '. . . this has been going on for a week . . . he is trying to be "unseen" . . . he withdraws like this every so often . . . there are times when he will spend most of the day sleeping.'

Durng SSR, even though in his interview he indicated that he did not like SSR, he was usually observed reading. This behavior was similar in other areas as well. At the writing center, he usually finished his task quickly and went on to the follow-up activity without bothering other students. He did well in creative writing activities. Several of his stories indicated that he had a good sense of story and wrote well.

During classroom observations, except for the days when he seemed to be having problems at home, Brad appeared to be a good student. He was not at-risk academically. His good friend Travis, another student in the study, said 'He (Brad) does fine cause he's quick. He's smart. It's like he's just lucky . . . like in soccer and the ball will just come to him and in school, he'll be the first or second or third to get his work done.'

Discussion

Brad finished his interview by saying, 'I feel great about school but I don't know how school feels about me'. Not only was he an example of how students can move from being at-risk to not being at-risk but also of how difficult those labels are to loose. Observations indicated that he was experiencing little if any difficulty with his school work, yet he was uncertain about what kind of a student he was in the classroom. In addition, he had made improvement in all academic areas and his test scores were above average, yet his teacher was hesitant to take him out of the LD program. She felt that he might regress in the fourth grade and it was difficult to put students back once they were taken out. She did not want to take this risk. It appeared that the system perpetuated labeling.

Even though his mother did not talk much about the home environment and attributed his difficulties in school to a visual/memory problem, the home environment did appear to contribute to his lack of self-confidence that affected his progress in school. In addition, the emotional strife that seemed to go on in the home did cause Brad to be less effective in school on the days it occurred. That it didn't affect his learning more can be attributed to the communication system that had been developed between the home and the school. Brad's mother had been able to develop a trust with the school and shared the home problems with Brad's teachers because of this trust. These problems were then taken into account when Brad had problems in school that related to the home environment. The knowledge the teachers had about him helped them work on the problems and not make them worse as happens in some cases. Brad's case illustrates the importance and the necessity for good communication between the home and school and the need to develop a trust level between the two so that it can occur.

Jerry

Jerry was in the third grade at Plaza School, and considered at-risk for academic and social reasons. Ms. Green felt that he was functioning academically at least one year below grade level and that he had a poor self concept. Ms. Jones talked about his academic problems but seemed most concerned with his social and personal problems. Both teachers and the aide used the term 'unusual' when they described him. Ms. Jones saw it as strange and unusual how everyone 'picked on him'. Ms. Green called him an unusual child. The aide said that he was unusual and that he kept ' . . . to himself most of the time'. They also described him as loving, kind and sensitive with all his emotions 'up-front'.

Jerry was difficult to communicate with and this contributed to the school personnel's perceptions of his problems. Ms. Green had a 'lot of trouble understanding and getting to know' him. The aide felt that 'he just shuts himself out' and the nurse described him as 'very, very quiet' and 'very, very difficult to talk to'. The counselor had tried to communicate with him on several occasions and said that 'it's very seldom that you get anything in depth'. When he spoke with her, he took a long time to begin to talk and seemed uncertain when he did. Jerry and his two sisters were new to the school that year. No records were brought with them, nor were records received from the last school that their father said they attended. The father volunteered little information when he registered Jerry at Plaza. It was deduced that Jerry had attended school in Kentucky the preceding year, and during the study Jerry said he had attended kindergarten in Germany. Other than that, little was known about his previous schooling. His date of birth was given as 24 September 1977, which made him a year older than most of the students in his class, but no one at Plaza School knew whether he had repeated a grade.

School personnel said that his mother was 'oriental', 'Korean or something' and 'Vietnamese'. It was never determined. His father, an Anglo, had been in the military. Jerry was born at a military post in the Midwest. He was the middle child with an older sister in fifth grade and a younger sister in first grade. (Both were also considered at-risk by school personnel.) School records listed his father as a salesman for a tool company, but was unemployed at the beginning of the study. Later, the father told the counselor that he was working long hours across town in construction.

Parents and Home Experience

Jerry's house was located in the area from which children were bussed to Plaza School. His home was very small and appeared to need repairs. Entrance was gained through the side door as furniture in the living room blocked the front door. The side door opened into the kitchen which was small and had only one cupboard. Jars of vegetables and other food items sat on the counters. The living room was also small and filled with two davenports (which might have been used for sleeping) and a large dresser for clothes on which sat a TV set. During the first informal interview, the mother appeared very uncomfortable and seemed to have difficulty using English to communicate. She continually glanced at the TV which she had not turned off. Jerry's mother gave permission to include Jerry in the study without any comments or questions. She did appear to understand what was discussed. She said that her husband said Jerry could be included in the study. She added that Jerry's father was working at a new job, and suggested that Sunday would be a better time to visit when he was home. No other information was gained from her concerning Jerry or the family. While attempted a number of times, a second interview, which was to include the father, was never scheduled. Later, the family moved to another area of town. When attempts were made to locate Jerry and his family it was determined that he and his two sisters had been withdrawn from school without a follow-up address.

There was limited contact between the school and the home. Both of his teachers stated that they had tried to get his parents into the school many times, but only his mother had come once. They had tried calling home, but no-one answered. They sent notes home, but none were returned. The nurse was able to get the father to talk to her on the phone by threatening to call the Child Protection Agency for medical neglect if he did not. The counselor was unable to hold a special education staffing to put the younger sister in a resource room because the parents would not come in and sign the Individualized Educational Plan (IEP). The counselor summed up these problems when she said that 'they were very difficult to get any communication from . . .'

School Personnel Perceptions of Jerry

When asked to name students considered at-risk, Jerry was the first student named by both Ms. Jones and the classroom aide. The teachers also indicated that his case was the only one they had taken to the Teacher Assistance Team (TAT). During the first formal teacher interviews, Jerry's teachers focused much of their discussion on his social problems, although they were concerned with his academic problems. Ms. Green thought he was 'functioning probably beginning second grade' but that his problems were 'more social than academic'. She felt that he had a 'very poor self concept' and was concerned that he had no friends.

Ms. Jones assessed his reading skills to be about first grade level and his writing development was at an early phonetic stage. This did not seem to interfere with his inability to communicate in writing as she added that 'he just pours out his feelings'. Ms. Jones was most concerned with his home situation and the social problems he was having. The aide was puzzled with the inconsistency in his ability to retain information. She said, 'one day he can really understand what we're doing and then . . . he doesn't understand a thing that was told to him the day before'. She was concerned with his unwillingness to participate and the amount of school he had missed. She thought that his lack of attendance might be one reason for his problems.

The teachers felt that he had not been readily accepted by the other students in the classroom. Not only was he ostracized by classmates but by other students in the school. Earlier in the fall, he had been beaten up after school while walking home with his older sister. An investigation indicated that this occurred because he was defending his older sister who was also ostracized by students in her classroom. Ann, another at-risk student, thought the kids wanted to fight him because 'they lived in an old house and they weren't able to provide that much for him'. Others agreed. The classroom teachers along with school personnel were concerned with the living conditions in his home. Ms. Jones felt 'they lived in a heavy poverty situation'. Ms. Green thought that there was not a lot of care given to the children and that the personal hygiene was poor. The nurse had not been to the home but relayed comments from the school social worker who had said that the 'home was a disaster' and 'it was kind of like the slums you would see in China . . . the worst home he's ever been to in his life'. The counselor repeated the same story and added that they had attempted a number of home visits but had never been received. She said, 'the door is not answered or they're not there'.

Both the school nurse and counselor had spent a considerable amount of time working with Jerry and his sisters on their social as well as physical problems. As an example, they made sure that the children had received their immunization shots. They also arranged for a doctor's appointment when the oldest girl had several untreated ear infections. The youngest had been severely burned the previous year and had scars that were 'at least a good half inch thick' according to the nurse who arranged for the Crippled Children agency to work with the parents. Jerry had two serious blackouts and went to the nurse. In each case the school personnel felt that they received little if any cooperation from the parents. Once during the year, they did get the mother to come to school for a conference. The conference had been scheduled with the father but she came instead. All the children's teachers had concerns and wanted to talk with their mother. During the conferences, each had difficulty communicating with her and weren't sure if she understood what they were saying. She asked no questions. The counselor was later able to talk to the father on the phone. She discussed with him the teachers' concern with Jerry's lack of communication skills. The father told her that it was probably because he didn't have time for Jerry and that his mother didn't speak English very well. Later the counselor asked the children how they communicated with their mother. They answered that they didn't, they 'just kind of go ahead and do things'. The counselor concluded that they just weren't a very verbal family and lacked social skills for that reason.

By January, Jerry's teachers felt that he was beginning to improve. He had adjusted somewhat to the 'system' in the classroom and appeared to be managing better academically and socially. Ann had become friends with Jerry and his sisters. She said, 'he is a very nice boy'. The teachers felt that he seemed to be concentrating more and gaining a 'wealth of information' although it was still difficult for him to 'get it out'. In February, the pattern began to reverse. He started missing school and when he was at school the teachers didn't think he appeared 'to be into it'. Ms. Green said that 'even though he could hardly read at the beginning of the year, he had made progress in reading but now he was slipping'. Both teachers noticed this change in behavior. After being absent one Monday, Jerry came to school with two black eyes and bruises on his hands and arms. (His eyes remained black for over a week.) This was not the first time Jerry had appeared at school with injuries. He usually told them that he had a bike accident. This time he wouldn't tell the teachers what happened. They sent him to the nurse. One of the first remarks he made to the nurse was, 'I don't care what you say, my father didn't hit me'. The counselor got involved. The sisters were questioned. All three were hesitant to talk about the incident. Jerry later told the nurse that he was afraid of what would happen at home if he told. His final story was that his mother had hit him with a wrench when she was mad, although this story was never confirmed. The incident was reported to the Child Protection Agency (CPA). CPA personnel talked to the children, but were not successful in contacting the parents before they moved and withdrew Jerry from Plaza School.

In the final interview with the classroom teachers, they felt that although he had made improvements, he was still only low average academically. They thought that he would always be at-risk because of his home situation. Ms. Green was concerned that he would probably 'slip back' in a new school and become the class 'dunce/jerk'. She felt this hadn't happened in their classroom because they had spent considerable time helping Jerry with social skills and in developing social relations with the rest of the class. Both felt that he should be in a Learning Disability program.

Classroom Observations of Jerry

Jerry was a tall boy, larger than most of the other students in the classroom. His physical appearance was unusual as he appeared Anglo except for his eyes which reflected his mother's oriental heritage. Students in the room did not seem to relate to him but he did not relate to them either. He seemed to have little in common with most of the students. He also had difficulty relating to his teachers and seldom greeted them when he entered the classroom. He usually had a sad look on his face. He came to school in clothes that were unclean and too small. On several occasions, he appeared to need a bath and had an unpleasant body odor. During school he could often be observed staring off into space with a far away look on his face.

Classroom observations substantiated that Jerry had academic problems. During Silent Sustained Reading (SSR), he was rarely observed reading. He would turn pages, look at the pictures or just sit and stare. He was never reprimanded for this behavior. He seldom raised his hand to participate nor did he take part in activities. During the large group instruction period in the morning he had difficulty keeping up with the group and staying on task. He often did not finish his work or would miss the follow-up instructions while he attempted to complete a task. He did not give the appearance that he was bored or unmotivated. It just seemed that his mind was on other things. He often lacked the skills needed to successfully complete the activity. His sporadic attendance did not help the situation.

The following description of an observation, made during a reading activity, illustrates some of the above behavior. As usual, the teacher read the group assignments and the students moved to the different activity centers. Jerry was staring into space when she read the names, and did not hear what group he was to be in. When his classmates went to the centers, he wandered around the room. Ms. Jones intervened and sent him to the reading center. He could not find a book and just stood there. He didn't seem to know what to do. By this time all the other students had begun the task. The aide gave him a book, he sat down, stared into space and then began to 'read' (his eyes moved across the page but he did not appear to be actually reading). He yawned, turned one page, then another. He watched the other children. He turned pages forward, then turned them backwards. Several children finished reading the assigned story and got the follow-up activity sheet. Jerry got a sheet. He must have felt that enough time had passed to make it appear that he had read the story. He did not work on the sheet but again sat and stared. The researcher checked to see what his problem might be, and was told by Jerry that he had 'trouble with some of the words'. His attempt at reading for the researcher supported his statement. When the activity was over, his paper was still sitting, unfinished, on the table.

Jerry's Perceptions of School

Jerry left Plaza School before he could be formally interviewed. However, his words, recorded in field notes and in his writing, revealed many of his thoughts and feelings. He seemed aware of his social problems and lack of friends, and wore his heart on his sleeve. For example, during a letter writing lesson in the fall, one student wrote him a letter that read: 'you are the dumbest in the class'. Jerry's response to the student was as follows: 'you broke my heart'. The student later apologized.

One day, while reading a story about a man's life, Jerry shared with the researcher a glimpse into his life. He said that in kindergarten in Germany, when the kids played with him, he always had to be the bad guy. He added, 'You know, I always have to be the bad guy when I play with the kids'. Another day, during a reading lesson, Jerry raised his hand when the aide asked the students who among them wished they were in junior high. She asked him why. He said, 'Cause then I would be almost finished with school. Then I could get a job and be out in the open'. The aide went on to talk about money. Jerry turned to the researcher and said that his mom always takes his money but 'sometimes he hides it from her'. When the story moved to a birthday party he revealed that he had never had a birthday party. He said, 'Never had a birthday cake and I have lived nine years'.

Discussion

Jerry represents a dilemma for schools; one that is increasing in magnitude, particularly in neighborhoods that spawn social problems. While the school felt that it could make a difference in Jerry's life and set out to do so, it had no control over what happened to Jerry outside school. This is clearly not a problem in most cases – in fact, it would be unacceptable if schools had such control – but in Jerry's case, what happened to him outside school was destroying his chances for a normal life in the future. Jerry was indeed at-risk. Although he had social and academic problems, the school seemed to concentrate more on his social problems. Before much academic or social growth could be seen he was pulled out of Plaza school, placed in another school and taken out of the second one before the school year ended. There was, therefore, no coherence in his educational program or in school environment. He was probably removed from the school because the staff had contacted the Child Protection Agency concerning the suspected abuse. The school had no other recourse. And as happens in many such cases, according to school personnel, a family move occurs soon after such reporting. Thus, the school's response to his abuse appeared to add another problem to those he already had and contributed to his high levels of transiency. One is unable to predict what will happen to Jerry in the future.

References

Anderson, C. S. (1985) 'The investigation of school climate' in AUSTIN G. R. and GARBER H. (Eds) *Research on Exemplary Schools*, New York, Academic Press.

Anderson, L. M., Stevens, D. D., Prawat, R. S. and Nickerson, J. (1988) 'Classroom task environments and students' task related beliefs', *Elementary School Journal*, 88, 3, pp 281–95.

Ashton, P. and Webb, R. (1986) *Making a Difference: Teachers' Sense of Efficacy and Student Achievement*, Longman, New York.

Atkin, J., Bastiani, J and Good, J. (1988) *Listening to Parents: An Approach to the Improvement of Home/School Relations*, New York, Croom Helm.

Bacharach, S. B., Conley, S. and Shedd, J. (1986) 'Beyond career ladders: Structuring teacher development systems', *Teachers College Record*, 87, 4, pp 563–74.

Ball, S. J. (1981) *Beachside Comprehensive: A Case Study of Schooling*, Cambridge, Cambridge University Press.

Baratz, J. and Baratz, S. C. (1982) 'Early childhood intervention: The social base of institutional racism' in YETMAN N. R. (Ed) *Majority and Minority: The Dynamics of Race and Ethnicity in American Life*, 3rd edn, Boston, M A, Allyn & Bacon, pp 415–25.

Barr, R. and Dreeben, R. (1983) *How Schools Work*, Chicago, IL, University of Chicago Press.

Berger, E. H. (1987) *Parents as Partners in Education: The School and Home Working Together*, Columbus, OH, Merrill.

Berlak, A., and Berlak, H. (1981) *Dilemmas of Schooling*, London, Methuen.

Birksted, I. (1976) 'School performance: Viewed from the boys'. *Sociological Review*, 24, 1, pp 63–77.

Boersema, D. B. (1985) ' "Hey teacher! Who am I, Anyway?": Teacher determination of student identity', paper presented at the annual meeting of the American Educational Research Association, Chicago, April.

Bogdan, R and Biklin, S. (1982) *Qualitative Research for Education: An Introduction to Theory and Methods*. Boston, MA, Allyn & Bacon.

Borko, H. and Niles, J (1987) 'Descriptions of teacher planning: Ideas for teachers and researchers' in RICHARDSON-KOEHLER, V. (Ed) *Educators' Handbook: A Research Perspective*, New York, Longman.

Borko, H. and Shavelson, R (in press) 'Teacher decision making' in JONES B. and IDOL L. (Eds) *Dimensions of Thinking and Cognitive Instruction*. New Jersey, Erlbaum.

Brantlinger, E. A. (1987) 'Making decisions about special education placement: Do low income parents have the information they need?', *Journal of Learning Disabilities*, 20, 3, pp 94–101.

Broman, S., Bien, E. and Shaughnessy, P. (1985) *Low Achieving Children: The First Seven Years*, New Jersey, Lawrence Erlbaum.

Brophy, J and Rohrkemper, M. (1980). 'Teachers' thinking about problem students', Research Series No. 68, Institute for Research on Teaching, Michigan State University, East Lansing.

Brown, R. (1986) 'State responsibility for at-risk youth', *Metropolitan Education*, 2, pp 5–12.

Buchanan, A., Schulz, R., and Milazzo, P. (1983) *Instructional Risk Reduction: An Alternative to Instructional Remediation*, Washington, DC: National Institute of Education, (ERIC Document Reproduction Service No. ED 251 419).

Buttran, J., Kershner, K. and Rioux, S. (1987) *Special Education: Views from America's Cities*, Philadelphia, PA, Research for Better Schools. Inc.

Campbell, S. M. (1985) *'Kindergarten entry age as a factor in academic failure'*, paper presented at the annual meeting of the American Association of School Administrators, (ERIC Document Reproduction Service ED 251 495).

Carnegie Task Force on Teaching as a Profession (1986) *A Nation Prepared: Teachers for the 21st Century*, New York, Carnegie Forum on Education and the Economy, Carnegie Foundation.

Carrier, J. (1986) *Learning Disability: Social Class and the Construction of Inequality in American Education*, New York, Greenwood Press.

Casanova, U. and Howard, E. (1987) *Culture and Education: Survey of the Literature and Research Recommendations*, Tucson, Bureau of Applied Research in Anthropology, University of Arizona.

Chalfont, J. and Pysh, M. V. (1981) 'Teacher assistance teams: A model for within-building problem solving', *Counterpoint*, Council for Exceptional Children.

Clark, C. M. and Peterson, P. L. (1986) 'Teachers' thought processes'. in WITTROCK M. C. (Ed) *Handbook of Research on Teaching*, 3rd edn, New York, Macmillan.

Clark, R. (1983). *Family Life and School Achievement: Why Poor Black Children Succeed or Fail*, Chicago, IL, University of Chicago Press.

Clay, P. L. (1981) *Single Parents and the Public Schools: How Does the Partnership Work?*, Columbia, MD, National Committee for Citizens in Education.

Cohen, M. (1987) 'Improving school effectiveness: Lessons from research' in RICHARDSON-KOEHLER, V. (Ed) *Educators' Handbook: A Research Perspective*, New York, Longman, pp 474–90.

Coles, G. (1987) *The Learning Mystique*, New York, Pantheon.

Comer, J. P. (1980) *School Power: Implications of an Intervention Project*, New York, Free Press.

Cook-Gumperz, J. (1986) 'Introduction: The social construction of literacy' in COOK-GUMPERZ, J. (Ed) *The Social Construction of Literacy*, Cambridge, Cambridge University Press.

Cooper, H. and Good, T. (1983) *Pygmalion Grows Up: Studies in the Expectation Communication Process*, New York, Longman.

Corcoran, T. (1985) 'Effective secondary schools' in KYLE, R. (Ed) *Researching for Excellence*, Washington, DC, Government Printing Office.

Cross, R. (1984) *'Teacher Decision-making in Student Retention.* Paper presented at the annual meeting of the American Educational Research Association, New Orleans, April, (ERIC Document Reproduction Service ED 252 930).

Cummins, J. (1979) 'Linguistic interdependence and the educational development of bilingual children', *Review of Educational Research*, 49, 2, pp 222–51.

Cummins, J. (1982) 'Tests, achievement and bilingual students', *Focus* (newsletter of the National Clearinghouse for Bilingual Education), 9 (entire volume).

Cummins, J. (1984a) *Bilingualism and Special Education: Issues in Assessment and Pedagogy*, San Diego, CA, College-Hill Press.

Cummins, J. (1984b) 'Wanted: A theoretical framework for relating language proficiency to academic achievement among bilingual students' in RIVERA, C. (Ed) *Language Proficiency and Academic Achievement.* Avon, England, Multilingual Matters, Ltd.

Cummings, J. (1986) 'Psychological assessment of minority students: Out of context, out of focus, out of control?' in WILLIG, A. and GREENBERG, M. (Eds) *Bilingualism and Learning Disabilities*, New York, American Library Publishing Co., Inc.

Dahllof, U. and Lundgren, U. P. (1970) *Macro- and Micro Approaches Combined for Curriculum Process Analysis: A Swedish Educational Field Project*, Goteborg, Institute of Education, (mimeo).

Davies, L. (1983) 'Gender, resistance and power' in WALKER, S. and BARTON, L. (Eds) *Gender, Class and Education*, Lewes, Falmer Press.

Diaz, S., Moll, L. C. and Mehan, H. (1986) 'Sociocultural resources in instruction: A context-specific approach' in CALIFORNIA STATE DEPARTMENT of EDUCATION (Ed) *Beyond Language: Social and Cultural Factors in School Language Minority Children*, Los Angeles, CA, California State University.

Doyle, W. (1980) *Classroom Management.* West Lafayette, IN, Kappa Delta Pi.

Doyle, W. (1986) 'Classroom organization and management' in WITTROCK,

M. *Handbook of Research on Teaching*, 3rd edn, New York, Macmillan, pp 392–431.

Duke, D. L. (1979) 'Editor's preface' in DUKE, D. L. (Ed) *Classroom Management* (78th Yearbook of the National Society for the Study of Education, Part 2), Chicago, IL, University of Chicago Press.

Duffy, J. (1981) *Theory to Practice: How Does it Work in Real Classrooms?* Research Series 98, East Lansing, MI, Institute for Research on Teaching, Michigan State University.

Dutcher, N. (1982) 'The use of first and second languages in primary education: Selected case studies', staff working paper 504, Washington D.C., World Bank.

Educational Resources Information Center (ERIC) (1987) *Thesaurus of ERIC descriptors*. Phoenix, AZ, Oryx Press.

Elmore, R. (1983) 'Complexity and control: What legislators and administrators can do about implementing public policy' in SHULMAN L. and SYKES G. (Eds) *Handbook of Teaching and Policy*, New York, Longman, pp 342–69.

Enright, D. S. and Tammivaara, J. (1984) *Tell Me More: The Elicitation of Interview Data in the Microethnographic Study of Multicultural Elementary Classrooms'*, paper presented at the annual meeting of the American Educational Research Association, New Orleans, April.

Epstein, J. (1986) 'Parent's reactions to teacher practices of parent involvement', *Elementary School Journal*, 86, 3, pp 227–94.

Erickson, F. (1985) *'Toward a theory of student status as socially constructed'*, paper presented at the annual meeting of the American Educational Research Association, Chicago, April.

Fletcher, J. M. and Satz, P. (1984) 'Test-based versus teacher-longitudinal follow-up', *Journal of Pediatric Psychology*, 9, 193–203.

Fraatz, J. M. B. (1987) *The Politics of Reading*, New York, Teachers College Press.

Fullan, M. (1985) 'Change processes and strategies at the local level, *Elementary School Journal*, 85, 3, pp 391–422.

Garmezy, N. (1974) 'The study of competence in children at-risk for severe psychopathology' WITTROCK M. C. (Ed) *Review of Research in Education*, Itasca, IL, F. E. Peacock.

General Accounting Office (1981) *Disparities Still Exist in who gets Special Education*, report to the Chairman, Sub-committee on Select Education, Commission on Education and Labor, House of Representatives. Washington, D. C., U. S. Congress.

General Accounting Office (1987) *Bilingual Education: A new look at the research evidence*, Washington D. C., US Congress.

Genishi, C. (1979) *Code-Switching: A Review of the Literature and Comments on Future Research*, report to the National Institute of Education, Department of Education, Austin, TX, University of Texas.

Glaser, B. and Strauss, A. (1967) *The Discovery of Grounded Theory: Strategies for Qualitative Research*, Chicago, IL, Aldine Publishing Co.

Goldenberg, C. N. (1986) '*Roads to reading: Studies of Hispanic first graders at risk for reading failure*,' unpublished dissertation, University of California, Los Angeles.

Good, T. (1986) 'What is learned in elementary schools' in Tomlinson T. M. and Walberg H. L. (Eds) *Academic Work and Educational Excellence*, San Francisco, CA, McCutcheon, pp 87–114.

Goodlad, J. I. (1984) *A Place Called School*, New York, McGraw-Hill.

Goodman, K and Goodman, Y. (1981) *A Whole-language, Comprehension-centered Reading Program*, Tucson, AZ, College of Education, University of Arizona.

Graham, S. (1984) 'Teacher feeling and student thoughts: An attributional approach to affect in the classroom', *Elementary School Journal*, 85, pp 91–104.

Granger, L and Granger, B. (1986). *The Magic Feather: The Truth About 'Special Education'*, N York, E. P. Dutton.

Gumperz, J. (1982) *Language and Social Identity*, Cambridge, Cambridge University Press.

Gumperz. J. and Hernadez-Chavez (1972) 'Bilingualism, bidalectalism and classroom interaction' in Cazden C. B., John V. P. and Hymes D. (Eds) *Functions of Language in the Classroom*, New York, Teachers College Press.

Hakuta, K. (1986) *Mirror of Language: The Debate on Bilingualism*, New York, Basic Books.

Hakuta, K. (in press) 'Language and cognition in bilingual children' *Advances in Language Education*.

Hakuta, K and Diaz, R. M. (1985) 'The relationship between degree of bilingualism and cognitive ability: A critical discussion and some new longitudinal data' in Nelson K. E. (Ed) *Children's Language, Vol. 5*, Hillsdale, NJ, Lawrence Erlbaum.

Harter, S. and Connell, J. (1984) 'A model of the relationship among children's academic achievement and their self-perceptions of competence, control, and motivational orientation' in Nicholls J. (Ed) *The Development of Achievement Motivation*, Greenwich CT, JAI, pp 219–50.

Hawley, W. D. and Rosenholtz, S. with Goodstein, H. and Hassenbring, T. (1984) 'Good schools: What research says about improving student achievement' special issue of *The Peabody Journal*, Summer.

Hoffman, L. W. (1979) 'Maternal employment: 1979', *American Psychologist*, 34, pp 859–65.

Holmes Group Executive Board (1986) *Tomorrow's Teachers: A Report of the Holmes Group*, East Lansing, MI, Holmes Group.

Huberman, A. M. and Miles, M. (1984) *Innovation Up Close*, New York, Plenum Press.

Hunter, M. (1976) *Prescription for Improved Instruction* E1 Segundo, CA, TIP.

Ingersoll, G. M., Scamman, J. P. and Eckerling, W. D. (1988). 'Impact of student mobility on student achievement in an urban setting' paper presented at the annual meeting of the American Educational Research Association, New Orleans, April.

Irvine, J. J. (1988) 'An analysis of the problem of disappearing black educators, *Elementary School Journal*, 88, 5, pp 503–13.

Johnson, S. M. and Nelson, N. (1987) 'Conflict and compatibility in visions of reform, *Educational Policy*, 1, 1, pp 67–80.

Kash, M. M. and Borich, G. D. (1978) *Teacher Behavior and Pupil Self-concept*, Reading, MA, Addison-Wesley.

Keogh, B. and Daley, G. (1983) 'Early identification: One important component of comprehensive services for at-risk children', *Topics in Early Childhood Special Education*, 3, pp 7–16.

Kessler, C. and Quinn, M. E. (1987) 'Language minority children's linguistic and cognitive creativity' *Journal of Multilingual and Multicultural Development*, 8, pp 173.

Kjolseth, R. (1982) 'Bilingual education programs in the U.S.: For assimilation or pluralism?' in TURNER P. R. (Ed) *Bilingualism in the Southwest*, 2nd ed., revised, Tucson, AZ, University of Arizona Press.

Kugelmass, J. W. (1987) *Behavior, Bias and Handicaps: Labelling the Emotionally Disturbed Child*, New Brunswick, NJ, Transaction Books.

Laboratory of Human Cognition (1981) *Culutre and Cognitive Development*. CHIP Report 107, La Jolla, CA, Center Human Information Processing, University of California, San Diego.

Lambert, W. E. and Taylor, D. M. (1986) 'Cultural and racial diversity in the lives of urban Americans: Hamtramck/Pontiac study', preliminary draft, Toronto, Canada, McGill University.

Lampert, M. (1985) 'How do teachers manage to think?' *Harvard Educational Review*, 55, 2, pp 177–98.

Lazarus, B. (1985) '*Getting a special education identity: How an experienced teacher decides*', paper presented at the annual meeting of the American Educational Research Association, Chicago, April.

Lentz, F. E. (1983) '*Behavioral approaches to the assessment and remediation of academic problems*, paper presented at the annual convention of the American Psychological Association, Anaheim, (ERIC Document Reproduction Service ED 244 183).

Levin, H. M. (1987) Proposal to Rockefeller Foundation for a conference on accelerating the education of disadvantaged students, Palo Alto, Stanford University.

Lightfoot, S. L. (1978) *Worlds Apart*, New York, Basic Books.

Lightfoot, S. L. (1978) 'Exploring family-school relationships: A prelude to curricular designs and strategies' in SINCLAIR R. L. (Ed) *A Two-way Street: Home School Cooperation in Curriculum, Decision-making*, Institute for Responsive Education.

Lilienfeld, A. M. and Lilienfeld, D. E. (1980) *Foundations of Epidemiology*, New York, Oxford University Press.

Litcher, J. and Roberge, L. P. (1979) 'First grade intervention for reading achievement of high risk children', *Bulletin of the Orton Society*, 29, pp 238–44.

Little, J. W. (1981) *School Success and Staff Development: The Role of Staff Development in Urban Desegregated Schools*, final report to the National Institute of Education, Contract Number: 400–79–0049. Boulder, CO, Center for Action Research.

Lutz, F. W. (1981) 'Ethnography: The holistic approach to understanding schooling' in GREEN J. L and WALLAT C. (Eds) *Ethnography and Language in Educational Settings*, New Jersey, Ablex.

McCann, R. A. and Austin, S. (1988) At-risk youth: Definitions, dimensions, and relationships', paper presented at the annual meeting of the American Educational Research Association, New Orleans, April.

McNeil, L. (1987) 'Exit, voice and community: Magnet teachers' responses to standardization', *Educational Policy*, 1, 1, pp 93–114.

Marshall, H. and Weinstein, R. (1984) 'Classroom factors affecting students' self-evaluations: An interactional model', *Review of Educational research*, 54, pp 301–25.

Mead, G. H. (1934) *The Works of George Herbert Mead, Vol. 1, Mind, Self and Society*, Chicago, IL, University of Chicago Press.

Medway, F. (1979) 'Causal attributions for school-related problems: Teacher perceptions and teacher feedback', *Journal of Educational Psychology*, 71, pp 809–18.

Mehan, H., Hertweck, A, and Meihls, J. L. (1986) *Handicapping the Handicapped*, Palo Alto, CA, Stanford University Press.

Meighan, R. (1986) 'Other minorities: Those with special needs' in MEIGHAN R. (Ed) *A Sociology of Educating*, London, Holt Rinehart & Winston.

Melaragno, R. J., *et al.* (1981) *Parents and Federal Education Programs, Vol. 1: The Nature Causes and Consequences of Parent Involvement*, Santa Monica, CA, University of California Press.

Mercer, J. R. (1973) *Labelling the Mentally Retarded*, Berkeley, CA, University of California Press.

Mergendollar, J., and Marchman, V. (1987) 'Friends and associates' in RICHARDSON-KOEHLER V. (Ed) *Educators' Handbook: A Research Perspective*, New York, Longman, pp 297–328.

Metz, M. H. (1987) 'Teachers' pride in craft, school subcultures, and societal pressures', *Educational Policy*, 1, 1, pp 115–34.

Meyer, J. W. and Rowan, B. (1978) 'The structure of educational organizations' in MEYER M. J. *et al.* (Eds) *Organizational Environments and Organizations*, San Francisco, CA, Jossey Bass.

Milazzo, P., Buchanan, A., Escoe, A, and Schulz, R. (1981) *Method for Analyzing District Level IAI Bases to Identify Learning Opportunity Risks*, Washington, DC, National Institute of Education, (ERIC Document Reproduction Service No. ED 251 418.

Miller, P. S. (1988) 'Teaching efficacy as a mediating variable in teachers' decisions to refer students for special education services', paper presented at the annual meeting of the American Educational Research Association. New Orleans, April.

Miramonte, O. (1987) 'Oral reading miscues of Hispanic students: Implications for assessment of learning disabilities', *Journal of Learning Disabilities*, 20, 10, pp 627 32.

Moll, L. C. and Diaz, S. (1987) 'Change as the goal of educational research', *Anthropology and Education Quarterly*, 18, 4, pp 25–8.

National Commission on Excellence in Education (1983) *A Nation At risk: The Imperative for Educational Reform*, Washington, D.C., U.S. Department of Education.

National Education Association (1982) *Productive Relationships: Parent-School-Teacher*, Washington, D.C., NEA.

Nelkin, D. (1985). 'Introduction: Analyzing risk' in NELKIN D. (Ed) *The Language of Risk*, London, Sage Publications.

Ogbu, J. U. (1980) 'Anthropological ethnography in education: Some methodological issues, limitations and potentials' in GIDEONSE H. D., KOFF R. and SHWAB J. J. (Eds) *Values, Inquiry and Education*, Los Angeles, CA, Center for the Study of Evaluation, University of California at Los Angeles.

Ogbu, J. U. (1982) 'Minority education and cast' in YETMAN N. R. with STEELE C. H. (Eds) *Majority and Minority: The Dynamics of Pace and Ethnicity in American Life*, Boston, MA, Allyn & Bacon.

Ortiz, A. A. and Maldonado-Colon, E. (1986) 'Reducing inappropriate referrals of language minority students in special education' in WILLIG A. and GREENBERG H. (Eds) *Bilingualism and Learning Disabilities*, New York, American Library.

Ortiz, A. A. and Yates, J. R. (1983) 'Incidence of exceptionality among Hispanics: Implications for manpower planning, *NABE Journal*, 7, 3, pp 41–53.

Page, R. (1987) 'Teachers' perceptions of students: A link between classrooms, school cultures and the social order', *Anthropology and Education Quarterly*, 18, pp 77–99.

Pelissier, C. (1985) *On becoming a pariah: A case study in the social construction of student status'*, paper presented at the annual meeting of the American Educational Research Association, Chicago, April.

Pheasant, M. (1985) 'Aumsville school district's readiness program: Helping first graders succeed', *Oregon School Study Council Bulletin*, 28, 6, (ERIC Document Reproduction Service No. ED 252 967).

Phoenix High School District (unpublished, n-d). *At-Risk Factors*, Phoenix, AZ.

Popkewitz, T. S., Tabachnick, B. R. and Wehlage, G. (1982) *The Myth of Educational Reform*. Madison, WI, University of Wisconsin Press.

Purkey, S. and Smith, M. (1983) 'Effective schools: A review', *Elementary School Journal*, 83, 4, pp 427–53.

Ramirez, J. D. and Marino, B. J. (1988). 'Classroom talk in English imersion: Early-exit and late-exit transitional bilingual programs' in JACOBSON R. and

FALTIS C. (Eds) *Language Distribution Issues in Bilingual Schooling*, Multilingual Matters Ltd.

Rich, D. (1987a). *Teachers and Parents: An Adult to Adult Approach*, Washington, D.C., National Education Association.

Rich, D. (1987b). *Schools and Families: Issues and Actions*, Washington, D.C., National Education Association.

Richardson-Koehler, V. (1988). 'What works does and doesn't', *Journal of Curriculum Studies*, 20, 1, pp 77–9.

Richardson-Koehler, V. and Fenstermacher, G. (in press) 'Graduate programs of teacher education and the professionalization of teaching' in WOOLFOLK A. (Ed) *Beyond the Debate: Research Perspectives on Graduate Teacher Preparation*, Englewood Cliffs, NJ, Prentice Hall.

Rogoff, B. and Wertsch, J. (1984) *Children's Learning in the 'Zone of Proximal Development'*, San Francisco, CA, Jossey-Bass, Inc.

Rubin, S. E. and Spady, W. G. (1984) 'Achieving excellence through outcome-based instructional delivery, *Educational Leadership*, 41, 8, pp 37–44.

Rueda, R. and Mehan, H. (1986) 'Metacognition and passing: Strategic interactions in the lives of students with learning disabilities', *Anthropology and Education Quarterly*, 17, pp 145–65.

Ruiz, R. (1984) 'Orientations in language planning', *NABE Journal*, 8, 2, pp 15–34.

Rutter, M. (1983) 'School effects on pupil progress: Research findings and policy implication' in SHULMAN L. S. and SYKES G. (Eds) *Handbook of Teaching and Policy*, New York, Longman, Inc.

Schatzman, L. and Strauss, A. (1973) *Field Research,* Englewood Cliffs, NJ, Prentice-Hall, Inc.

Schell, T. J. (1975) *Labelling Madness*, Englewood Cliffs, NJ, Prentice-Hall.

Sergiovanni, T. J. (1985) 'Landscapes, mindscapes and reflective practice in supervision, *Journal of Curriculum and Supervision*. 1, 1, pp 5–17.

Sevigny, M. (1981) 'Triangulated inquiry' in GREEN J. and WALLAT C. (Eds) *Ethnography and Language*, Norwood, NJ, Ablex, pp 65–86.

Shavelson, R. and Bolus, R., (1982) 'Self concept: The interplay of theory and methods', *Journal of Educational Psychology*, 74, pp 3–17.

Shavelson, R. and Stern, P. (1981) 'Research on teachers' pedagogical thoughts, judgments, decisions and behavior', *Review of Educational Research*, 51, pp 455–98.

Sigmon, S. B. (1987) *Radical Analysis of Special Education: Focus in Historical Development and Learning Disabilities*, Lewes, Falmer Press.

Sinclair, R. L. and Ghory, W. J. (1981) 'Parents and teachers together: Directions for developing equality in learning through environments in families and schools' in Sinclair R. L. (ED) *A Two-way Street: Home School Cooperation in Curriculum Decision-making,* Amherst, Mass., Institute for Responsive Education.

Slavin, R. (1983) *Cooperative Learning,* New York, Longman.

Smith, M. L. (1983)*How Educators Decide Who Is Learning Disabled,* Springfield, IL, Charles C. Thomas Publishing.

Snider, W. (1987) 'Study examines forces affecting racial tracking', *Education Week,* 7, 10, pp 1–20.

Spivack, G., Marcuso, J, and Swift, M. (1986) 'Early classroom behaviour and later misconduct', *Developmental Psychology,* 22, p 124–31.

Spivack, G. and Swift, M. (1977) ' "High risk" classroom behaviors and later misconduct', *Developmental Psychology,* 22, pp 124–31.

Spradley, J. (1979) *The Ethnogaphic Interview,* New York, Holt, Rinehart & Winston.

Stacy, E. W. (1981) 'On defining at-risk status, *Evaluation and Program Planning,* 4, pp 363–75.

Stallings, J. and Krasavage, E. (1986) 'Program implementation and student achievement in a four-year Madeleine Hunter follow-through project', *Elementary School Journal,* 87, 2, pp 117–38.

Stevens, R. and Phil, R. O. (1982) 'The remediation of the student at-risk for failure', *Journal of Clinical Psychology,* 38, 2, pp 298–301.

Stromberg, P. (1986) *Symbols of Community,* Tucson, AZ, University of Arizona Press.

Tangri, S. and Moles, O. (1987) 'Parents and community' in Richardson-Koehler V. (Ed) *Educators' Handbook: A Research Perspective,* New York, Longman.

Tugent, A. (1986) 'Youth issues in prominence on national agenda', *Education Week,* 6, 2, pp 9–13.

Ulibarri, D., Spencer, M. and Rivas, G. (1981) 'Language proficiency and academic achievement: A study of language proficiency tests and their relationship to school ratings as predictors of academic achievement', *NABE Journal,* 5, pp 47–80.

Vellutina, F. R., Steger, B. M., Moyer, S. C., Harding, C. J. and Niles, J. A. (1977) 'Has the perceptual deficit hypothesis led us astray?', *Journal of Learning Disabilities,* 10, pp 375–88.

Vygotsky, L. S. (1978) *Mind in Society,* edited by Cole, M. *et al,* Cambridge, MA, Harvard University Press.

Walker, E. and Emory, E. (1983) 'Infants at risk for psychopathology: Offspring of schizophrenic parents', *Child Development,* 54, 1, pp 269–85.

Wehlage, G. G. and Rutter, R. A. (1986) 'Dropping out: How much do schools contribute to the problem', *Teachers College Record,* 87, p 364–92.

Weick, K. E. (1982) 'Administering education in loosely-coupled schools', *Phi Delta Kappan,* June, pp 673–76.

Wells, G. (1987) 'Language in the classroom: Literacy and collaborative talk', paper for the Center for Applied Cognitive Science and Department of Curriculum, Ontario, Canada, Ontario Institute for Studies in Education.

Werner, E., Bierman, J. and French, F.(1971) *The Children of Kauai: A Longitudinal Study from the Prenatal Period Through age 10,* Honolulu, University of Hawaii Press.

Wilcox, K. (1982) 'Ethnography as a methodology and its application to the study of schooling: A review' in SPINDLER G. (Ed) *Doing the Ethnography of Schooling*, New York, Holt, Rinehart & Winston, Inc, pp 454–88.

Wiles, J. and Bondi, J. (1981) *The Essential Middle School*, Columbus, OH, Charles E. Merrill.

Willig, A. C. (1986) 'Special education and the culturally and linguistically different child: An overview of issues and challenges' in WILLIG A. and GREENBERG M. (Eds) *Bilingualism and Learning Disabilities*, New York, American Library Publishing Co., Inc.

Willig, A. and Greenberg, M. (Eds) (1986) *Bilingualism and Learning Disabilities*, New York, American Library Publishing Co., Inc.

Wolcott, H. (1982) 'Mirrors, models and monitors: Educator adaptations of the ethnographic innovation' in SPINDLER G. (Ed) *Doing the Ethnography of Schooling*, New York, Holt, Rinehart & Winston.

Wong-Fillmore, L. with Valdez, C. (1986) 'Teaching bilingual learners' in WITTROCK M. (Ed) *Handbook of Research on Teaching*, 3rd ed, New York, Macmillan, pp 648–85.

Woods, P. (1986) *Inside Schools: Ethnography in Educational Research*, London, Routledge & Kegan Paul.

Yin, R. K. (1984) *Case Study Research: Design and Methods*, Beverly Hills, CA, Sage.

Index

absenteeism 5, 36
Atkin, J. 92, 96
at-risk behavior, blame for 121–2
'at-risk', meaning of 1–14
at-risk status
  interactive model of 138–42
  stability of 33–6
at-risk students
  demographic information on 19–21
  identification and treatment of 16,
    133–6, 141–2
  by teachers 35, 36–8
  numbers of, identified by teachers 19,
    34
  schooling of 40–61
  classification, fragmentation and
    production in 55–7
  community, coherence and individual
    development in 57–60
  teachers' definitions of 16, 17–19
  types of 134–6
  context dependent 134, 135, 142, 152
  masked 134, 135–6, 142, 152
  readily identifiable 134, 141–2, 151
  severe 134–5, 142, 152

Bastiani, J. 92, 95
behavioral risk factors 4
Berlak, A. 119, 122
Berlak, H. 119, 122
Biklen, S. 9
biological risk factors 4
Bogdan, R. 9
Brantlinger, E. A. 91

case studies of at-risk students 21–33,
  167–264
centers 128
Child Protective Services 1, 22, 28, 87,
  90, 147
Child Study Team 100, 101, 102, 109
classrooms 63–78, 140, 148–50
  academic organization of 65, 77
  dilemmas in organization and
    management of 122–3, 125–33
  ecology of 70–2, 77
  environment 148
  influences on 70–7
  school and school district effects on
    72–6, 78
  social organization of 65, 77, 125
  and students requiring extra help 149
  teacher beliefs and expectations in
    76–7
  view of knowledge in 148–9
clinical psychology 4
Coles, G. 7
Comer, J. P. 96
communication, parent-teacher 94–6
compensatory programs 4, 5
computer-assisted instructional system
  (CAI) 41, 123
constructivist schooling 49, 74
Control vs. Autonomy 123
Cummins, J. 99

Danforth Foundation 42
data analysis 13
demographic risk factors 4
demographics of families 83–5

deprived, labelling as 9
desegration 45–6
disadvantaged children 3
Doyle, W. 70, 71
dropping out, 4, 5

educable mentally handicapped (EMH) 109
Education Week 3
'effective schools' movement 44, 46
Emory, E. 4
emotionally handicapped children 115
English as a Second Language (ESL) 59, 69, 109
English Language Proficient (LEP) 14
epidemiological model 3–7, 33
Epstein, J. 89
ERIC: *Thesaurus of Descriptors* 3
Erickson, F. 8, 16, 78, 120
'Essential Elements of Instruction' (EEI) 42
expectations of parents and teachers 89–96

family characteristics 93–4
Feurestein 144
foster homes 18
Fraatz, J.M.B. 126, 153
'full frontal' strategy 92

Glaser, B. 9, 13
Goldeberg, C. N. 135
Good, T. 126
Goode, J. 92, 96
grouping 127–8

Head Start program 4
Hertwick, A. 8, 40, 91, 103, 119
high-risk students 3, 55
home environment 2, 80–97
    demographics 83–5
    teacher information about 86
    teachers' perceptions of 80, 85–8
homework 128–9, 150
Hunter, Madeleine 42

identification of at-risk students 16, 133–6, 141–2
    context effects on process 120–1
    by teachers 35, 36–8
individual education plan (IEP) 103, 106
interactive model of at-risk status 138–42
interactivity theory 7–8

K-3 programs 41

knowledge, view of 148–9
Kugelmass, J. W. 102, 115

labelling, effect of 6, 16
Lampert, M. 122, 131
language
    in the classroom, choice of 129–30
    and learning disabilities 108–15
language therapy 59
learning disabilities (LD) 98–117
    interactivity theory of 7–8
    labelling procedures 100–4
    and language 108–15
    role of teachers in 102–4
    and schooling of at-risk students 105–8
    theories and practices regarding 99
learning disabled (LD) students 9
    identification and treatment of 13
Lewis 144
Limited English Proficiency (LEP) 53, 98, 109, 135
linguistically different status 6
low achievement 3, 5
'lower track' students 60–1

'marginally at-risk' students 18
Mead, George Herbert 119
Mehan, H. 8, 40, 91, 103, 119
Meighan, R. 99
Meihls, J. L. 8, 40, 91, 103, 119
mentally retarded, labelling as 9, 99
Mercer, J. R. 80, 85, 144
Miller, P. S. 102
minority status 4, 6
Miramonte, O. 113
miscommunication, parent/teacher 91–2, 94–6

Nation at Risk A, 42
National Education Association 96
Nelkin, D. 7

Office of Civil Rights 41
Outcomes Based Education 42, 50, 51, 54, 55

Page, R. 8, 61
parent interviews 11, 81–2, 161–2
parents' expectations 89–96
perceiver, role of 80
perceptions
    parents', of the school 81
    teachers' and parents', of student competence 88–9

teachers', of the home 80, 85–8
Popkewitz, T. S. 43, 49, 52, 55, 56
poverty 4–5
pull-out programs 126–7

referrals 102–3, 104
remediation 112
risk factors of school failure 4

'school climate' 44
school district 41–3, 123, 141
  accountability requirements and
    testing programs 144
  effects on classrooms 72–6, 78, 141
  mandates 143–4
school faculty 146–7
school failure
  explanations of 40
  indicators of 81
  poverty and 4–5
school organization and management
    122–3, 125–33
  dilemmas in
  control vs. autonomy 123
  form vs. substance 130–1
  individual or group 126–30
  test vs. teaching for deep
    understanding 131–3
  district influences on 72–6, 78, 141
school psychologist, role of 104
school records 86
school success
  epidemiological model of 3–7, 33
  explanations of 40
schools
  change in 142–3
  dilemmas in 124–33
  effective, for at-risk students 143–52
  environment 144–6
  and parents 81, 147
  and social agencies 147–8
'self-esteem' 56

Sigmon, S. B. 118
  Radical Analysis of Special Education 133
Slavin, R. 127
Smith, M. L. 8
social construction 118–37
  of at-risk status 119–22
social constructivist model 7–9, 33,
    118–19, 121–2
socioeconomic risk factors 4
socioeconomic status (SES) 6
Speakers of Other Languages (SOL) 110,
    115, 136, 150
special education 4, 59
specialists, classroom 127
speech/hearing therapy 59
social agencies 147–8
Spradley, J. 9
Strauss, A. 9, 13
student interview 11, 163–5
'Success Schools' 46
suspensions 5

Tabachnick, B. R. 43, 49, 52, 55, 56
Teacher Assistance Team (TAT) 48, 100,
    101, 102, 108, 147
teacher interviews 11, 16, 82
  first 155–7
  principal 160
  second 158–9
teacher/pupil ratio 149
teachers' expectations 89–96
'technical schooling' 43, 52, 72
tests, classroom 131–3

underachievement 3

Walker, E. 4
Wehlage, G. 43, 49, 52, 55, 56
Weick, K. E. 42
Wells, G. 112
Willig, A. C. 108